HEY: WHY BOTHER? 7

TRUTH: THE UNDERLYING REALITY 11

GOD: THE IMMOVABLE OBJECT 53

ASK MY PASTOR!

HE KNOWS THAT STUFF

A quick-start guide to what Christians believe

> "ARE YOU NOT IN ERROR BECAUSE YOU DO NOT KNOW THE SCRIPTURES OR THE POWER OF GOD?"
>
> MARK 12:24

"If you do not listen to Theology, that will not mean that you have no ideas about God. It will mean that you have a lot of wrong ones—bad, muddled, out of date ideas. For a great many of the ideas about God which are trotted out as novelties today, are simply the ones which real Theologians tried centuries ago and rejected."

C.S. Lewis, *Mere Christianity*

ASK MY PASTOR!
HE KNOWS THAT STUFF

written by Alan Root Robertson © 2013
Scripture passages taken from the NIV, Copyright 1984,
used by permission of Zondervan, all rights reserved

SOMEDAY AVAILABLE FREE AT THE WEBSITE, www.alanrootrobertson.com
sermon notes based on the chapters
downloadable doctrine chart pdf
downloadable intro videos
small group materials

SOMEDAY TO BE **FOR SALE** AT THE WEBSITE, www.alanrootrobertson.com
multi-whole-family community group curriculum!
giant wall chart review tool
"Scripture pictures" flashcards
intergenerational CDs, DVDs and books
more copies of THIS book, including Kindle and iBook!

. . . .

ABOUT THE AUTHOR

Alan Root Robertson is a big-picture type, always fascinated by the panoramic view of life and faith, 'cause he thinks context helps. For 30+ years, he's traveled the nation as an evangelist and a musicianary. His call includes kids and families. He's been privileged to be present at the moment when thousands of kids have said yes to the call of the Holy Spirit in salvation. He's all about **downloading the nuts and bolts of our common Christian thing** in songs, sermons, and crusades.

Alan's love of teaching has made him *have to be* a lifelong learner. Along the way, he's noticed that **a ton of us don't know what we believe or why we believe it**. And we really don't know how to even begin to remedy the problem; hence, this book which puts the basic non-denominational teachings of the Bible into the hands of those who sincerely want to know what's going on with their faith in Jesus Christ.

Alan is uniquely equipped for this job by his default mode for simplification, encouragement and his seeming inability to be serious for long stretches of time. Here in this book are **the basics of what believers believe**: an eagle's-eye view of the landscape of biblical doctrine. As the hymn says, *"How firm a foundation, ye saints of the LORD, is laid for your faith in His excellent word!"*

ASK MY PASTOR – HE KNOWS THAT STUFF

Great, a dry book about a dry subject: doctrine. We want to laugh, to dance, to pass the time and get relief from our problems. We want to be entertained. But God meant our lives to be a hugely satisfying adventure, not just an existence ... to be the overcomers, not the overcome. If knowing more about a stupid cell phone can unlock riches unknown, what do you think knowing more about Almighty God might do? Are we living to die, or dying to live?

¬set up
HEY: WHY BOTHER?
is ignorance really bliss?

Christianity seems to have become a professional sport. We hire a church staff to act like Christians all through the week so the rest of us can go about our business. We buy tickets for those highly scripted Sunday events by dropping money in a collection plate that passes through the crowd, and we then sit back and evaluate how well our team is doing. The pastor is showing marked improvement, the worship leader's still struggling, while the Sunday school teacher? Let's just say they're not keeping us *entertained*. We think of trying that other church on the corner. They serve soy milk lattes in the sanctuary.

Apparently, we Christians are judged solely by occasional church attendance and maybe not even that. We're no longer expected to know what we believe and why. We're not even sure what God expects of us anymore, we're so busy telling God what *we* expect. We said a sincere prayer when we were in high school, and we were told our ticket was punched. We were good to go, yet we still have the feeling we're missing something. Sunday mornings, we drive past people reading morning newspapers at the coffee shop and we wonder what it would be like to dare to sip expensive hot drinks in tee shirts and sunglasses at an outside table every Sunday instead of having to show up and evaluate the church staff.

We think we oughta be happy and successful because, after all, God's reputation is on the line and we don't want Him to be embarrassed. We're nagged by the suspicion that we fall woefully short of pleasing Him, so we double our efforts to produce lives that look OK on the outside. We're supposed to be doing and believing something or other, but it's complicated and confusing. We can't even agree on Bible translations: forget being salt and light. We've just sorta checked out.

What? You have a question about Christianity? Sorry, no clue. Ask my pastor, we <u>pay</u> him to know that kind of stuff . . .

We talk about movies, we talk about sports, we talk about the weather, we talk about restaurants and cars and clothes. My friend and former pastor Ron Ferguson rephrased a Chesterton axiom when he said, "Everything matters except what *matters*." We want to think of ourselves as deep, but our conversations take us no further than the shallow end of the conversation pool. But each of us, deep down inside, want to talk about, and <u>be</u> about, the things that really *do* matter.

Everybody's got an opinion, and thanks to social media, everybody can benefit from knowing what ours are. It's a great time to be alive because apparently nobody's opinions are wrong. Unless your opinions should happen to come from the Bible. Then those most certainly are wrong: bigoted, out of date, intolerant and horrifically, embarrassingly wrong! If you think that's an overstatement, try this: Stand up and declare, "God hates divorce!" Or maybe, "Ten percent is only a minimum suggested beginning amount of money for giving!" Or the ever popular, "If you follow Jesus, expect your life to be really hard!" These are some of God's opinions. There're bunches more where those came from. Don't like 'em? Then I guess you can go make your own time/space continuum any way *you* like! But we'd better at least know what his opinions *are*, don't you think?

This book is about God's opinions revealed in Scripture. What does God think about stuff? What's he revealed in the Bible? These revelations are the stuff of Christian <u>*doctrine*</u>. Do we even know these things anymore?

Doctrine has been relegated to the domain of theologians and it should never have been. It's is the coin of the realm of the Kingdom of God and thus ought to be the birthright of every one of his children. Ignorance of doctrine frustrates our desire to mature and produce the fruit of an effective and victorious life. I mean, come on. Are we scared to have our own beliefs challenged by the Scriptures? Maybe we should be! Maybe we might have to alter or ditch some of them!

Doctrine attempts to tackle questions about which we ought to be curious. Charles Spurgeon said doctrine answers such questions as: why do we exist? How can we know anything? How much can we know? Who is God? What's wrong with the world? How is God going to fix it? How do we reconnect with Life? Is God just?

What does God expect of us? What's the key to belonging to His family?

Doctrine is like a swimming pool: it takes the "deep things of God" and puts them in a handy, comprehensible box—a tub where we can touch the bottom and the sides and not feel like we're in over our heads. As fun as the ocean is, have you noticed people would rather actually *swim* in a swimming pool? No one wants to be helicopter-dropped in the middle of the vast bottomless ocean. Doctrine provides a safer way to come into the always overwhelming world of God's thoughts and actions, helping us systematize His revelation so we can better know what He's like and what He expects of us.

Doctrine is the theological equivalent of a "fixed point." Surveyors and astronomers sometimes designate a fixed point as a stationary observational position from which to begin to map the landscape or the constellations. A benchmark. A null point. A point of reference. An unmoving belief system platform from which to judge the veracity of the ideas flying all around us.

Doctrine is a storage place for concepts about God. When you have to organize a large room full of stuff, it's helpful to have shelves with labels. We can take one of God's revealed truths and roughly categorize it by placing it on a shelf with other revealed truths like it. It will be there when we need it.

Doctrine provides context for the vocabulary we come across in the Bible, guarding us from gross error. Sharing a vocabulary is not enough unless we also share a dictionary. In the dictionary, "fast" means both rapid and stationary. "Bark" is either something you can touch or something you can hear. And "bad" can mean defective, unpleasant, decayed, diseased, guilty, worthless, immoral or even surpassingly good. The point is, words without *context* can often give the opposite idea of what was intended.

Doctrine decodes the messages that bombard our senses. If you don't know the code, the colors of the traffic lights mean nothing. If you come up to a light with 5 lights in a circle (pink, orange, blue, magenta, and purple), what will you do if the magenta light is on? Stop? Go? Wait? Freak out? The point is, we need the code.

The doctrines in this book are generally ones about which most Christians *agree*. My bias is conservative evangelical with a touch of liturgical charismatic flavoring. I've tried to compensate, but you'll have to adjust your screen for that slight skew! Any book written by human beings will fall short, and this one certainly does. The reason I wrote it is because the church is constantly tossed about by changing tides of societal pressures. Doctrine can serve as an anchor to keep us from drifting.

Jesus said, ***"You know these things; you're blessed if you DO them."*** It's crucial that we *do* whatever we know to do; yet we must "know" first before we can then "do!" May this book help us celebrate the commonwealth of the wisdom and the knowledge and the love that is found in Jesus Christ, and in Him alone.

If you could experience a life without any truth, what do you imagine it would be like? Obviously at that point, everything you believed would be of no value whatsoever. Nothing would be reliable. Everything, and I mean everything, would simply be a cheat and a fraud. Maybe we under-appreciate the vital role of truth in our lives. It's kind of like oxygen: we don't think about it, but we sure do miss it when it's not there!

¬chapter one
TRUTH: THE UNDERLYING REALITY

listen: can I tell you a secret?

"The secret things belong to the LORD our God, but the things revealed belong to us."
Deuteronomy 29:29

Everyone loves a secret. Everyone loves to *blab* a secret. Everyone loves to *hear* a secret blabbed. Well?! God's been blabbing a ton of secrets. He calls it *revelation* truth. Is there any conceivable reason that we might not listen?

Luke 8:10 says, ***"The knowledge of the secrets of the kingdom of God has been given to you."*** This is stupendous stuff. This is Indiana Jones, Marco Polo, Christopher Columbus magnitude. Secrets of the Kingdom? Given? To us? Is that a past-tense verb Jesus uses? You'd better believe it, pal. It's no small matter. Will we pay attention to this gift? Will we leave this gift under the tree? Will we chase after lesser gifts and ignore this one?

For good reason, we honor truth above all things. Even when it's painful, we want the truth. We adjure our court witnesses to stick to it. We expect our philosophers to seek it. We want our songwriters to explore it. We demand our children tell it. We hate lies and liars more than we hate anything.

Truth destroys lies as light destroys darkness. Truth battles destructive heresy as Lysol disinfects toilet bowls. Truth fills up our lives the way good, hot, honest food satiates a hungry man. Truth connects with us in our deepest place, reminding us of what we already suspected but perhaps hadn't yet come to realize. Truth is like cool water to our thirsty souls. Truth is the most solid, satisfying thing we know. So why would we settle for anything less than the absolute truth?

I don't know. You tell me!

• EVIDENCE

how many blatant, barefaced signposts do we require?

"WISDOM CALLS ALOUD IN THE STREET, SHE RAISES HER VOICE IN THE PUBLIC SQUARES; AT THE HEAD OF THE NOISY STREETS SHE CRIES OUT, IN THE GATEWAYS OF THE CITY SHE MAKES HER SPEECH: HOW LONG WILL YOU SIMPLE ONES LOVE YOUR SIMPLE WAYS? HOW LONG WILL MOCKERS DELIGHT IN MOCKERY AND FOOLS HATE KNOWLEDGE?"
PROVERBS 1:20-22

If our senses are working at all, we know there's a God. We know He's powerful and masterful. We know He's vast in His imagination and creativity. We know that He's beyond our ability to figure out. We know that He's purposeful and unstoppable in whatever He decides to do. All this just by standing still and experiencing our surroundings. All this without ever cracking open a Bible. God definitely wants us to know a lot about Him.

We of the western world have a procedural custom that comes from Greek and Jewish culture by way of the Roman Empire. We try to lay aside our feelings and emotions and attempt to be rational about things. To *think* rather than react based on hormones or outside stimuli. We place an emphasis on our determination to gather the facts, and based on our assessment of the veracity of those facts and their claims, to act accordingly. Modern science was formulated by Western civilization.

In this light, the "if it feels good, do it" motto of the 60s in America is a vile regression from Western thought, so much so that the generation that subscribed to that empty philosophy have become bankrupt, both rationally and morally. Sadly, it is these 60s people in our time who are in elected office and Hollywood, steering the culture with disastrous results—perhaps unintended, perhaps not. Still, who cares what they intend if the result is the same?

Naturalism, gnosticism, animism, legalism, dualism, materialism, multiculturalism, secular humanism, and new-age demonic spirit-guides are more often the norm than we might want to think. These are irrational beliefs. To buy into them, a person must push away the witness of creation, their own conscience, their mind, the Bible and the Holy Spirit. The worst kind of deception is self-deception, but I think in the case of our relationship to God's truth, it's the only kind of deception the devil ever needs, because it works so well.

Into this tangle of wrong thinking comes the witness of *evidence*, obvious clues left everywhere. All around, in every language of sensory experience, we get a billboard of truth that calls us to the right road. In the end, no one will be able to say they never knew that God is who He says He is, nor can they credibly claim that their search for truth yielded no answers. When we stand before God, ignorance is one excuse that just won't wash.

Evidence ought to be something that changes the way we think. Perhaps it won't change the way we feel, but it definitely should affect our mindset. If I know my business associates are cheating scumbags, I may still like them and want to stay friends, but it's unlikely I'll loan them money. When evidence is produced it ought to redirect any decision-making process. Evidence influences. Evidence shapes. Evidence persuades. Evidence convicts.

Evidence does not leave us where it found us. It calls us to a make a choice. It demands an assessment of our present course. We sidestep evidence at great cost. God has left us scads of evidence about Himself. What will we do now that we know what we know? There are four possibilities: *ignore* the evidence, *contest* the evidence, merely *assent* to the intellectual veracity of the evidence, or *act* upon the evidence.

Ready? Choose.

1 meaning
does it make sense that anything makes sense?

"WHAT MAY BE KNOWN ABOUT GOD IS PLAIN TO THEM, BECAUSE GOD HAS MADE IT PLAIN TO THEM."
ROMANS 1:19

God's not playing hide and seek with us. If we can't see Him, it's because we refuse to look. Perhaps our observational abilities have been seared like a steak on a sizzling grill. We persist in rationalizing our wrong behavior, and the warning signals of God's truth no longer reach us as easily as they used to. It's as if we're calmly resting our hands on a hot stove because our pain response has been deadened. But the truth remains. Everyone knows the truth. Truth is plain as the nose on your face. God is for real, God is in charge. God makes the rules not us. We turn our backs on Him at our own peril.

Meaning must exist, or else we'd have no idea that it didn't! Do you get that? I'm not sure I do, but it's true. Meaning is what we call *self-evident*.

Let me try again. Meaning must exist before someone could possibly posit that it doesn't. Meaning must be real, because if it weren't, we'd never know that it might not be. I mean, plug in your own explanation here and see what YOU get. Hah! It's not so EASY, is it? Even the attempt to talk about meaninglessness is difficult to accomplish in a meaningful way!

I know Solomon said *everything* was meaningless, but he wasn't sawing off the rational branch he was standing on. When he spoke of "meaning," he was using the word as a synonym for "purposefulness." It couldn't be otherwise. How could Solomon possibly bemoan the lack of something that wasn't bemoan-able due to it's not being there? This is getting so weird. Even here, there is a clue to the truth.

To even *say* that everything is meaningless proves the reality that everything does in fact have meaning. As Jon Foreman of the band Switchfoot says, *"The shadow proves the sunshine."* Meaninglessness is not the problem. It's not possible for life to be meaningless, because if it were, we would be unable to wonder if it were.

So we have positive proof of the existence of meaning. What does this tell us? Meaning is not accidental, nor is it evolving. Meaning can only be recognized by sentient, conscious, aware beings, so it must proceed from a sentient, conscious, and aware Being. Don't read too much into this. We aren't yet even close to the God of the Bible or His goodness or creativity or power or love. We've only said this: our ability to wonder about meaning is a solid fact of the existence of Someone from whom meaning itself emanates.

This is such a telling fact that agnostics either have to ignore it or fall on their knees. To an agnostic or a neo-Darwinist, meaning is a pink elephant in the room. Once we admit that life has meaning, we must admit that there is a bigger Someone of some sort if we want to keep a shred of our intellectual viability. And if one admits to the existence of meaning, there's a tiger loose in the house. There's no telling what's going to happen now.

God might be good, might be maniacal, might be loving, might be sadistic, might be compassionate or might be out for only Himself. But you can't say that He doesn't exist and call yourself perceptive. Can you?

The existence of meaning lets us in on a secret: there's more to the universe than just what we can see or what we can observe in a petri dish or describe with a thermometer or a telescope. There is something alongside us in this universe that enriches things with significance and consequence. There's a _point_ to life, whatever that point is. And the question of what is the ultimate point of the universe haunts us deep inside our soul.

Meaning just <u>IS</u>. It exists with no help from any of us. And, my friends, it absolutely must _originate_ from Someone who <u>IS</u>.

2 mind

are you aware that you're self-aware?

"WHO ENDOWED THE HEART WITH WISDOM OR GAVE UNDERSTANDING TO THE MIND?"
JOB 38:36

Scientists cannot produce a brain.

Oh sure, they can make a computer circuit that will produce calculations based on an algorithmic program and bake it into a silicon chip. No emotions, no morality, no memory of joy and laughter. No sense of _self_. No longing, no regret. In the future, we will continue to produce toys that look and act deceptively more like ourselves, but bear in mind:,_deceptive_ is the operative word.

Our brains are just a collection of fat cells with connective pathways. How in the world did Someone make that into a mind, into a soul? Do we understand the implication of "mind"? Look at me. I asked you a question.

The fact that we _have_ a mind points to the inescapable conclusion that we _came from_ a Mind. Mind does not come from mindlessness. Our mind comes from THE

Mind. Descartes said, *"Cogito ergo sum."* Since we're all Latin scholars, I don't really need to translate that, but I'll do it anyway just to show that I can use Google: "I think, therefore I am." Sure, thinking proves we exist, but it also proves that THE BIG THINKER exists. Beyond "I think therefore I am" is this inescapable proposal: "We think . . . therefore *God* is."

We would not be able to think unless God exists. Dr. Ravi Zacharias, the Christian apologist, was once asked by a student during a Q&A: "Do I exist?" To which the good doctor replied, "Whom shall I say is asking?" Love it.

Can we wonder if mind exists? Then, ergo and ipso facto, it does. And equally ipso facto, eons of mindless evolution of fatty tissue does not account for the existence of mind. Mind comes from mind. It's not mindless nor is it accidental. The presence of our mind reveals the presence of God's mind. I'm belaboring this point because it is routinely overlooked in our world. The smartest people can (and standardly *do*) miss this pedestrian and glaring reality. So I don't apologize for belaboring it.

The mind has the distinction of being the only body part Jesus ever added into a quotation of Old Testament scripture! In the Shema, Moses says in Deuteronomy 6:4 and 5, **"Hear, O Israel, the LORD our God, the LORD is one. And you shall love the LORD your God with all your heart, all your soul and all your strength."** In explaining the most important commandment, Jesus said, **"Love the LORD with all your heart, all your soul, all your MIND, and all your strength."** We are obviously to go all out in our love and service to God, but *why on earth would Jesus add the word "mind" here?*

First, I honestly don't know. Second, I'm fairly sure it wasn't because Moses didn't hear correctly the first time. My guess is that Jesus was speaking to a Western culture that valued mind in a way unprecedented in civilizations to this point. After all, both the Greeks and Romans were slowly overrunning the land of Israel.

We in America have deep roots in Israel, Greece and Rome. Western civilization and the Enlightenment have elevated rationality to a new level. We are to apply not only our hearts, our souls and our bodies to loving and serving God, but also our *minds.*

Make of that what you will. Our minds are perhaps the most amazing creation of our Amazing Creator. For those of you (like Charles Darwin) who prefer that the *eye* should be the most miraculous body part God made, I won't argue, but the mind is right up there. Our present day supercomputers are poor mockeries of something God made in a nanosecond on the sixth day of His creation. Watery protoplasm that houses personality, memory, cognitive ability, learning, reasoning, awareness, recognition, input processing, language management . . . the list is endless. And don't forget the mind's ability to appreciate beauty, create poems and paintings, impose itself over our sense of self-preservation, and laugh at jokes.

Our minds mimic the Great Mind that fashioned them.

3 causality
does a universe just happen by accident? really?

"WHEN I ACT, WHO CAN REVERSE IT?"
ISAIAH 43:13B

God is the First Cause. He's where everything originates. Even evil does not exist on it's own; there's no balanced yin yang in the universe. Evil is the result of God's gift of free will gone sour. Evil is a product of the Creator giving creatures permission to make decisions outside of His own will and purpose. There isn't anything that God did not ultimately cause. His actions are the initial determinant power fed into the closed system He instigated.

He started all of this. All of it.

Sometimes truth is discovered through the application of logic. If I see a man in a suit carrying a briefcase riding a transit to the city, I can logically deduce he is a businessman instead of a farmer. This deduction is based on assumptions and conclusions I can draw in my mind. Or since I know that a car was designed and manufactured, not the result of random sun rays bouncing off inanimate materials accidentally leached into a pool of water, I can assert that human beings of greater complexity and functionality than a car have been designed and manufactured. They have a Cause. Simple enough. This is not rocket science.

If I see a room with shelves of ordered books, arranged furniture, and plugged-in light fixtures, I don't think, "Wow, what a coincidence. It must have been star beams!" Similarly, if I see a universe with discoverable scientific principles, I see a system that must have a Principle Establisher. If I see a universe with ordered orbits I must conclude that it was put in place by an Orbit Designer who prefers certain orbits and can bring them about and maintain them. If I discover that there are personalities in people that I meet, I arrive at the deduction that a Personality is at work in the universe. If I see beauty in the world around me, there must exist a Lover of Beauty who caused it and triggered the appreciation of it in me.

It is in fact *illogical* to not believe there is a God. It's embarrassing how many legitimate lines of reasoning must be disregarded to do so. There are smart atheists like Christopher Hitchens (now dead) and clever atheists like Richard Dawkins (who will someday die), but there are no <u>wise</u> atheists. Psalms 14:1 explains why: **"*The fool has said in his heart, 'No God for me.'*"**

Someone calculated that the last time a single person could know all of what can be known was sometime around 1850. Even if an atheist were to know nine-tenths of everything there is to know in all the world, that little one-tenth they did not know should give even an atheist pause before pronouncing that God is fictional. Frankly, we don't even need a tenth of all knowledge to catch the aroma of God's presence. Just watch ants go about their daily business. Now *there's* a sermon! Even old Solomon was impressed with them in Proverbs 6:6.

The thing is, every event has a cause. As the brilliant philosopher Julie Andrews sang in <u>The Sound of Music</u>, "Nothing comes from nothing: nothing ever could." Causality is only logical. That's why it amazes me when evolutionists and big bang believers say that Christians are backward rubes! Come on! How clueless do you have to be to ignore the inviolable law of causality? You might be clever, but you can't possibly be *smart*.

If the principle of causality holds, then there are many corollaries. Causality requires a First Cause, we call him God. Causality requires a First Cause full of purpose and design, since what He caused is full of purpose and design. Causality requires a First Cause who is concerned about us, since He fashioned a planet with the perfect size, temperature, composition, and everything needed to support life. And causality requires a First Cause who is willing to reveal Himself to us, which is what science attempts to accomplish: map the fingerprints of the First Cause.

The logic of causality, when applied, should comfort us in ways biblical theology might not even be able to do!

4 conscience

that tiny angel hovering over your shoulder

"When Gentiles, who do not have the law, do by nature things required by the law, they are a law for themselves, even though they do not have the law, since they show that the requirements of the law are written on their hearts; their consciences also bearing witness, and their thoughts now accusing, now even defending them."

Romans 2:14-15

In this passage, Paul instructs the Christians in Rome that no one can credibly claim, "Nobody told me! I never knew how God expected me to behave! I'm off the hook because no one ever read me the rules!" Bah-lony! The fact is, we *all* know what's right and wrong. Jew and Gentile. Ancient and Modern. Eastern and Western. Educated and Ignorant. God's rules are written on our hearts.

That's inarguably true and we know it. Case closed.

If we think about it, we didn't really even need the Ten Commandments, since they're already part and parcel of our very nature. Who doesn't already agree with the Ten Commandments? Respect authority? Check. Hands off what belongs to others? Check. Do the right thing? Check. This is stuff we all reinforce with our kids, but no one really needs to be taught. We know these laws without being told. We call this phenomena *conscience*. Like noses, everybody (and every body) has one.

Conscience comes as software preinstalled on our hard drive. It automatically loads when our computers boot. No one has to tell us it's wrong to steal. No one argues that lying is a virtue. While people may disagree about when it's alright to fight, nobody values a coward or a thug.

Conscience is not, as the Darwinists would have us believe, an evolved instinct to preserve the species, since quite often what our consciences tell us to do might short-circuit our chances of survival.

Conscience is uncomfortable, since most of what we *feel* like doing is frowned upon by our conscience. Conscience is inconvenient. Inescapable. Bothersome. Cold water. Conscience is the goody-two-shoes party-pooper you wish you'd left behind. We just want it to shut up.

Have you ever seen the cartoons where a tiny angel sits on one shoulder and a tiny devil on the other? Often, the angel and the devil look exactly like the character on whose shoulder they appear, and they argue with each other. The angel is our conscience, the devil is our own will. Hence the idiom "our better angels," coined by Abe Lincoln. The conscience is a built-in gyroscope that keeps us flying right.

Should we break in line? Should we help old ladies? Should we kick cats? Should we tell the truth? Should we dump our garbage in someone else's yard? Should we encourage people to break their promises? Should we laugh at the sufferings of others? Should we flaunt authority? Are these questions hard? Of course not. We all have consciences and we don't have to get out life's rulebook and look up the answers to these questions.

Right and wrong is easy. Not at all easy to *do*, but easy as pie to figure out!

In the Garden of Eden, God declared that after eating from the Tree of the Knowledge of Good and Evil, Adam and Eve were now like Him in the sense of knowing right and wrong. Knowing right and wrong is part of the "fruit," if you will, of The Fall. We now have the *responsibility* of making right choices, and guess what? We don't. All have sinned and fall short of the glory of God. Nobody chooses right. It's not that we're ignorant, it's that we're _rebellious_. Our consciences should protect us from our boneheaded decisions, but instead they only rag on us after we flame out and bomb in our behavior. If we don't know the Mosaic Laws, it doesn't let us off the hook for our sins, because God's laws are part of our inner code—in our consciences. We know right. We do wrong.

Tabula Rasa is a lie; there's no such thing as being born with a clean slate. We don't reach the age of one without ignoring our conscience about something. "Warped" comes as close as anything to describing our native state.

Sorry, I guess. Especially if you're a humanist! Get a better cosmology, pal.

5 witness of creation
ever been overwhelmed by the wonder of the world?

"The heavens declare the glory of God; the skies proclaim the work of his hands. Day after day they pour forth speech; night after night they display knowledge. There is no speech or language where their voice is not heard. Their voice goes out into all the earth, their words to the ends of the world."
Psalms 19:1-4

Creation just *preaches*. Wherever you look, everything that has been fashioned by the hand of God declares the glory of it's Maker and Master. Ever studied how our eyes process light and distance and movement? How they recognize familiar features? How they focus near and far without conscious effort on our part? How the stereo imaging they're capable of keeps us from ricocheting off walls? Even the spiritually confused Charles Darwin looked at the eye and saw a major problem with proposing an accidental solution to the problem of the origin of species. And the eye is easy. Don't get me started on how our throats know to send air to the lungs but food to the stomach as they come down the same chute.

In many ways, we're at a disadvantage in our age of computer screens, movie screens, TV screens and hand-held-device screens. Why would I say that? *Because we spend our time in front of secondhand information.* Much of what reaches our perception is already hearsay. We don't smell the strong aroma of wet dirt, don't see the distant grey blue of the hills, don't hear the brave song of the house wren, don't marvel at the myriad starry points of fierce light in the night sky. We're cut off from creation which sings a continual song of it's Creator.

There's no surer way of feeling like big stuff than frying a planet-load of virtual space aliens with a joy stick and a down-arrow key. And there's no better way to get a real read on how small and fragile we are than to sit on your back porch and watch a thunderstorm sweep in over the neighborhood. We need to get away from a backlit screen and sit quietly watching a backlit sky.

Naturalism is the belief that there is no Creator, that this nebulous force/concept of "nature" produced the cosmos and everything in it by accidentally using just the laws of science. The naturalist is widely respected in our society, so much so that to gainsay a naturalist means that you must be anti-science! Don't get me started on that one. So which will it be, believe your own lyin' eyes that tell you the universe was created by God, or the textbook in which the naturalist explains that everything came about naturally by mere natural accidents in an infinite natural universe? Careful. You don't want to be called anti-science, do you?

We place a ton of confidence in scientific truth in our society, which is fine up to a point, but then we badly misplace that same confidence in the scientists themselves. When a scientist claims the Bible can't be true because of something they discovered, before we do anything else, we should consider the possibility that the scientist is wrong. After all, a scientist is a human being with grant money to apply for, a party line to toe, an agenda to defend and a distinct bias brought on by long study in atheistic higher education. And the Bible? Well … it's *the Bible*.

Take evolution: an example of a scientific theory. Where's the data set? What are the assumptions necessary to fill in that data set? What is the rationale for making those assumptions? Is the theory of evolution proven? Is it even provable? What would it take to prove it? Can it be replicated? Falsified? Can it accurately predict a future event? Is evolution science or is it philosophy?

There's a tendency in our society to categorize the Bible as faith and to categorize scientific theory as fact. The reality is quite the opposite. We can more reliably count on the findings of the Bible than on the theories of macroevolution, man made global warming or cooling, alchemy, phlogiston, spontaneous generation, the four humors, vitalism and atomic particles known as gluons. In case you missed some of those things, they used to be the "facts" of science. They really did.

If a space alien experienced both witch doctors and naturalistic scientists, they might conclude that there's no *practical* difference. Both receive blind acceptance by their respective hangers-on and both achieve their "results" in ways none of the rest of us can follow. Naturalistic scientists don't deserve more (or less) respect than any other profession deserves. As sentient beings, we ought to apply our own tests as we assess the witness of the universe around us. Creation preaches to us in plain and inarguable sermons of the greatness and glory of God.

Watery tissue inside our skulls can receive stereoscopic sensory input from sounds, light and smells, process those signals, and determine such things as how good supper will be, whether or not a camera will require a flash, and how close an oncoming wall is to our face. Other tissue within our skulls can control the production of cells in our bodies, tell our teeth when to chew and when to open for certain vowel sounds while singing, cause our heart valve muscles to involuntarily pump blood through our bodies, and get our lungs to hold our breath behind a smelly tractor trailer on the highway. Still other tissues within our skulls can help us balance when we're standing up, understand abstract concepts like calculus and maps, and not only think something's humorous but instruct the abdominal walls of the trunk of our bodies to contract rhythmically in laughter. Tissue inside our skulls can remember, imagine, love, and solve complex problems. We've just begun to describe some of the phenomenal things skull tissue does, and yet, if you separate the skull tissue from what we simplistically call life, none of the functions can continue. Our Creator somehow animates the tissues in our skulls to do all these spectacular things. Skull tissue does skull-tissue-bending things.

We get so excited when our cell phone can react half intelligently to a clear vocal command. Did the cell phone get this ability from sun rays? From rocks in hot water? From exploding gas over eons of time? No? *Then why think skull tissue did?!*

Creation screams, "God made me! I am purposeful, beautiful and meaningful! I have the signature of my Maker! Pay attention and give the Creator great praise!" Creation makes a fool of a naturalist without really trying.

6 natural law
why does everyone seem to know certain things?

"FOR SINCE THE CREATION OF THE WORLD, GOD'S INVISIBLE QUALITIES: HIS ETERNAL POWER AND DIVINE NATURE, HAVE BEEN CLEARLY SEEN, BEING UNDERSTOOD FROM WHAT HAS BEEN MADE, SO THAT MEN ARE WITHOUT EXCUSE."
ROMANS 1:20

"Natural law" is not the law that governs nature, but *the laws mankind naturally ought to know and obey.* The dictionary defines natural law this way: a body of unchanging moral principles regarded as a basis for all human conduct. The Constitution of the United States plainly invokes "the laws of nature and of nature's God" as justification for the action taken by the British colonies in the Revolutionary War. There were no *national* laws that applied to a collection of colonies rejecting the rule of a mother country. Therefore, the writers of the Constitution appealed to a *universal* law acknowledged by all of mankind: natural law that comes from God.

As a corollary, those that blather on about "separation of church and state" must not realize that there would be no "state" if the framers did not appeal to natural law which proceeds from God Himself as the trump card over all other law. Natural law is the only universally recognized morality.

Natural law is self-evident and produces such "self-evident" truths as this: all men are created equal. By the very nature of our making, we are all God's creatures, equal in His sight and equally protected and constrained by the laws of nature and nature's God. The Constitution goes on to say that each of God's created people are endowed by their Creator with certain inalienable rights such as life, liberty, and the pursuit of happiness. These are rights that are immoral for a society to deny its citizens. A contract (such as citizenship) can abridge natural law and a person can sign away their commonwealth rights for a consideration, but this is not natural law. The new contract may circumscribe a new set of agreed behaviors, but these would not be *rights* under natural law, rights that are self-evident, rights that come straight from God. Rights not found under natural law include welfare, healthcare, gay marriage, abortion, a minimum wage, the Great Society and so on. These are the constructs of people determining how they will co-exist, not natural law.

The interesting thing about natural law is that people acknowledge it who do not live by it. When people are caught stealing, they never say it's okay to steal; they always explain why their particular case is the *exception*. They do not challenge natural law; instead, they rationalize why, in this special case, natural law does not apply. That in itself is a tacit admission of the jurisdiction and universality of the intrinsic morality of natural law.

No one taught societies this morality. It's understood, self-evident, inarguable. Oddly, these laws, while universally acknowledged, aren't universally *followed*. This is a fascinating conundrum. We all know what to do, whether or not we in fact do it. Cultures from around the world and throughout time have valued the same virtues and frowned upon the same transgressions. It's as if our individual consciences extended into society around us.

That's why Madeline Murray O'Hare in the 1960s was so successful in her diabolical takedown of prayer and the Ten Commandments in public: America was tired of being reminded that we do not abide by God's natural law. We now have people scream, "Separation of church and state!" when what they are really saying is, "God can't tell *ME* what to do, only the government!" But we can't just brush God off or make Him go away. He's a little too large. A little too in charge.

Here's the truth: everybody knows God has *lawful demands* of our behavior. Natural law is the universal morality that every society in every age has intrinsically known to be in force: marriage between man and woman, protection of the young, rights of private property, the right of standing before one's accuser to refute the accusation, honoring the elderly, telling the truth, not taking innocent life, doing what you say you'll do, being willing to fight to protect your family and your neighbors and your country from enemies, and so forth. There has not been a healthy and intrinsically good society where precepts such as these were not held virtuous and naturally expected of all people in that society.

Natural law proves the existence and goodness of The Natural Lawgiver.

7 miracles
doesn't God know He can't violate laws of science?

"JESUS DID MANY OTHER MIRACULOUS SIGNS . . . WHICH ARE NOT RECORDED IN THIS BOOK. BUT THESE ARE WRITTEN THAT YOU MAY BELIEVE THAT JESUS IS THE CHRIST, THE SON OF GOD, AND THAT BY BELIEVING YOU MAY HAVE LIFE IN HIS NAME."
JOHN 20:30-31

Jesus did miracles for a specific reason—so that a stubborn and stiff-necked people would know that *He is God*. Brokenness to wholeness. Water to wine. Sickness to health. Tormented to sane. Tempest to mirror calm. Lunchbox to banquet.

I've heard it said that the reason primitive people believe in miracles is because they don't understand science like we do today. Just stop it! There's never been anyone who thinks you can be born of a virgin. Nobody has ever thought you could step on the surface of a lake and walk unless it's frozen. And nobody has ever believed that it's natural to rise from the dead and be able to walk through walls and travel at the speed of thought.

But there *are* people all around us who sincerely believe that the universe came about from exploding hydrogen gas and life arose from rocks in hot water over time! These are the people who don't understand science! These are the people who believe in the wildly miraculous while mocking others for doing so. "Primitive" people would find them extremely amusing.

Some people can hear the gospel and just believe. Others want God to perform a miracle before they'll listen. A miracle is NOT a natural process we don't yet understand. *It's a contradiction to a natural process we know very well.* It's not a miracle for a match to light, or for a plane to fly, as amazing as those are. But it *would* be a miracle for a brilliant shining star to remain in place over a stable in Bethlehem Ephrathah and guide three wealthy and wise amateur astronomers from Arabia to the birthplace of a Baby who turns out to be the King of kings.

We can't chalk up the miracles in the Bible as being mass delusions or misunderstandings of ordinary processes we understand today. The Bible describes events that no one in their right mind would claim or believe ... unless they actually happened ... which they did!

Enoch really *did* go straight to heaven without dying. Noah really *did* survive the destruction of the antediluvian world in a wooden boat God told him how to build. The Red Sea really *did* part to let the Israelites walk through on dry ground and came back together to drown the Egyptian army. The walls of Jericho really *did* fall. Joshua really *did* stop the sun in the sky. The Assyrian king Sennacherib really *did* attack Jerusalem and woke up to find 185,000 of his soldiers had died in their sleep.

Elijah really *did* stop the rain for three years and really *did* call fire down from heaven. Isaiah and Ezekiel really *did* see God on His heavenly throne and angels covered with eyes and flying with gyroscopes.

The disciples really *did* watch Jesus heal crowds of sick, blind, crippled and demon-possessed people and raise Lazarus to life after three days of being dead and decaying in a tomb. They also talked and touched Jesus for 40 days after they saw Him dead and buried—neither ghost nor zombie—but so full of life that He rose up to heaven one day as they were watching Him. Miraculous indeed! It doesn't matter how much you know or don't know, miracles still happen.

God is in the miracle business. It's nothing for Him to make time go forwards or backwards, to cause damaged cells to be repaired in the blink of an eye or for the stars of heaven to flame out and fall to earth. God works miracles with both His hands tied behind His back.

Miracles insult and invade our complacent and cynical sensibility. They bear unmistakable witness to our miracle-working God who made the inviolable rules of the universe and then, at His whim and fancy, stomps gloriously all over them.

Speaking of miracles, have you heard of the Scriptures?

• THE SCRIPTURES

where do we find truth in black and white?

"THEN WE WILL NO LONGER BE INFANTS, TOSSED BACK AND FORTH BY THE WAVES, AND BLOWN HERE AND THERE BY EVERY WIND OF TEACHING AND BY THE CUNNING AND CRAFTINESS OF MEN IN THEIR DECEITFUL SCHEMING. INSTEAD . . . WE WILL IN ALL THINGS GROW UP INTO HIM WHO IS THE HEAD, THAT IS, CHRIST."
EPHESIANS 4:14-15

There is truth that cannot be trumped. Transcendent truth. Ultimate truth. Unchanging, reliable, stable truth that doesn't bend and sway with the winds of passing fads. That truth is found in the Bible. What the Bible says is absolutely right for Adam, for Moses, for St. Peter, and for you and me. On the truth meter, the Bible not only pegs, it breaks the needle off and keeps going around.

Why do we say that the Bible is authoritative? Because Psalms 138:2 says, **"You have exalted above all things your Name and your Word."** In John 10:35, Jesus proclaims: **"Scripture cannot be broken."** Saying, *"It is written,"* Jesus quotes Scripture continually to crowds, to His disciples, and to the Scribes and Pharisees. He employs it to triumph over the temptations of Satan. Jesus equips His own army with the Scriptures in Ephesians 6 by giving them *"the sword of the Spirit, which is the word of God."* Jesus seems to think the Bible is uniquely, powerfully true.

Charles Spurgeon, that great preacher, said that the Bible is like a lion. You don't have to defend a lion, just let him out and he'll defend himself. That's another way of saying that Bible truth is *self-validating, self-supporting, self-authenticating*. We recognize the truth when we hear it because truth reverberates deep inside. It has a familiar ring to it, even if we've never read it before. Biblical truth is indomitable, relentless, unstoppable.

For example, secular humanists tell us we're born as innocent as little lambs—that human beings are basically good. That's just not true. Not to be harsh but . . . *it's a lie*. The Bible, in marked contrast, says that we're all morally bankrupt from birth and that we came into this world ready to make our own rebellious choices. That's the unvarnished truth. Even if we may not want to believe it, the Bible turns on a light deep inside us, and the Holy Spirit verifies it as only He can. When we hear biblical truth, no one needs to tell us it's right. *We already know it's true.*

Hey! Question. If we don't rely on the Bible to provide truth, what's our next option? Trust our own brilliant intellect? Rely on someone else? Listen to the fantastically beautiful people who make ads and movies or the insanely cool singers who perform our favorite music? Believe the politicians? Our friends? Trees? Pets? Dice? Tea leaves? Horoscopes? Modern science? Ancient mystics? Where exactly would we look to find authority?

Truth is found in the Bible like it's found nowhere else. Second only to Jesus Himself in unveiling the glory of God, the Bible is an inspired source of wisdom and revelation truth unmatched in all the world around us. It's the best selling book of all time with no close second. It's the most translated, most quoted, most read, most influential, most beloved of all books ever read.

Why would that be if it's just another collection of stories? Why would our American system of jurisprudence be based on it? Why is our western culture saturated by it? Why are the walls of our buildings carved with it? Why would modern U.S. presidents want to be seen on camera carrying it into church? Why do preachers preach from it? Why do people take oaths while resting their hands on it? Why would people give their lives so that others could have it in their own language and read and believe it? Why would we quote and memorize and honor this book above all others? Why would God so miraculously preserve it for us?

Why indeed. Do we usually leave our birthday presents unopened?

1 apostles
how big an army does it take to conquer the world?

"THEY DEVOTED THEMSELVES TO THE APOSTLES' TEACHING."
ACTS 2:42A

Why would the early church "devote" themselves to what Peter and James and other apostles were saying? They must have been serious about the letters we find preserved in the New Testament. Didn't those guys know that doctrinal study is only for salaried professional Christians? Wouldn't their time have been better used producing after-school programs and feeding the hungry? And isn't the word "devoted" a little heavy handed? We should check with the original Greek wording there. The translation surely has to be something more like "they intended to listen to the apostles' teaching, but they found it was really hard with all the other things they had to do, and anyway that was the job of their pastor." I'm not sure why Acts 2:42 is even in my Bible. *Just kidding!*

Actually, I'm not wondering at all. It's there for a transparent purpose: we also should "devote" ourselves to the apostles' teaching. Often in the Bible, the word devote connotes an irreversible giving over of a life as an act of worship. For us today, the apostles' teachings are preserved in the New Testament scriptures. And the apostles continually quoted from the Old Testament. (Check the references in the center column or at the bottom of the page in your Bible!)

Think about what Jesus did: He sent us firsthand instructions through His apostles. Because Jesus selected, trained, and commissioned the apostles, it's that very *apostolic authority* we look for in determining what is and what isn't orthodox scripture. These apostles were men whose qualifications for office we'll never know. The paperwork is missing, probably because they never actually applied for the job. The fact remains that they lived and ate and slept and laughed and cried with Jesus for all three years of His earthly ministry.

The eleven faithful apostles and the apostle Paul were dispersed throughout the nations to inaugurate the Great Commission, going into all the world and making disciples, baptizing in God's name, and teaching obedience to everything Jesus said. Then according to eyewitness accounts, 10 of the original 12 plus the apostle Paul died horrible deaths in carrying out this calling. The book of Acts records the death of the apostle James—"put to the sword" by King Herod.

According to church tradition, the others were stabbed to death, hurled from the top of buildings, boiled in oil, beaten to death with clubs and whips, tortured and crucified. Not one of them recanted the gospel. Not one of them said, "Hold it. It's not true. We just made it up. No sense in being *tortured* for a myth we invented! I take it all back. Remove me from your list of people who call themselves followers of Jesus of Nazareth." No sir. Each one of them braved the worst that wicked men could dish out with their firm conviction that Jesus is who He personally told them He was, who He continually demonstrated Himself to be; whose teachings *are* worth living for and in the case of the Apostles, worth dying for too.

The New Testament is a collection of books and letters, gathered into one volume. How did we know which books or letters had the divine mark on them? It boils down to a single question: Is the book unquestionably of apostolic origin? To be canonized, the early writings had to be authentically associated with an apostle somehow, some way. No book that was not clearly connected with one of Jesus' disciples was considered for inclusion in the New Testament canon.

The instructions of the apostles are the teachings we call "doctrines," and these doctrines are what give us the direction we need to grow and become increasingly more useful to Jesus for His Kingdom work. If it's in the New Testament, we can confidently say that it's in the teaching of *the apostles*, who learned it straight from Jesus. Even Paul who never met Jesus during His earthly ministry, still learned His doctrine by direct revelation from our Lord. Read Galatians 1:12. Nothing is supposition or hearsay. We learn what Jesus said from the people to whom Jesus spoke, and we learn what Jesus did from the people who were there and saw it happen.

This is pretty basic stuff, but I didn't know it until recently. Oh, *you* did? Well if you're so smart, which apostle wrote Hebrews? What's the recipe for manna? What was Mrs. Noah's first name?

So you don't know *everything*. Your shoelace is untied.

2 doctrine

what are the fundamentals of our faith in Christ?

"YOU MUST TEACH WHAT IS IN ACCORD WITH SOUND DOCTRINE."
TITUS 2:1

First, *doctrine is not just for theologians*, although theologians use it constantly. They use it as shorthand to keep from having even longer conversations than they do already. They can simply say, "When you boil it down, it's a kind of sovereignty/theophany thing," and they know exactly what they're talking about. "Covenant" is a doctrine they not only understand in English, but in Hebrew, Greek, Aramaic and Arabic. Still, doctrine is not the sole property of the scholarly.

For us, doctrine is not shorthand, but a kind of conversation starter. If you heard someone utter a phrase such as, *"That book has a quasi-millennial pneumatological supralapsarianist slant to it,"* you and I would want them to explain. We don't use doctrine as shorthand, but rather as a doorway into discussions about the things of God. We use it as a file folder in which to gather our ideas about who God is and how He works. ("That's very *covenantal*.") We use it as identification. ("I'm kind of *Arminian* on that one.") And we use it to pick up very large ideas with a single word. ("We are a *fallen* people.") Doctrinal study is not only useful in our conversation, it's requisite for our spiritual growth. If you found someone who was using their computer for nothing more than to crack walnuts, you might tell them to read the manual a little more carefully.

Second, *doctrine is not denominational*, although denominations use it to beat each other up. Pre this, post that, sprinkle, dunk, wine, grape juice, transubstantiation, purgatory, baptism of the Holy Spirit, tongues, liturgy, freedom, instruments, no instruments, women in ministry, hats in the sanctuary —the church has argued doctrine through the ages, and as a result, we're denominationalized to the max. Correct doctrine is important, with no caveat. But it should never be weaponized for use on Jesus' family.

All of our denominations are fine if they're no more than flavors of the one faith (Ephesians 4:5-6: ***"One Lord, one faith, one baptism; one God and Father of all"***). But we should know better than to set ourselves up as the sole arbiters of doctrinal correctness. Paul said in Romans 14 that the stronger ones in the faith should not exercise their theological freedom in such a way as to hurt those who are weaker. In other words, our doctrine should never bind us. *We can be free within our own constricting doctrine*, and that freedom includes the liberty to give grace to other's doctrine.

Third, doctrine is not esoteric, although esoterics—wait a minute, I've got no idea where I was going with that. Trying to make three points like a real preacher I guess. Never mind esoterics. We don't care about them anyway. Just remember that doctrine is *not* the sole property of theologians or of any of our myriad denominations. Don Finto says, "No church has the ball."

So that's a little of what doctrine is NOT. Here's what doctrine *is*. It's a way to pick up large helpings of scriptural truth with a word or a few words. It's a condensation of a lot of nuanced and complex information about God, just as a gallon of maple syrup comes from 50 gallons of maple sap. Doctrine is a doorknob: easily grasped, yet it opens the way to a much larger and mysterious reality behind the door. Doctrine is what every sermon and Sunday school lesson really ought to be about. Doctrine is the ABCs and the multiplication tables of Christianity. Doctrine is a security check on all ideas. Doctrine is a flashlight in a dark forest of seeming contradictions. Doctrine is a Sherpa guide through the high mountain passes of God's thoughts.

So what about *sound* doctrine? Sound doctrine is doctrine that passes muster with the Holy Spirit. If I say God wants His people to drive fuel efficient cars, you can guess this is *not* coming from the Holy Spirit. What about if I say that it's okay to get drunk on Saturday nights as long as you're safe in church Sunday morning? No sale? Good for you. If I say God has an undyingly unique love for His people the Jews and you say that's sound doctrine, you're right. What if I say we've got to rebuild the Temple in Jerusalem and reinstitute the sacrifices prescribed by Mosaic Law? I hope that you'd tell me this is lousy doctrine, since Jesus' sacrifice on the cross cancels any need for further temple sacrifice. Now the redeemed children of God have become His dwelling place.

Sound doctrine is hard to define, like the flavor of a banana. But you know it when you run into it. It's doctrine that has the stamp of God's approval, witnessed in our hearts, testified by centuries of practice and teaching within the family of God. *We bring it to mind, and remind each other of it whenever we can.* For 2,000 years, the family of God has been reminding each other of the Trinity, the creation, The Fall, The Flood, the inspiration and revelation of Scripture, the Law of Moses and the Law of the Spirit of life in Christ, blood atonement, the cross and the empty tomb, the return of the King, and the renewal of all things—reminding each other of the gospel truth couched in sound doctrine.

Bypassing the serious study of doctrine is easy: just completely ignore your Bible!

3 scripture
why would God have this stuff written down?

"NOW TO HIM WHO IS ABLE TO ESTABLISH YOU BY MY GOSPEL AND THE PROCLAMATION OF JESUS CHRIST, ACCORDING TO THE REVELATION OF THE MYSTERY HIDDEN FOR LONG AGES PAST, BUT NOW REVEALED AND MADE KNOWN THROUGH THE PROPHETIC WRITINGS . . ."
ROMANS 16:25-26

The word Scripture means "the writings." God spoke to people and they wrote it down. And ever since, God's people have used the Scriptures when they talk truth with each other. Hey, the writers of the *New* Testament constantly, and I mean *constantly*, cite the *Old* Testament! The Apostle Paul loved it when people checked his preaching out with the Old Testament scriptures, as the Bereans did in Acts 17:11.

When Jesus announced the start of His ministry, He quoted from Isaiah where the writer prophesies, **"The Spirit of the LORD is upon me."** In dialog with His opponents, Jesus used the Scriptures to baffle and antagonize as well as to pose thorny questions and provide thoughtful answers. The Pharisees and Sadducees wondered where He got His extensive knowledge of the Bible, not realizing that He had personally dictated the whole thing in the first place!

Can we take the Bible literally? Stop it. Yes, of course. But what about the metaphorical language? Oh, I see the problem: we think that metaphors are a misdirection, a fake-out. But the Bible uses metaphors as place holders for ideas too big for us to grasp. We metaphorically call Jesus the Good Shepherd. We don't mean He's a smelly man in a bathrobe who stays out all night with a herd of sheep. That kind of shepherd is an illustration of Jesus. But calling Jesus a shepherd doesn't imply He's NOT a shepherd either. The pictorial language stands for a reality that is *more* true, not less.

For instance, the fact that Genesis 1 uses metaphor doesn't mean it's merely a bedtime story, or, as some say, that evolution is the science while Genesis is the context. Good grief. Metaphors in the Bible are accurate descriptors of realities too big to fit into language. Did God *literally* create the earth. Yes! Did He *literally* do it in six days? Well, there's a reality beyond our understanding, but that doesn't invalidate the truth of six days, rather, it augments it. The use of metaphor does not signal a half truth in the Bible, but a truth on an even grander scale. Not sure I got that point across. You may have to ask God to explain this one—I tried!

We've all heard people say this stuff: "There are a million interpretations. You can make the Bible say anything you want. Some of the worst atrocities in history have been committed in the name of the Bible." Blah blah. Yada yada. Some just don't like biblical authority. But sincere people also say these things, so to them we have four replies.

One. There are many interpretations of Scripture, but the major doctrines aren't up for grabs. The Bible is the all-time champion of clarity because of the Holy Spirit helping the writers write and the readers read.

Two. You can't make the Bible say *anything you want* unless you're willing to be intellectually dishonest. The Bible *doesn't* say that human sexuality is evolving. It *doesn't* say that it's okay to kill unborn babies. It *doesn't* say that Christians are perfectly behaved. It *doesn't* say that God let's people into heaven if they're good. People accuse the Bible of saying stuff that it just doesn't. That's not the Bible's fault, is it?

Three. Atrocities are committed using whatever excuses people can grab, including the Bible. The wheel has enabled innumerable atrocities. Shall we get rid of the wheel?

Four. People who claim the Bible can't be clearly understood haven't approached it with a humble, teachable heart! We first ask the Holy Spirit to reveal truth. THEN we read.

Our Bible is traditionally subdivided like this. Genesis through Deuteronomy make up "**The Law**" or the Pentateuch, written by Moses. Joshua through Lamentations make up "**The Writings**" and include philosophy, poetry and history of the Jews.

Isaiah through Malachi make up "**The Prophets**" including both prophecy and history. Matthew through John make up "**The Gospels**" which present eyewitness accounts of Jesus' 33-year earthly ministry. "**The Acts of the Apostles**" is the authorized chronicle of the early church. Romans through Jude are "**The Epistles**" (which are NOT the wives of the Apostles), the letters of the apostolic leaders of the early church. Finally, "**The Revelation**" is an apocalyptic vision given to the Apostle John.

In the Bible, the mind of God is revealed, at least all we can begin to grasp with the brains we've got now. Apparently, what's in the 66 books of the Bible is all we need to know to make it victoriously through this world and into the world to come. No wonder Christians through the ages have uniquely treasured the Bible. No wonder our churches build their foundation upon the Bible alone. "Sola Scriptura," the exclusive reliance on biblical authority, was both Luther's and Calvin's point of no compromise!

God reveals truth in many ways, but the Bible gives us a unique benchmark from which to calculate the veracity of all other revelations.

4 canon
who gave which writings the right to be right?

"[JESUS] WAS TAKEN UP TO HEAVEN, AFTER GIVING INSTRUCTIONS THROUGH THE HOLY SPIRIT TO THE APOSTLES . . ."
ACTS 1:2B

The Bible is the standard measurement of truth. What about if something comes along that contradicts the Bible, something exciting and new? I'll tell you what happens in that case: believe your Bible. How simple is that!

Say I want to build a house and you're going to help, along with some of our friends. We have a blueprint, but we don't all agree on what we mean by an inch or a foot. When you bring me your 2" by 4", it's shorter than everyone else's. When someone else bring me a 6" pipe, it's way too big to fit. Without agreement on measurements, we're sunk, defeated before we start. When we finish the house, it looks like a Picasso painting of a nightmare. In order for us to have a prayer of building a functional house, standardized measurements are imperative. Close enough is *not* close enough.

So it is with truth. If we are going to establish what is unquestioned, we need some standardized book that contains reliable measurements. The church fathers long ago determined that the books in your Bible are the ones God meant to be there.

Canon, with one *n* in the middle, means "ruler" or "measuring stick." The canon is the standard by which the books of the Bible were measured for inclusion and all others for exclusion. The Old Testament canon was essentially set by the time Jesus was quoting it in His teachings. Merely the fact that our Savior used the Old Testament canon and treated it as authoritative should be enough of a recommendation. But there's no doubt that from earliest times, the apostles regarded the majority of the Old Testament canon as beyond dispute. The Christian church began with a set of recognized, standardized, authoritative books of the Old Testament.

This is not to say that there aren't a few discrepancies. Apocryphal books accepted by the Catholic canon are not included in the Protestant canon. There are three major versions of the Old Testament we have: the Hebrew Bible, the Greek Septuagint (reputed to have been done by 70 scholars, hence the *"sept"* part), and the Latin Vulgate (*"vulgus,"* for the "common" man). These are not identical in their selection of canonical books. Make of that what you will, but know that the overwhelming majority of the Old Testament canon is absolutely agreed on.

Hey, if you want to get touchy about it, Jude quotes the archangel Michael and the patriarch Enoch from unknown source books, which may be one of the reasons it took so long for the church to recognize Jude as canonical himself, even though Jude is the brother of both James and Jesus! Any controversy is comparatively minor.

Ephesians 2:20 says the church is founded on the Apostolic teachings. Those teachings were preserved in letters and accounts that were written or orally passed on by those who had been with Jesus. Other writings had infiltrated the church and were making the rounds, claiming to be the real deal. If you're going to die for a letter or a book, wouldn't it be nice to know that it was authentic Scripture from God and not some half-baked correspondence from a pretender? So the church fathers came up with the New Testament canon—those books that bore the mark of apostolic authority. Acts 4:13 records this unique and defining characteristic of the Apostles: ***"They took note that these men had been with Jesus."***

The first listing of the New Testament canon was in the early part of the second century AD, including the four gospels and much of the rest of the New Testament. Hebrews, Jude, James, Revelation and some of the shorter epistles took longer to be acknowledged beyond doubt. The final canon was established and it was in general acceptance by the end of the fourth century. That's a lot of information. The thing to remember is that to be included in the New Testament, a book had to be sourced to an apostle.

They just . . . *smell* right. There's an unmistakable aroma about them. They hold together miraculously, with shockingly few apparent contradictions (we say "apparent" because contradictions in the Bible appear exactly where our understanding disappears). Our Bible is made up of 66 books and not one of them is a stinker.

Well, maybe Song of Solomon. Just kidding. That book does kind of creep me out though. I can just see the letters coming in to the editor.

5 authority
where do you go to get your truth?

"THE GRASS WITHERS, THE FLOWER FADES; BUT THE WORD OF OUR GOD SHALL STAND FOREVER."
ISAIAH 40:8

The Bible tells us authoritatively what's happening in heaven, why there's such a place as hell and who has to go there, what a seraphim is and what it's capabilities are, how to worship God the way He requires, what to do about money we have or don't have, how to deal with friends and enemies, how to pray and get results, who the devil used to be and what he's been doing lately, why bad things happen to good people, what to do when you're sick or sad, why a tiny city like Jerusalem is the center of the universe, what will happen at the end of time, who gets to return with Jesus when He comes in power and glory to make everything in the world right again and … oh, you get the idea.

The doctrine of biblical authority has two challengers. Some *outside* the faith say the Bible is just another book, and it's packed with contradictions. And some *inside* the faith believe the Bible is not the *only* standard of truth, but that the pronouncements of the church fathers are also authoritative. We'd better look at both of these bumps in the road.

Let's deal with those within the faith first. The Bible is universally accepted as authoritative within the Christian faith, but for some, the Bible is not the *sole* authority—for instance, with the Catholic wing of the family of God. For a Catholic, the Pope has a big say in what we should consider authoritative. I have no doubt that the Pope is a God-fearing man, unique and set apart, and yet I cannot quite give him the allegiance I save for the Bible. Call me crazy!

Others within the church have said the early church didn't have Bible,s so obviously they had to rely on oral tradition. Wrong. The early church may not have had the New Testament canon until the fourth century, but that doesn't mean they didn't have the Bible. The early church considered the Old Testament the authoritative Word of God and as such read from it in their meetings along with the letters from the apostles that were copied and passed around. As the apostles and those who knew them died, God preserved the Old and New Testaments together for those like us who would come to faith in Christ later.

Now as for those outside the faith who trivialize the Bible, I admit that I used to be one of them. The simplest explanation for my change of heart is that before I was born again the Bible was a letter that was written to someone else, and now that I'm a child of God, it's a letter written to me. Now I "get" the Bible.

But perhaps some outside the faith don't even *want* to understand the Bible. They doubt the authority of anything outside themselves. To the one who says there's no right and wrong, I ask, "How do you know if you're right about there being no wrong?" To the one who says there are no absolutes, I ask, "Oh? Absolutely?" To the one who says there's no ultimate authority, I ask, "Oh yeah? By what ultimate authority do you say that?" I hope you're appreciating the irony dripping from this paragraph.

If we refuse to rely on Scripture for truth, then what WILL we turn to? New ideas simply because they're not the old ones? Our feelings that go up and down constantly? Our own brilliance, proven by the way everyone can't wait to hear what we have to say? Maybe our pop culture icons, those beautiful buffoons? Horoscopes we could write ourselves with equal accuracy? Science that changes every few years? Clever academics who make stupid wild guesses? What's our source of absolute truth if not the Scriptures? If not the Bible, then what?

The thing is, the Bible is reliable, trustworthy, dependable and supreme truth in one handy book. It speaks with a ring of authority to every corner of our lives. If the Bible is not our authority on truth, we are treading water in a sea of unreliable opinions and will, at some point, sink.

6 inspiration
didn't imperfect men write the Bible?

"YOU MUST UNDERSTAND THAT NO PROPHECY OF SCRIPTURE CAME ABOUT BY THE PROPHET'S OWN INTERPRETATION. FOR PROPHECY NEVER HAD ITS ORIGIN IN THE WILL OF MAN, BUT MEN SPOKE FROM GOD AS THEY WERE CARRIED ALONG BY THE HOLY SPIRIT."
2 PETER 1:20-21

When we say the Bible is inspired, we mean that it comes straight from the Spirit of God. *Inspire, conspire, perspire, respire* and *spirit* all have the same root that means "breath" or "breathed." God breathed life into Adam who became a living soul. He breathed truth into the Scriptures and they became life-giving sustenance for our spirits. We use the word "inspired" sometimes to mean that someone has produced something so great God must have directed it. Well? The Bible is all that and more. Papered. Pedigreed. Passed down from on high. The Bible is a record of the very words of God, straight from His heart and mind.

The Bible is doubly inspired, for not only did God breathe the Scriptures to the ones who wrote them, but He can breathe the Scriptures *again* to us as we read them. We're able to hear what God is saying to us today in the words He inspired thousands of years ago. The same one who initially spoke the original words in the hearts of the writers now speaks them once more in our hearts as we open the book (the very hardest thing to do) and read (the next hardest thing).

This is why we pray before we begin to study the Bible. We ask God to reveal again to us today that which He first revealed to those long ago. Of course He promises to do just that. In Matthew 7:7, Jesus says that if we ask and keep on asking, it will be given; if we knock and keep on knocking, the door will be opened; if we seek and keep on seeking, we will find. In John 16:13, Jesus tells His disciples that He's going to send the Holy Spirit who will guide them into all truth.

1 John 2:27 says, ***"As for you, the anointing you received from him remains in you, and you do not need anyone to teach you."*** John tells the believers that they have an *anointing* from God that teaches them what the Bible is saying. Strange? Not so much. That anointing is simply the presence of the Holy Spirit. In the Old Testament, the anointing was embodied by pouring olive oil on the recipient's head. However, the Old Testament anointing was unique and transitory, given for a specific purpose and then the anointing lifted.

Attention! Something has changed and here it is: now under the New Covenant, the anointing does not lift and is not transitory. It *remains*, as the scripture above tells us! When we pick up a Bible to read and hear from God, we don't have to be recommissioned with another pouring of anointing oil and another solemn ceremony. The Holy Spirit is right where He was the last tim—living in God's children. Living in you and in me.

That's why those who say the Bible is only a history book are flat-out wrong. The Bible resembles a history book in the same way a sweaty, worked-up, terrifying, armed-to-the-teeth-and-fighting-mad in the flesh pirate resembles a cardboard storybook about pirates. When we hold a Bible in our hands, we're holding the real living, breathing thing—a modern day miracle. The very words breathed by God, passed down through the millennia by the diligence of the faithful and the purposes of Him who breathed those words to begin with.

Imagine having all the knowledge of the universe crammed into a book you can slip into your pocket or download to your phone. Imagine having the very wisest of the wise men waiting for your call day or night. Imagine having the secrets of the ages ready for you anytime you feel like opening up the treasure chest that holds them.

Ever wanted to see the cheat sheet on a really tough test? In the test of our lives, the cheat sheet is the Bible, with all the answers that really matter written down for us, inspired by the great Teacher of the classroom of life. We have been given the answers to the great questions of life, questions like: who made this universe, why did He do it, where are we going, and what can it all mean?

If Genesis tells us Adam became alive when God breathed into him, His inspiration today can surely make the Scriptures alive to us.

7 inerrancy
isn't the Bible full of mistakes and contradictions?

"ALL SCRIPTURE IS GOD-BREATHED."
2 TIMOTHY 3:16

When we say the Bible is *inerrant*, with no mistakes, uninformed people say, well how about all the translations that disagree? They miss the meaning. By "inerrant," we mean *mistake free in the original manuscripts*. Our modern versions of the Bible can be widely dissimilar to each other. So what? Inerrant means the *writers* of the Bible got it right, not the translators. Yes?

Actually, we mean the Bible as originally written is more than just correct, it's *absolutely perfect*. Subsequent copies (transcripts) may have minor discrepancies, and none of those discrepancies affects a single major doctrine, but that doesn't change the inerrant nature of the Bible. It's error-free, faultless, flawless, matchless, incomparable, inimitable.

Obviously, Biblical inerrancy is a matter of faith, like the resurrection. But it's no more a leap of faith than trusting an abstract science like mathematics. Math is supported by underlying axioms which cannot be proven and must be taken on faith. Accept these axioms, and math "proves" itself. As mathematician Dr. A.G. Hamilton writes, "Mathematics is a mixture of intuition, analogy and logic." Interesting. Dr. Hamilton is telling us that mathematics, a precise and exact science, is supported by three abstract disciplines!

Do you see that even trusting in mathematics, that no-nonsense bedrock of so many other sciences, is like trusting in biblical inerrancy? It's a step of faith. Once accepted, it proves reliable. Inerrancy is axiomatic. *Unprovable*, but once accepted it becomes reliably dependable.

So. What are the axioms, the unprovable assumptions of Biblical inerrancy? There are at least three. First, God *can* reveal Himself. Second, God *wants to* reveal Himself. Third, God *has* revealed Himself in a way that we can understand in the Bible.

If those are all true, then the Bible is as dependably trustworthy as anything we know, and even more so because, given our axioms, the one who guarantees the Bible's reliability is God Himself. Those who say the Bible is full of error are really saying that God has miserably failed in His capability, His desire or His accomplishment. I wouldn't want to be the one saying that to God's face!

Some would say that the only way we know the Bible is absolutely true is because the Bible claims to be absolutely true and the Bible, being absolutely true, is absolutely true when it claims to be absolutely true. This is, of course, a tautology (cool word, huh?), and it's a problem. But it's not a difficult problem. I can't verify if a particular yellow road sign is accurate, even though it looks okay to me, but if I put my trust in it and it proves to be trustworthy, I begin to have faith that the other yellow road signs will prove true and act accordingly.

If someone you know to be free and loose with the truth tells you something, you take it with a grain of salt. But if someone with an unimpeachable reputation for veracity tells you something, you tend to trust it. We can't prove that the Bible is inerrant, it's a matter of faith, but if we put your weight down on the words of the Scriptures, we find that those words are dependable. The Bible has an unimpeachable reputation for truth telling, built over the millennia in the hearts of countless believers who have relied on it and found it completely trustworthy.

Like the wise man who built his house on a rock, we can build our lives on the Bible, and when the storms of life come, our lives will not collapse in ruin, but stand the test and endure.

The copies may be blurred, the translations may be a little out of focus, but the inerrancy of the original Scriptures is God's satisfaction-guarantee to those who approach the Bible with a humble, teachable heart. If we understood the doctrine of inerrancy, we'd trust our own opinions less and rely on God's opinions found in His Holy Word more.

• THE HOLY SPIRIT

how do we know that we know what we know?

"THE SPIRIT IS THE TRUTH."

I JOHN 5:6B

Jesus promised that He'd never leave us, Matthew 28:20. Not long after that, He left us. Surprise! He was taken up into heaven. He'll remain there until the end comes. So what gives? What's happened to His promise? He kept it, of course.

Jesus is with us now as the Holy Spirit, the Spirit of Truth. Jesus, limited by His human body, touched a limited number of people in His earthly ministry. The Holy Spirit can be with everyone, everywhere, all at the same time, all the time. Constantly, no matter where we go or what we do. He leads us into all truth according to John 16:13, and as the passage above says, He *is* Truth.

We don't discover truth because we're sincere or persistent or smart. Truth discovers *us* because Truth is hunting us down relentlessly. Truth is a train and we're tied to the track. We're in Truth's crosshairs. On Truth's hit list. Truth loves us and wants us to get to know Him.

And here's the greatest truth: the Spirit of Truth wants us to know that God made us in order that He could have a *relationship* with us. We'll never hear more astounding news. The Master of the Universe created us to share a wonderful friendship with Him. How do we know beyond doubt this is true? Because the Holy Spirit testifies in our hearts.

There are agnostics and skeptics who blather that nobody can KNOW anything. They try to convince themselves that skepticism is simply realism: to believe in the love of God is like believing in Santa Clause. They laugh at the naiveté of us poor shlubs who have taken a "blind leap" into Christianity. They call us weak-minded, delusional, childish, and impractical. We may be all that, but what about them? Talk about weak minded and all the rest. They've pushed away the truth they know instinctively, according to Romans 1:19: **"What may be known about God is plain to them, because God has made it plain to them."** You can close your eyes and say there's no sun, but you'll still get sunburned. Nobody denies God and lives to tell the tale.

The Holy Spirit's modus operandi is to reveal truth to humankind. That's simply what He does. Like a hound dog pointing to a raccoon in a tree, like a map directing a traveller, like the sun lighting up a dark world; the Holy Spirit takes the things of God and makes them known to us. Who can resist the truth? Rephrase that question using what we now know: who can resist the Holy Spirit? Where would be a safe place to hide from the Spirit of God? High up? Deep below? Far away? David posed this question in Psalms 139:7 and concluded that it just couldn't be done: **"Where can I go from your Spirit? Where can I flee from your presence?"**

Truth is going to run us down and shake our world like a terrifying earthquake. Truth will find us no matter where we hide. We can stuff our fingers in our ears and sing the "Star Spangled Banner" at the top of our lungs, but when we stand before God at the judgment, no one will be able to say they didn't know. That they had no idea that God is the rightful Master. That everyone should obey Him. That we have rebelled and tried to establish our own lower case "k" kingdoms where we're in charge. That we should have lived for *His* glory and *His* Kingdom and so entered into *His* joy.

Everybody knows, nobody doesn't know. God's judgment on the proud and unrepentant will surprise no one at all. We have a mighty witness to the truth who testifies to each of us: the Holy Spirit.

To a dark and confused world, the Holy Spirit heralds the irresistible, irrefutable, irrepressible truth because truth is who the Holy Spirit *is*.

1 guide
need help with the direction of your life?

"BUT WHEN HE, THE SPIRIT OF TRUTH, COMES, HE WILL GUIDE YOU INTO ALL TRUTH. HE WILL NOT SPEAK ON HIS OWN; HE WILL SPEAK ONLY WHAT HE HEARS; HE WILL TELL YOU WHAT IS YET TO COME."
JOHN 16:13

Would you like to raft down a breathtaking river as it winds through the purple haze of the deepest gorge in North America, feeling the terrifying power of the churning water, passing bighorn sheep, brown bears, and bald eagles while the madness of the everyday world seems far away and insignificant in comparison? Well my friend, take a ride down the Snake River in the great northwest. It doesn't just lazily wind around, it *screams* tortuously, zigging and zagging as it ricochets down the narrow canyon walls. The sluice in which it thunders? It's called Hells Canyon because the rock walls are red and jagged and nearly perpendicular while the river rages deeply down inside. The surface of the river is often smooth, but that's because there is such an enormous quantity of water swiftly flowing over the deadly boulders below. At any point in your journey, you could be thrown from your raft and the inexorable pull of the water would drag you down, beating you against the hidden rocks below and pouring water into your lungs.

Ummm . . . You should probably take a guide.

Come to think of it, life is like Hells Canyon. At any point, while admiring the scenery, we could be tossed overboard and powerful currents might drag us down and beat the life out of us. There's no question that our lives need a Guide! We've been freely given the very Guide we need—the Holy Spirit of God.

We have to remember that Galatians 4:6 and other passages clearly teach that the Holy Spirit is Jesus Himself. Don't think on that too hard because your mind can't get it, just believe it! It's true. The Holy Spirit knows exactly what we're going through because Jesus has gone through exactly what we're going through. And more. Loneliness? Jesus was deserted by His home town, His family, His closest friends and the leaders of the synagogues and the Sanhedrin. Hunger? Jesus went 40 days without food. Sadness? Jesus is called by the prophet Isaiah, "A man of sorrows, familiar with suffering." Hebrews talks about the loud groans that were often the prayers of Jesus. Pain? Isaiah 52:14 tells us that Jesus was beaten so badly at His trial that you couldn't see that it was still a human being standing there. Have you heard the word "excruciating," and did you realize the root word is *crux* or *cross*? The cross is the most horrific agony ever devised by the perverted mind of fallen man, and Jesus went to hang on the cross with a willing heart—for you and for me.

There is nothing that will come into our lives that Jesus doesn't know about first hand. And no circumstance He's not been victorious over even while going through it. Jesus conquered *death*, for crying out loud! You could make a good case that death is a very tough circumstance. So tell me. Who lives inside each Christian? Jesus Himself. But pay attention: 1 Peter 1:11 calls this presence the **"Spirit of Christ."** The Holy Spirit. The Holy Spirit knows everything we're going through. Everything. By experience.

This is the Guide we've been freely given. One who knows our most elemental needs, our deepest heartaches, and our most fundamental yearnings. One who knows us better than we know ourselves, who wants better for us than we want for ourselves. One who's familiar with our life story, indeed knows it better than we who have lived it; who sees ahead on the road of life and prepares us for what is to come, who knows the road behind and is helping us deal with that too.

He is the best companion we could ever want: never tiring, ever present, full of fierce joy, an inexhaustible supply of the strengthening bread of life and the source of refreshing living water. Watching over us, allowing us to drop His hand and choose wrongly, yet never abandoning us to our own deplorable choices, whose very presence is fortifying, comforting and reassuring. One who cannot be ambushed by the unexpected, cannot be overwhelmed by the predatory, cannot be tricked or beaten by the diabolical. A sure and unerring Guide. Our friend and our God.

Have you been settling for a lesser life coach?

2 advocate

ever wish someone were unrelentingly on your side?

"IF GOD IS FOR US, WHO CAN BE AGAINST US? HE WHO DID NOT SPARE HIS OWN SON, BUT GAVE HIM UP FOR US ALL HOW WILL HE NOT ALSO, ALONG WITH HIM, GRACIOUSLY GIVE US ALL THINGS?"
ROMANS 8:31-32

The word used in John 14:26 to describe the Holy Spirit is from the Greek: "*paraclete*." *Para* means adjacent to, or beside. *Clete* means called. The Holy Spirit is God alongside the ones He has called. God has called us and given us a mighty traveling companion.

Paraclete really has no one word in English that does it justice. "Counselor" is used in the NIV, which in the sense of a defense lawyer is accurate, but counselor is also used to denote a psychiatrist which is not even close. In other versions the word "helper" is used, one who aids us; but that's less than paraclete; helper sounds more like a downline employee. Least useful perhaps would be the translation *"comforter,"* because while the root meaning of *com-fort* is "with strength" which is perfect, that definition for comfort is hopelessly out of date. These days, comfort suggests fuzzy blankets and buttery foods. The translation of paraclete is a real problem.

Perhaps the best single word for paraclete is *"advocate,"* the prefix "ad-" means "with" and "-vocate" means "voice." So the word means "one who stands up and speaks up for us," a champion who fights for us. The Holy Spirit rescues and defends us, pleads and upholds our case, speaks to the Father on our behalf.

Judgment Day should strike fear in every heart. If the facts of our righteousness were all that were being considered we'd be sunk. We'd have no confidence in our own lukewarm goodness when blinded by the burning holiness of God Almighty. Unable to face the horror of God's judgment, justly frightened people will try to medicate their fear in many different ways. Some use anesthetics, or depressants, or stimulants. Some even use television, which is all three combined! Some push the thought of judgment away with a great effort and some do it unconsciously. Some cowards run from it, some skeptics choose to disbelieve it.

Yet the coming judgment of the world will not be deflected or slowed or stopped by our coping mechanisms. The Holy Spirit is even now convicting the world of sin and righteousness and judgment, John 16:8. Those responding to the convicting power of the Holy Spirit at Pentecost cried, "We've been cut to the heart, what shall we *do?*" Peter told them, ***"Repent and be baptized into the name of Jesus, and you will receive the gift of the Holy Spirit."*** Receive the Paraclete! Receive the one who comes alongside us in power and deliverance.

Job knows Him well, for he says in Job 16:19, ***"Even now my Witness is in heaven; my Advocate is on high. My Intercessor is my friend as my eyes pour out tears to God; on behalf of a man he pleads with God as a man pleads for his friend."*** The moment will come when we find ourselves alive before the Judgment Seat of the God: the One who has been wronged, the righteous God whose laws have been trampled, the God who is holy and all powerful, the God who has promised to rain down judgment on the unrepentant wicked. At that moment, we will not stand alone. Supporting our trembling knees and quaking heart will be the Paraclete.

The Almighty who sits on the Judgment Seat is the same God whose Spirit will defend us in that day. Successfully pleading our cause: our Advocate, bulwark, vindication, our sure salvation, our rock and our fortress, our victory! The Holy Spirit, the Paraclete—God's power which has come to walk with us.

And not only will the Paraclete be with us on that Day when the great and the small stand before Judgment Seat, but He is with us *right now*. As Satan hurls his fiery arrows of accusation at us, the Paraclete gives us His armor to shield us. "You are a sinner!" screams the devil. The Paraclete gives us our victorious response: "It's true that I *was* a sinner, but now because of God's grace and Christ's victory at the cross and the empty tomb, I am no longer a sinner, but I am in truth a child of God. Born again with a new name, a new nature, and a new birthright. *Take it up with Him* if you think you're up to it."

Great news! God is our biggest fan.

3 revelation
how can we know the stuff that we can never know?

"THEN HE OPENED THEIR MINDS SO THEY COULD UNDERSTAND THE SCRIPTURES."
LUKE 24:45

Revelation produces truth that can't be found any other way. For instance: you're unlikely to have any idea about what I ate for breakfast five days ago unless I *reveal* it to you. In the same way, there's much about ourselves, about the world we live in, and about God Himself that we simply cannot know unless God reveals it to us through the Scriptures by His Holy Spirit. That just rubs secular humanists the wrong way, and I'm *really* okay with that.

It's ironic that the Darwinists and the materialists and the humanists say that *Christians* are closed-minded and anti-science! That's funny. They themselves have slammed the door shut on God's revelation, closing their minds off to most of the incoming light of available knowledge. In actuality, the people who are *most* open to hearing new ideas are those whose faith in Christ is secure through long study of the Scriptures. You can't scare someone with rising floodwaters who's got a helicopter, and new ideas don't frighten the one who is grounded in the truth. Strangely, at times the people *least* open to new truth can be academics and naturalists. Go figure. Offering an objection to some hyper-educated naturalist's ideas can be like offering a bucket of water to the Wicked Witch of the West.

The greatest example of revelation truth is the initial act of creation. Although there was only one eyewitness to the actual event, it's pretty easy to reach the conclusion that this cosmos was fashioned by a powerful and competent Creator. In avoidance of this plain revelation, secular humanists deny the miracle of creation and instead set up a primordial explosion of gasses of unknown origin and unknown composition and unknown location to explain how the universe came to be. Then they affix to themselves the label of "smart"!

Hillaire Belloc's classic poem, "THE MICROBE", penned around 1900, absolutely lays it out.

> *"THE MICROBE is so very small*
> *You cannot make him out at all,*
> *But many sanguine people hope*
> *To see him through a microscope.*
> *His jointed tongue that lies beneath*
> *A hundred curious rows of teeth;*
> *His seven tufted tails with lots*
> *Of lovely pink and purple spots,*
> *On each of which a pattern stands,*
> *Composed of forty separate bands;*
> *His eyebrows of a tender green;*
> *All these have never yet been seen --*
> *But Scientists, who ought to know,*
> *Assure us that it must be so.*
> *Oh! let us never, never doubt*
> *What nobody is sure about!"*

The Christian's knowledge rests securely on God's ability, His desire, and His brilliant accomplishment of the task of revelation. God is *revealed partially* in His creation. We can study the universe around us and see God. That's why an atheist scientist is so odd: how CAN one study the miraculous, meticulous design of creation and still totally miss the miraculous, meticulous Designer of it?

Besides the revelation of God discovered in the world around us, God is *revealed even more fully* in the Scriptures, the written word of God. We can read the Bible and easily see God, which is why Jesus laughed at the religious leaders who "searched the Scriptures" but could/would not see the one to whom the Scriptures point.

And beyond the revelation we have received in creation and the Scriptures, God is *revealed perfectly* in Jesus Christ. There's no part of God that's not revealed in Jesus; accurate down to the detailed minutia of God's intrinsic God-ness. When we see Jesus, we're looking straight at God Himself. No wonder Jesus was flabbergasted when Thomas looked straight at Him and asked to see the Father! Talk about not seeing the forest for the trees.

Revelation truth is the greatest truth we have, when God is the source of the revelation. Have you ever wanted to ask Thomas Jefferson what it was like to craft the Declaration of Independence? Quiz Handel about writing *The Messiah*? Check with Moses on his feelings on parting the Red Sea? It would be great to sit down with these guys and hang out. That's exactly what the Maker of heaven and earth invites us to do. Anytime at all. Observe Him fashioning the universe, humbling the nation of Egypt, stopping the motion of the sun in the sky, determining the level of the oceans, leading the Israelites through the dry bed of the Red Sea and the Jordan River, preserving the lives of His servants thrown into a blazing furnace without a single scorch mark, causing strong fortresses to collapse, raising up world powers and casting them down, directing the invisible angelic army of light that contends with the powers of darkness. How would we know these things unless God told us?

One of the perks of being God is that you get to perform unimaginable miracles, and then you get to gather your children around you and reveal it while they gaze up at you in fascination and awe.

4 omnipresence
do you wonder if God has abandoned you?

"WHERE CAN I GO FROM YOUR SPIRIT? WHERE CAN I FLEE FROM YOUR PRESENCE? IF I GO UP TO THE HEAVENS, YOU ARE THERE; IF I MAKE MY BED IN THE DEPTHS, YOU ARE THERE. IF I RISE ON THE WINGS OF THE DAWN, IF I SETTLE ON THE FAR SIDE OF THE SEA, EVEN THERE YOUR HAND WILL GUIDE ME, YOUR RIGHT HAND WILL HOLD ME FAST."
PSALMS 139:7-10

Would you like to have lived back when Jesus was on earth? Be able to watch Him turn water into wine, heal the sick, walk on water and raise Lazarus from the dead? Yeah? Well, not me, and I'll tell you why. Very few actually got to hang out with Him back then. There was just one of Him and however many of everyone else: there was only so much of Him to go around. If you wanted to talk with Jesus, you had to . . . well, you *couldn't*. He was constantly busy. He had only 12 disciples and really there were just three of those who were super close to Him. He had Mary and Martha and Lazarus as friends, too. Your chances of being Jesus' friend then were pretty skimpy. If you knew Jesus back then, you were like a lottery winner.

Fast forward to Pentecost. All of a sudden, we've got all-the-time year-round access to Jesus through His Holy Spirit. Are you going to the grocery store? Jesus would love to go with you. Waking up in the middle of the night? Jesus is right there, alert and wide awake. Do you need to take a long trip to a faraway place? Jesus has the time and He's ready to go anywhere with anyone. I ask you, is it better to have lived during the time of Jesus' earthly ministry or now? No contest.

This presence of God is not the stuff of mystical monks and mountaintop maharishis. You don't have to check out of the world to experience total immersion in God's nearness. Seriously, I've been in the middle of an airport with hundreds of strangers all over the place, and yet I've felt the closeness of Jesus that you might think you'd have to go by yourself to a lonely Rocky Mountain meadow to get.

Jesus doesn't want us living to be alone with Him, though that's great. He wants us to be constantly *aware* of His presence in our lives wherever we are. *"Continually,"* as in 1 Thessalonians 5:17. Not simply daily—moment by moment by moment.

Brother Lawrence (he only signed his first name!) wrote a book called <u>Practicing The Presence</u>. We should be constantly realizing God's presence. God's continued presence in our lives is a fact and to see it we only need God to open the eyes of our hearts. The question "What would Jesus do?" misses the wonder of His presence with us minute by minute. Why would we wonder what He might do *when Jesus is right here with us?* We can *ask* Him. The catchy acronym WWJD (What Would Jesus Do) might more correctly be JWDYWDITSSYHACTM (Jesus, What Do You Want Done In This Situation Since You're Here And Can Tell Me).

We're not talking about a rosy feeling or a divine "spark," or any sort of vibration. No, no, no. Jesus is a *person*, the Holy Spirit is a *person*, the heavenly Father is a *person*, not a spark or feeling or vibe! While it's true you can get a feeling from a person; you *cannot* get a person from a feeling! Reread this paragraph and think about it. It's fireworks.

Sometimes we'll know God's nearness even though He doesn't seem to be saying or doing anything. His presence can't be mistaken. You won't have to ask if it's Him; He's inimitable. It's healthy to talk about these experiences of God's presence with mature Christians to make sure you don't go off the deep end. Nothing you will experience about God will ever go against the clear teaching of the Bible.

A parishioner once told pastor John Wimber that the service had gotten a little too wild, and didn't he think they should be more "biblical," to which Wimber replied, "Have you *read* the Bible?!" The presence of God is unpredictable but always biblical!

The Holy Spirit is the presence of God. We cannot constrain Him, but He has decided we will contain Him—living in our hearts, in our day to day lives. As the Holy Spirit, God Almighty is *with us all the time*. He's our Creator and Master, and on top of that, He's the best friend we'll ever have. Let's live constantly aware of His moment by moment presence with us.

Moses told the Lord God, "If your presence doesn't go with us, we don't want to go."

5 conviction
does anyone really not know what God expects?

"HE WILL CONVICT THE WORLD OF GUILT IN REGARD TO SIN AND RIGHTEOUSNESS AND JUDGMENT: IN REGARD TO SIN, BECAUSE MEN DO NOT BELIEVE IN ME; IN REGARD TO RIGHTEOUSNESS, BECAUSE I AM GOING TO THE FATHER, WHERE YOU CAN SEE ME NO LONGER; AND IN REGARD TO JUDGMENT, BECAUSE THE PRINCE OF THIS WORLD NOW STANDS CONDEMNED."
JOHN 16:8-11

There's an age-old courtroom tactic called ignorance of the law. "Sorry, Judge, I didn't know you expected me to stop at that red light." That's why the law had to come up with the age-old courtroom response: ignorance of the law is no excuse. In the same way, no excuse will do the trick when we're under conviction from the Holy Spirit. God has produced evidence about our behavior that He wants to help us deal with. That's where conviction is different from guilt. Guilty people want to hide from God. When we come under conviction, we want to find God. We're drawn to His heart.

Pilgrim's Progress is rated the second most beloved book of all time among Christians, after the Bible. It tells the allegorical tale of Pilgrim as he travels from his sinful worldly life to the heavenly realms and describes all the adventures that befall him. A moving story with a power-packed message. In the beginning, the Pilgrim is wracked by _conviction_ of his own sin. Conviction is depicted as a burden strapped to his back, weighing him down. In desperation he runs out of his home crying tears of repentance and finds himself at the foot of the cross, where his burden is released and rolls into the empty tomb, never to be seen again.

What a picture Bunyan paints! After responding to the conviction of the Holy Spirit, the Pilgrim is ready to begin his journey of faith which will end at the joyful crossing of the river of death and on to the gates of the Celestial City. Conviction is a gift of grace. Conviction is the beginning of our way back to God's joy and peace.

At Pentecost, the gathered crowd listened to Peter preach Christendom's first sermon. Peter told them that although they had put Jesus to a cruel death on the cross, the heavenly Father had raised Him to life and made Him both Master and Messiah. When they heard this, they were "cut to the heart" and cried out, "What shall we do?" Beautiful! This is conviction at its very best. You and I can read the words of Peter, close the book, and go on with our lives; they could not. God was calling them to surrender in repentance. Conviction leads to salvation.

As we said, there's a huge difference between conviction and _guilt_. Guilt is just an annoying racket. Conviction is a quiet knowledge that something is wrong in our relationship with God. Guilt comes from the accuser of our souls, Satan; he wants to make us think God will never take us back. But conviction is proof that God is, in fact, very willing to take us back. Conviction is from the Holy Spirit; drawing our hearts to God's heart. Jesus, in His undying love for us, sends conviction.

Do you see the distinction? Guilt is something we must *overcome*. Conviction is something we must *embrace*, knowing that it's meant for our good. The quicker we agree with God, the quicker His forgiveness can reach us. The faster we find our way back to the right road, the sooner He can fill our hearts with real life. Conviction is confirmation that God loves us. Did you hear that?

Conviction comes from the word *convince*. The prefix *"con-"* means "with." The root word *"vince"* means "victory!" When the Holy Spirit convicts us, it's to line us up with *Christ's victory* at the cross and the empty tomb, where He triumphed over the darkness. He wants to make us partakers of His victory. Conviction is not punishment! Not at all! It's God's gracious invitation to share the glorious victory of Jesus Christ.

We become overcomers in Christ when we surrender to the Holy Spirit's work of conviction. I like that.

6 wisdom
how can we decide which choice is right?

"For the LORD gives wisdom, and from his mouth come knowledge and understanding . . . Then you will understand what is right and just and fair; every good path. For wisdom will enter your heart . . ."
Proverbs 2:6, 9 and 10

Wisdom is much more than just having knowledge. It's *the ability to decide what's best* between options. Not what you thought, maybe? Being knowledgeable is merely the capacity to pack information into a brain. Some people are quick-witted, but that's not wisdom either. Wisdom doesn't necessarily come with age—a child can be wise and an old person foolish. Wisdom is a *gift*. The Holy Spirit gives it.

God says Solomon was the wisest man who ever lived. In 1 Kings 3, God tells the newly crowned Solomon that He'll grant him any wish. Solomon asks for the gift of wisdom. God is delighted with his request: **"I will give you a wise and discerning heart, so that there will never have been anyone like you, nor will there ever be."**

Solomon was a great judge because he could listen to conflicting courtroom evidence and pick out the truth. He famously told two women who claimed the same baby to cut the child in half. One woman said fine, if she couldn't have the child, no one would. The other cried out not to hurt the child and renounced her claim. So, the wise Solomon discerned the baby's true mother. Solomon asked God for the ability to chose rightly for his kingdom. 1 Kings 3:9 records his prayer. ***"Give your servant a discerning heart to govern your people and to distinguish between right and wrong."*** Too bad he didn't ask for wisdom in his private life.

King David was also wise. In Psalms 119:99, he wrote that he had ***"more insight"*** than all his teachers and in 119:104, that he hated ***"every wrong path."*** How did he get that astounding insight? The whole psalm proclaims that David spent his time meditating on God's statutes. Meditation is not curling up in a ball and trying to reach something inside us. To the middle eastern mind, meditation is to speak the truth out loud. David often told himself the truth from God's laws and statues. By following God's instructions he became wise; he was able to chose correctly.

Jesus has all wisdom. Isaiah 11:2 ***"The Spirit of the LORD will rest on him, the Spirit of wisdom . . ."*** Jesus is wise because He's God, but He laid down His rights as God to take up our flesh. Isaiah tells us that Jesus' wisdom comes not intrinsically, innately from Himself but because He has the Spirit of wisdom, the Holy Spirit, *resting* on Him. This same Holy Spirit has been given to us, living inside us because we're God's. This is the sense of 1 Corinthians 2:16, ***"We have the mind of Christ."***

Proverbs 3:19 says God created the world by wisdom. Proverbs 4:7 says wisdom is supreme. Proverbs 31:30 praises the wise woman and says beauty is fleeting, but wisdom will remain. Proverbs 9:12 says wisdom will reward us. Proverbs 16:16 says it's better than gold. Proverbs 24:14 says wisdom brings hope and gives us a solid future. Proverbs 28:26 says it will keep us safe. Proverbs 3:13 pronounces a blessing on the one who finds wisdom. Proverbs 9:10 says that to rightly fear God is the beginning of wisdom. Proverbs 8:14 says wisdom brings counsel, sound judgment, understanding and power. You know what? I think I like wisdom.

James 1:5 talks about wisdom and says that if we lack it, we should ask God, and He will give it gladly. In other words, if we don't know which way to turn, which path to chose, we only need to turn to God, ask and listen. We ask God for it for a very good reason: He's the only one who has it in the first place.

If you have kids, you want them making wise decisions about what career path they will chose, whom they will marry, how they'll manage their lives, how they'll raise their kids. Well? God the Father is no different than us. He wants wise children and will gladly grant their request when they ask Him for wisdom.

Wisdom is not knowing everything there is to know, it's the ability to discern what is the correct choice in the path that lies ahead.

7 worship
what do we possibly have to offer God?

"God is spirit, and his worshipers must worship in spirit and in truth."
John 4:24

Worship has been defined bunches of ways. To "kiss toward" is one definition. To give "worth-ship" is another. To "prostrate oneself" is yet another. I'm not sure how I would define it, but that doesn't mean I don't recognize it when I see it.

Worship is *our only reasonable response* to the absolutely overwhelming and nearly incapacitating holy greatness of God.

A painting can be worship. A job well done can be worship. Raising a child diligently can be worship. Being silent when we shouldn't speak can be worship. Dancing can be worship. Taking care of someone else can be worship. Waiting for something can be worship. Speaking truth in a truth-resistant situation can be worship. Giving time to a person society doesn't value can be worship. Staying in an uncomfortable post can be worship, moving out of a comfort zone can be worship. Taking a step of faith, singing all by yourself, doing everything well, honoring your parents, telling someone humbly what God speaks to your heart can all be worship. In all these ways, we react to God's amazingness with different expressions of worship. It can take many forms but the initiation comes from God Himself.

We *respond* to the wonder of who He is and what He's done.

God instructed Israel about worship. He told them specifically what to do and specifically what not to do. These regulations were not to make everything complicated. It's because God is never haphazard; there's a right and wrong way to approach Him in worship. Every person, every utensil and piece of clothing had to be cleansed before being used. The worship vessels, including the vessels called priests, had to be dipped in unblemished blood. Things had to be done in sequence, for God is a God of order. Things had to be done with a pure heart; God can't stand fake or phony. Things had to be done at certain times, because God said so, which is always the best reason. Simple obedience equals worship.

We, like the Israelites, are called to worship God. Not only that, we are all designed with the *need* to worship Him. If we don't direct that worship in a holy and right way to God alone, we will send it in a wicked and wrong way somewhere else.

Need an example of the wrong way to worship? Satan once held a privileged high place in the worship of God, but he wanted to swap places with God and be the center of attention. In Isaiah 14:14 Satan said, "*I will ascend to heaven; I will raise my throne above the stars of God; I will sit enthroned on the mount of assembly, on the utmost heights of the sacred mountain."* So enamored was Satan with receiving worship that he burned his mind and heart away trying to take into himself the white-hot glory of God. Satan lost his lofty place; in fact, he lost everything. He continues to this day to serve God, but only as a shoe serves a foot, not as a son serves a father. Someday God will discard that old shoe, but until that day comes, the shoe will be unwillingly but inexorably used for God's purposes.

Taking his cue from 1 Peter 5:6, the great basketball coach Don Meyer said, "It's our job to humble ourselves and God's job to exalt us. If we insist on doing God's job, then He'll have to do ours."

We need to learn and turn from the folly of Satan's pride. God has a different relationship planned for us. God loves us as His children and He has decided that someday He'll turn everything He owns over to us. He wants us to draw near to His heart, as He protects us in Christ Jesus from the unbearable heat of His glory. What Satan coveted—to be like God—God has reserved for us, in Jesus. We won't become like God by trying to set ourselves above Him, but by bending our knee and humbling our hearts. As we gaze upon Him in worship, we're increasingly transformed into His likeness.

It's a universal law: we become like what we worship. You maybe don't believe that? Consider Psalms 115:3-8, *"Our God is in heaven; he does whatever pleases him. But their idols are silver and gold, made by the hands of men. They have mouths, but cannot speak, eyes, but they cannot see; they have ears, but they cannot hear, noses, but they cannot smell; they have hands, but cannot feel, feet, but they cannot walk; nor can they utter a sound with their throats. Those who make them will be like them, and so will all who trust in them."* This principle applies to those who worship the one true God. We will "be like Him." Humble yourself before the Almighty, and He will lift you up! Lifted up means to share the place where He is, as the saints and the seraphim already do.

Humility before God is only sensible, because when we lower ourselves, He'll raise us up. He has invited us to His table, to His house and to His heart, and humility before Him is the key to making ourselves receptive to that invitation. He'll give us the strength to stand in His presence, the strength to stand anywhere. We can stand before powerful people or before the vicious onslaught of the spiritual forces of wickedness. If we learn to fall down before God in worship, we'll be able to stand when He destroys the world at the end of time.

Worship is really nothing more than healthy heart alignment.

Deal with it. God is large and in charge, and he's not going anywhere. People can misunderstand Him and slander Him. People can insulate themselves against Him. People can structure their thinking to exclude Him. People can lie about Him, try to discredit Him and even attempt to ignore Him, but it's a losing battle to mix it up with God. He's the 800 pound gorilla in whatever room He's in.

. . . .

¬chapter two
GOD: THE IMMOVABLE OBJECT
who does God think he IS anyway?

"REMEMBER THIS, YOU REBELS . . . I AM GOD, AND THERE IS NO OTHER; I AM GOD, AND THERE IS NONE LIKE ME."
ISAIAH 46:8-9

Nobody wins a fight with God. But many will win the game of life because they've surrendered to Him ... bowed their knee to His supremacy over their own will. God is beyond us. God is outside our ability to "get." God is someone we believe in, not someone we've figured out. He's someone we trust, not someone we keep in a box. One day we'll understand Him better, but eternity will pass before we even *begin* to fit more of Him inside our brains. And we'll need better brains to do it.

We know He's good. We know He loves us. We know He'd go to any length to rescue us. We know that He Himself is the greatest adventure we'll ever have. Many try to construct a world without Him. God constructed this world to contain those silly people, in the hope they'd turn to Him and become part of His family.

Maybe read those last couple of sentences again. It's hard to comprehend that God loves people who have no use for Him, that He cares more about them than He cares for His own prestige and welfare. Proof? The incarnation and the cross.

God won't go away. Nobody can push Him around, no one can make Him disappear by not believing in Him as if He were Peter Pan's Tinkerbell. We might as well come to terms with Him; *His* terms are the only ones available in the end!

He's like that giant pink paisley elephant singing loudly over there with neon blue sunglasses, a yellow polka dot dress, and a red parasol —good luck ignoring HIM.

• THE KINGDOM
what do we call that thing a king reigns OVER?

"THERE BEFORE ME WAS ONE LIKE A SON OF MAN, COMING WITH THE CLOUDS OF HEAVEN. HE APPROACHED THE ANCIENT OF DAYS AND WAS LED INTO HIS PRESENCE. HE WAS GIVEN AUTHORITY, GLORY AND SOVEREIGN POWER; ALL PEOPLES, NATIONS AND MEN OF EVERY LANGUAGE WORSHIPED HIM. HIS DOMINION IS AN EVERLASTING DOMINION THAT WILL NOT PASS AWAY, AND HIS KINGDOM IS ONE THAT WILL NEVER BE DESTROYED."
DANIEL 7:13-14

The Kingdom exists wherever God's will is done. As the Lord's Prayer says, ***"Thy kingdom come, thy will be done."*** Kings always insist on having their way. Kings are not the kind to defer. Kings have this idea that they're in charge. And they pretty much demand that things run according to their wishes. The kings of men come and go. The King of Creation doesn't come and go. His Kingdom doesn't come and go either. His Kingdom is just like Himself: it's everlasting and will never be destroyed. That's why you and I want to be part of His kingdom! That's why we submit our lives to Jesus Christ, the King of Glory ... so we can be included in *that*.

Ephesians 1:11 says, ***"According to the plan of him who works out everything in conformity with the purpose of his will."*** It may at times look as if this world is spinning out of His control, but don't bet on it. Sure it's a big mess right now, but God cleans up messes all the time. Sure it's chaotic now, but chaos can't thwart God's order and purpose. Sure it looks like evil is winning right now, but good and evil aren't opposites. Evil is good that's been twisted. One day God will straighten out those twists. Evil is being allowed for a moment on the timescale of eternity, in order to train up the children of God and to bring glory to the name of Jesus. God always wins. No exceptions. Zero.

Americans have historically had a problem with authority, beginning with old King George of England. Live free or die. It's my party and I'll cry if I wanna. I did it my way. Nobody can tell me what to do. You're not the boss of me. And all that stuff. It's in our national DNA. We're a spunky kind of people.

Spunk is great. But if spunk becomes pride, it stinks like month-old garbage. There's one King who cannot be overthrown, one King who can weather any revolt. His Kingship began before the creation, and will continue long after this world ends. Philippians 2:10-11: *"At the name of Jesus every knee should bow, in heaven and on earth and under the earth, and every tongue confess that Jesus Christ is Lord, to the glory of God the Father."* That word "every" means precisely what it says. Jesus is the King. Knees bow before kings, willingly or by force. God IS the boss of you! And me.

Complain if you want, but it won't change the fact. Kings will have our allegiance or our heads. God *always* gets His way.

For a brief time, by heaven's clock, we have two kingdoms at war on the planet: darkness and light. Did you hear that? Explains a lot, doesn't it? The kingdom of darkness is easily spotted. Open any newspaper, listen to any broadcast, visit any website that carries current events. Everywhere you turn in this fallen world, people are cheating, stealing, hating, wounding and murdering in thought and word and deed. Is that God's fault? Or is that to be expected in a dark world?

People are, as 2 Timothy 3 says, *"Lovers of themselves, lovers of money, boastful, proud, abusive, disobedient to their parents, ungrateful, unholy, without love, unforgiving, slanderous, without self-control, brutal, not lovers of the good, treacherous, rash, conceited, lovers of pleasure rather than lovers of God."* Words written two thousand years ago precisely describe today's kingdom of darkness. Paul wrote that these kind of people would appear in the terrible last days. I know Solomon says nothing is new, but people's evil behavior seems *escalated* these days, even if it's not new.

The Kingdom of Light, however, runs counter to the kingdom of darkness. The servant is greatest, the poor are truly rich. In the kingdom of darkness, money is power; in the Kingdom of Light, surrender to God's will is power. In the kingdom of darkness, beautiful people are admired; in the Kingdom of Light we admire beautiful hearts. In the kingdom of darkness, broken relationships are irreparable; in the Kingdom of Light there's not just forgiveness but there's *reconciliation*. The kingdom of darkness exists for a day; the Kingdom of Light is never ending. The dying gasp of the kingdom of darkness will be war against the Son of God, but the victorious Kingdom of Light will bring peace on earth. Darkness is surely passing, the light of the Kingdom of God is even more surely dawning.

When God's will is done in our personal lives, His Kingdom comes among us.

1 God is good
does God sometimes play cruel tricks?

"No one is good except God alone."
Luke 18:19

We learned it when we were little. God is great, God is *good*, let us thank Him for our food. It doesn't really rhyme, but we got the point. We were about to enjoy a meal because God's goodness is such that He provides us with what we need in quantities that more than satisfy the need. We thank Him because He's good to us. Good is exactly what God *is*.

Yet God's goodness can be a tough sell to those who are going through hardship, sorrow or suffering. Because of the problem of pain and the existence of evil, we have more doubts about God's goodness than probably anything else.

Be honest. Floods, fires, storms, earthquakes, sickness, cruel suffering, agonizing loss. Have you ever questioned God, wondering if He's perhaps asleep at the wheel? Sure. Me too. But did we ever stop to realize that we were basically wrestling with the question of God's *goodness*? Is God really good, or have we been sold a pile of junk?

We must come to grips with the fact that we live in a fallen, cursed world. Read Genesis 3 if you doubt it. We're separated by our sinful, self-willed rebellion from God's comforting, safe sovereignty. Living in such a world, nightmares should be our only reality. What is to stop someone from stealing, murdering, destroying? Evil people, demonic forces, death and destruction should be our normal experience in a world that has turned its back on God—a world where God has been shown the door and told not to come back. Our expectations are too high. We should count on life being ugly and brutish.

Considering the perverse world we live in, it's logical to conclude that we're doing too well! It could be worse. It *should* be worse. Much worse. For some reason, even though we have rejected the light, the light still shines. Somehow, the dire consequences of our wicked rebellion have been buffered, cushioned, insulated. It's not as horrible as it ought to be.

Would you prefer a world where evil was completely unchecked? I know I wouldn't. Yet in a depraved world, we are not abandoned by God. It's a God-*forsaking*, not a godforsaken world. Even while we live in a world where evil thrives, brought into being by our own wicked choices, we are daily still surrounded by God's goodness. The fact is easily demonstrated that He is unquestionably good and deals with His creatures in mercy and grace, not wrathful retribution.

When we say that a person is "good" we mean that they're okay—on the whole and on balance, not that they're perfect. But in God's case, the word "good" DOES mean perfect: *faultless*, blameless, pure, completely without anything remotely wrong. Because God is entirely good without a trace of anything else, there are such things as beauty and harmony and steadfast love. In short, there are the things that make life worthwhile which are a direct corollary of God's goodness. Because God is good, we can expect our future to be unimaginably better than our right now. Think about God's goodness and why it matters. You may find you're running out of brain space. God is not halfheartedly good; where goodness is concerned, God is irrevocably committed. ***"God is light; in him there is no darkness <u>at all</u>,"*** says 1 John 1:5.

When the ruler called Jesus "good" in Luke 18, he was merely saying he respected Jesus as a sincere and dedicated rabbi. Jesus knew what he meant, but responded by saying, "Don't use a word that should be reserved for God to describe someone who's just marginally better than you are. God is not just morally superior to you, He's *absolutely perfect* in His goodness. When you call me good, you must realize you're calling me something *only God is*. So by inference, you're calling me God. Don't use that word lightly." Not sure the ruler got what Jesus was saying, but we can get it. God *alone* is good.

And He isn't obligated to be like that. He could be any way He wanted to be. If you're God, you can pick your character style. Men have imagined impish gods, angry gods, lustful, greedy, sneaky gods, indifferent gods, insatiable gods. We think up really pathetic gods! God could be like our imagined gods if it suited Him. He could have decided to remember every one of our sins instead of choosing to forget them. He could have toyed with us, had fun at our expense, made sport of us and our pitiful ineptness, our bungling, our laughable pride. He might have hidden himself and laughed at us from a long way off. He could have destroyed us when we transgressed His will. But the real God is nothing like anybody we could have dreamed up. God's infinitely better than we deserve.

So many of our questions are answered by the assurance that God is good.

2 God is sovereign

who gets the final word on absolutely everything?

"I WILL HAVE MERCY ON WHOM I HAVE MERCY, AND I WILL HAVE COMPASSION ON WHOM I HAVE COMPASSION."
ROMANS 9:15, EXODUS 33:19

Sovereignty implies absolute authority and power. If we were to get a court summons, would we obey? Why? It's just a piece of paper for crying out loud. Why should a piece of paper call us to meek compliance? Well, that paper is issued by authorities who are empowered to toss us in jail. That's a picture of sovereignty. The sovereign God can do what He wants, when He wants, to whom He wants.

God doesn't have to ask anyone's permission, especially not yours or mine. He brought the world into being, and He can snuff the world out if He so chooses! Who can stop Him? Who can back Him down? Who can tell Him no? Who can shout "stop!" at God? Things will be done His way and no other way; that's what sovereignty means.

You've heard the difference between being in charge and being responsible. Being in charge means that you can write checks, while being responsible means that whatever goes wrong, it's your fault. God is definitely in charge. He writes and signs all the checks, meaning, it's His bank account that the universe runs on. He supplies the energy. He's the first cause. His power is the driving force. In Him we live and move and have our being.

And without a doubt, God is responsible for everything that happens. Ultimately. Whatever goes on, God could stop it if He wished to, and yet He allows stuff to happen we wish He wouldn't.

The question arises: "If God is so good and He's so powerful, how can He still allow evil? Maybe He's not as sovereign as you think He is." What if, dear genius, God is really smarter than we are, and those two options aren't the only ones? What if in His sovereign will God has a use for evil, at least for now? Our Sovereign God knows *exactly* what He's doing. God is responsible for the continuing menace of evil in the world. That's not a pleasant thought, but it's the truth. God in His sovereign wisdom has allowed evil for the present. But at the cross He has faced it down and destroyed it. God is sovereignly responsible. He alone has allowed evil to exist, and also He has personally dealt with the *consequence* of evil's existence.

Stunning huh? Be careful, though. God is not the *author* of evil. Nothing could be more wrong than to think God in any way has inspired or inaugurated evil. God didn't invent the cross or the gas chamber—that was us. God doesn't steal the commonwealth of the poor countries of the world. Their own rapacious rulers do that. God doesn't take pleasure in the death of anyone (Ezekiel 18:32). God's heart is broken because of the wickedness of godless men. God is not the originator of evil, not the architect of wickedness. He only lets it continue for a little while longer.

God didn't make the universe because He was bored and needed to pass the time. He made it with intentionality, for His own reasons, with His own ideas in mind. This is part of His sovereignty—His sovereign will. God's will is His plan and purpose that He alone decides. He has a blueprint that He's following and nobody can stop Him from accomplishing His will for the world He made. A wonderful thing we discover about God as we explore His will is that He has all kinds of great stuff in store for us in the coming ages. It's His will that we turn out to be like Jesus. It's His will to bring us safely to His house because we've put our faith in Jesus. It's His will that we should spend eternity in joy and endless delight. 1 Corinthians 2:9, ***"No eye has seen, no ear has heard, no mind has conceived what God has prepared for***

those who love him."

For some, the sovereignty of God is a problem because if He's sovereign, why are some *not* going to be saved? If He's sovereign, why does He need us to evangelize? If He's sovereign, does anything we do matter? If God is sovereign, is there still such a thing as free will? Great questions! All I can say is, if a sovereign God tells us that not everyone will be saved, that we should proclaim the Gospel every chance we get, that our actions have enormous consequences, and that even though He is sovereign He let's us chose to obey, I'm going to *table* my inability to understand God's sovereignty until I get a better brain. In the meantime, I'll trust Him.

There is a wrong reaction to God's sovereignty and that's to be *fatalistic*—to believe we're automatons acting out predetermined, scripted parts in a charade called life. Don't go there. That philosophy only wants to absolve its proponents from any responsibility for their bad choices! God's sovereignty doesn't make us puppets or Him our puppet master. He gave each of us the ability to choose to love Him back or to reject His love. Like the Trinity (or even electricity for that matter), we can still believe and engage with what we don't completely understand. There is an amazing relationship between God's sovereignty and our own free will that our minds have difficulty grasping. We can just accept the coexistence of the two seemingly contradictory doctrines, both as reality, because of our incredible Creator.

There's no one like our sovereign King, not even remotely. He's all-present, all-powerful, all-knowing. He thinks only about what's best for each of us. He knows what it's like to be human, to be frail, tired and tempted. He is merciful and gracious towards us. He is glorious and good. We couldn't ask for a more wonderful King to reign over us. It's only right to serve Him with gladness and with all our hearts, giving ourselves completely to obeying His all-surpassing will.

The reason we *know* Good wins in the end is because He can't do anything else.

3 God is eternal

know anyone who never began and won't ever end?

"NOW TO THE KING ETERNAL, IMMORTAL, INVISIBLE, THE ONLY GOD, BE HONOR AND GLORY FOR EVER AND EVER. AMEN."
1 TIMOTHY 1:17

We think eternity is endless, everlasting time. It's not. It's only *like* that. That's the closest description we can give for eternity, but that's not quite right. What it actually *is* is something we don't have the mental equipment to download. So we think of it in terms of time, but it's way beyond mere time. Eternity is *more*—more of everything good. More joy. More peace. More love. More comfort, more certainty, more excitement, more wonder, more delight. Everything that's terrific and amazing in ever-increasing more-ness. Buckle up, my good friends, it's going to be a crazy ride when we hit eternity! Get ready for more of what's great.

The average life span of humans before Noah seemed to have been about 800 years. It quickly dropped down to 40-50 years after The Great Flood. Modern medicine has propped up the average to around 70 or 80, but very few people who live past 70 have great "quality of life," whereas Moses at 120 enjoyed fabulous health, says Deuteronomy 34:7. Yet, however long we live, it's peanuts. As the old saying goes, *"Life is short, death is sure, sin the cause, Christ the cure."*

Can we imagine eternity from so short a lifespan? Even the oldest living things we know, Bristlecone Pines, only live a couple thousand years. That's not eternity! Death overtakes everything to which God gave life. Isaiah 40:6 calls man as feeble as the grass that withers at the end of the day.

The band Switchfoot has a song called *"Gone"* that says sooner or later, everything is *"Gone, like yesterday is gone, like history is gone; the world keeps spinning on, you're going, going, gone; like summer break is gone, like Saturday is gone, like Al Pacino's cash: nothing lasts in this life; my high school dreams are gone, my childhood sweets are gone; life is a day that doesn't last for long."* Don't love the world. It's gone before you can blink twice. This world is spinning down.

With a backdrop of lightweight moments that fly by, eternity comes at us like a couple tons of solid bricks. Eternity is the reality Jesus comes from. Eternity is where God the Father and the Holy Spirit live. Our own eternity began the day we were born again, but Jesus' eternity *has no beginning*. There never was or will be a time when He wasn't or won't be. Don't forget John 8:58 when Jesus famously announced to the Pharisees, ***"Before Abraham was, I AM!"*** Our eternity stretches out only into the future and only in Christ. God's eternity depends only on Himself and goes in every direction because He doesn't *exist* in time. Time is something He invented for *us* to live in. When eternity comes, we can't now understand what will happen to time. Time is not eternal, it is a created thing like us. Weird, huh?

Is evil eternal? Is Satan eternal? The answer is a resounding no. No present evil will escape the gravitational pull of the Lake of Fire, a little something God has cooked up for the wicked who hate God and refuse to be reconciled to Him. That's another thing about the two kingdoms of light and dark. The dark kingdom is like the Titanic. It may be fun for a while, but it can't last. But the Kingdom of light is like a giant intergalactic space-cruising luxury liner that renews itself and everyone in it each day. All analogies fall short, but you get the idea.

If you've ever experienced the presence of God, ever cried tears of joy and didn't know quite why, ever felt like dancing with no music playing, then, you know that getting closer to God is exciting stuff. Eternity is the ongoing continual process of getting closer to God, knowing Him better, experiencing Him more fully. And God is not like an onion! With an onion, the more you peel away, the smaller the onion gets and when you get to the inside, there's nothing. No, with God, the more you peel away, the *bigger* God gets, and when you get into His heart, there is *everything*. We'll have eternity to experience more and more the wonder of our God.

And that's just the beginning,. His plan gets better all the time. Tomorrow's amazing will be ten times better than today's ... guaranteed. Remember, it's always more of the good stuff, as much as we can possibly handle until we grow to be able to handle more and then God will give us more. Eternity is all wrapped up in Jesus Christ and the wonder of His mode of existence. He lives eternally, and He's promised that we who belong to Him will share in His eternal kind of life. Eternity seems to work just fine for Him!

Nothing else can last, unless it is properly related to the Everlasting.

4 God is omniscient

can God encounter something he wasn't expecting?

"FOR GOD IS GREATER THAN OUR HEARTS, AND HE KNOWS EVERYTHING."
I JOHN 3:20

If the universe is vast beyond knowing, and God's mind made it, what does that tell us about God's mind? We're not *able* to think His thoughts. We can't fit them into our skulls. It's not only that we're not all that bright, and we're definitely not as smart as we'd like to think; it's also that He's stupefyingly *brilliant*.

And tell me: why would we even *want* a God we could explain? Or for that matter, why would we want a God we could've thought up? Not that human people through the millennia haven't produced these kinds of small "g" gods, but you can get them for a dime a dozen anywhere you go. If you want a god who's only slightly smarter, easily manipulated, not quite ready for prime time, you definitely want a made-up one! The real God would disappoint you every time.

We can't trick God. We can't pull a fast one on Him. He's sharp! We can't hide anything from Him. He never says oops. He never experiences the unexpected. He knows too much: there's not one single thing He doesn't know. Absolutely nothing.

He knows the end from the beginning. He knows the future and the past—clear as day, every bit. He knows the square root of 3 to the infinite decimal place and can tell you in an instant. He knows the gravitational pull of Jupiter to the fractional ounce and its precise effect on our moon as well as on the orbit of Mercury. He knows the freezing point of water and the molecular structure it will assume as a solid below the atomic level. He knows every line of Shakespeare, every leaf on every tree that's ever grown, every atom in every constellation. He knows what everyone was thinking in the second grade on November 7th at 10:23 AM. He knows how hot the sun is 605,327 kilometers below the surface to a zillionth of a degree. He knows how long it took you to read this paragraph.

He's spinning the stars and moons and planets in space, and He doesn't even have to stand up to do it (Hebrews 1:3)! It's not even a strain. Why would we ever think that God needs our advice? We'd have to be really dumb to ever, ever think we're smarter than God.

Einstein is a complete doofus compared to God. Rocket science is light reading for God. God finishes impossibly tangled word problems in math before the teacher can finish posing the question. Did God know that you'd be alive and breathing right now? Yes. Does He know what your great grandchildren will be named, or if you'll even get to have them? Yes, of course He does. Does He know what really happened at Thermopylae Pass? Uh-huh. What Marco Polo had for lunch on his twelfth birthday? Yes, absolutely. Does He know the precise circumference down to the last micrometer of the largest star in the constellation called the Little Dog? You'd better believe it. The melting point, the ph, and the refractive vibration of an alloy made from 40.3% copper, 2.7% molybdenum, 8.45% zinc and the rest iron? Yes, yes, and yes. He's *always* known that. Except for the refractive vibration, I just made that up. But since it's God we're talking about, He probably knows that too.

Have you ever heard someone called a know-it-all? That's meant as an insult; it's razzing someone that they don't know as much as they think they do. In God's case, however, it's the other way around and upside down. He knows infinitely MORE than we think He does! He really does know it *all*. God can't be fooled or kept in the dark. We may think we're hiding something from Him, perhaps even keeping secrets from God for His own good, but we're kidding ourselves if we think He doesn't already know. He was there with us! He knows everything there is to know about us and *still* loves us. Just close your eyes, smile, shake your head side to side and say, "Wow!" I'll wait. Done? Okay.

There's another expression used for scholars and teachers: "So-and-so has forgotten more than I'll ever know." That means they know so much it's coming out their ears, and the knowledge they no longer have room for dwarfs what we'll ever learn. With God, that expression doesn't wash, because the only thing He forgets is our sin, and He does that because He decides to. His hard drive has infinite storage, instantaneous retrieval and needs no backup because it's indestructible.

Beyond his hyper-encyclopedic knowledge, God knows right where we are, what we're struggling with—mentally, emotionally, spiritually. Jesus knows our sorrows and offers to bear them with us. He hurts where we hurt. He knows exactly what what's-their-name did to us. He was there and remembers it with more clarity than we do. Not only did He go through all the same stuff and worse when He was on earth in a human body, but He knows just what it's like because *there's nothing He doesn't know about us*. God's omniscience is just a tiny part of his God-ness.

God knows what nobody else knows. That's a comfort to know.

5 God is almighty
can anyone or anything stand in God's way?

"IS ANYTHING TOO HARD FOR ME?"
GENESIS 18:14 AND JEREMIAH 32:27

Nothing is beyond God's ability to perform.

There was a juvenile question about whether God could make a rock so big that He couldn't pick it up. The answer is simple: of *course* He can make a rock too big for Him to pick up, and then He'd pick it up. Really, such an easy question when you have a God who can do the impossible. *Nothing* is too hard for a God of unlimited power and might. He can even make and pick up a rock He cannot make or pick up. Think on that, if you will, and see what you come up with.

The name God announces to Abraham in Genesis 17:1 is *El Shaddai* (*God provides, He is all sufficient*). Our English term, "God Almighty," comes from the Latin Vulgate translation of El Shaddai as God all-powerful (*"omnipotens:" the ability to overpower or to destroy*). While the English language doesn't have a single word that can do justice to the Hebrew name El Shaddai, the meaning still clearly shines through: God is our *everything*. He's all we need; He has unlimited power to meet our most desperate shortage. This is the name for God the patriarchs knew best, according to Exodus 6:3, **"I appeared to Abraham, to Isaac and to Jacob as God Almighty."**

God in His mighty power *provides* each of us with an escape route from any temptation (1 Corinthians 10:13). God *provides* **"seed for the sower and bread for the eater"** (2 Corinthians 9:10). He *provides* us with **"everything for our enjoyment"** (1 Timothy 6:17). Christ *provided* **"purification for our sins"** (Hebrews 1:3). He provides **"redemption for his people"** (Psalms 111:9). God gifts His church to *provide* for orphans and widows (James 1:27). Psalms 104 declares that God *provides* for every creature on the earth and in the seas. We have a hard time just taking care of our pets! God can spin the universe and feed all His creatures without breaking a sweat. That's the power of God in His provision.

One of the provisions God has in unending supply is power. God is all powerful. In other words, He never runs out, and always has all the power He needs for any situation. Once there was a ruler named Pontius Pilate who handed Jesus over to be crucified. Pilate thought *he* was all powerful and that peoples' lives were in his hands, but Jesus calmly reminded Pilate that he couldn't do a single thing if the power to do it hadn't been granted to him from God above. Power is ultimately God's. All power. Even, apparently, the power to put to death God in the flesh.

Satan is powerful, right? Aren't Satan and God fighting over the planet earth? Not at all! A creature of limited power like Satan has no shot against God Almighty. That's like a pea-shooter against a Galactic Destroyer. Satan isn't fighting *God*; he's fighting against the angels Michael and Gabriel! When God joins the fight, close the doors and gather up the hymnals, 'cause it'll be all over. Satan may think he's fighting God, but he'd better be glad he's not.

Have you ever seen a lightning strike up close? Had a brush with a tornado? Felt an earthquake turn the solid ground beneath you into quivering jello? Been nearly deafened by thunder roaring? These heart-stopping natural events are God's *toys*. He does these things with no hands and His eyes closed standing on one foot. He's the battery power that runs the universe. Never needs recharging ... never runs low.

Did you ever wonder how the moon goes around and around without crashing into earth or slingshot-ing off into outer space? How the stars hang in the night sky? How the universe sings and dances in perfect order? Wonder where the sun's energy originates from? Nothing comes from nothing! Wherever there is power, God granted it, for it is all His.

We never need to worry if God will come through, because Almighty is His name.

6 God needs nothing

do we somehow supply something God was missing?

"AND HE IS NOT SERVED BY HUMAN HANDS, AS IF HE NEEDED ANYTHING, BECAUSE HE HIMSELF GIVES ALL MEN LIFE AND BREATH AND EVERYTHING ELSE."

ACTS 17:25

We think that a ministry is something we do for *God*. But the plain truth is that God doesn't need us ... or Billy Graham or Mother Teresa or Saint Paul or Moses or Abraham. He can do it all with no help from anybody. But here's the way to look at this: if we want to get in on what He's up to, He'll let us think we're really important, like a 3-year-old helping her mother bake cookies. He wants us to have the *blessing* of ministering to others as long as we don't try to clutch at the *glory*. Glory isn't healthy for people; it's a dangerous byproduct of using God's gifts that we pass along to God for Him to render harmless. Kind of like recycling, we don't know what to do with glory. It burns us if we handle it, so we give it to someone with the capability of processing it. I don't know if you've seen what glory does to perfectly healthy people. Very few pop icons end up with lives that are not just . . . *ugly*. The <u>glory</u> goes to God, where it properly belongs, but the <u>blessing</u> of helping God in ministry can be ours. We're doing God no favors by glorifying Him. Truth be told, He doesn't *need* the blessing *or* the glory. Because He needs nothing.

But God must need our *money*, right? How else do things get done in this world? He gives us money so He can get it returned to Him in the offering plate, kind of a money-laundering scheme. Why take up the offering if God doesn't need it? I'll tell you why: the offering opportunity is for us, not for Him. God has no need of our treasure or our time or our talents. He's self-sufficient. You and I give to God because *we need to give!* That's why our God provides us the chances to participate.

Wait, He needs us to *appreciate* Him, doesn't He? Nope! He wants us to thank Him because it will bring *us* joy. Like glory and blessing and money, He doesn't need what we have. He's got it all already. All the thanks that human beings through the ages have ever expressed combined would not increase His cache ... make no discernible increase in His stockpile. He's complete in Himself, lacking nothing.

Still, He created us because He was sort of *lonely*, right? Wrongo! That's absurd. God is absolutely delighted with His own company. And why not? Who's more fun to be with than He is! He experienced abandonment at the cross, when He as the Father turned His back on Himself as the Son (try to put THAT in your brain without it exploding), but that's it. *God's got such an overabundance of love that He can lavish it on a whole world and never have less*, no matter how much He gives away. God has a glut, a surfeit, a superfluity, a superabundance, a *plethora* where love is concerned.

But surely God made us because He lacked something. What about *worship?* He can't sing praises to Himself. Where is He going to get worship if we don't give it to him? Well, Jesus said that if we were silent, the rocks would start up their own church service, but that's not the real answer.

The real answer is like the one about our offerings and tithes. He doesn't need our praise. We're the ones who *need* to praise Him. We were *made* to praise Him. We're *fulfilled* when we praise Him. 1 Peter 2:9, ***"But you are a chosen people, a royal priesthood, a holy nation, a people belonging to God, that you may declare the praises of him who called you out of darkness into his wonderful light."***

Have you ever given yourself totally over to worship and found yourself lost in God's presence, swimming in the river of God's joy? Worship connects us to the transforming power of the Holy Spirit. John Wesley describes a turning point in his life when he was "strangely warmed." Dwight L. Moody in his own words "had such an experience of His love that I had to ask Him to stay His hand." Charles Finney said he once had an experience with the Holy Spirit "that went through me, as it seemed to me, body and soul." We receive from God's presence so much more than we bring to His throne. We don't fill up God's bucket; *He fills ours.*

Ah, we might say, but now that He's become a human being, Jesus needs His family of brothers and sisters, though, doesn't He? The answer is still no. He doesn't need *anything*. He has decided that we're worth loving, contrary to all indications, and He has lavished His love and grace on us because that's just the way He's put together. *Not* because He needs us. Because He decided that He would. God's love is not a gimmick or a trick or a manipulative gesture or even an investment. It's a gift! Free and clear. No strings. No caveats. No ulterior motives.

Job 45:11 records God's rhetorical question: ***"Who has first given to me that I should repay him?"*** God owes no one anything whatsoever. Can we make Him love us more? No, though you wouldn't know that from a study of world religions. Making God love us more may be the root of all heresy! God loves us at max level right now; He has always loved us that way, even before He made us. We can only ever *return* the love He's given us, and when we return it, He STILL doesn't need it because He gave it out of His overabundance. He gave us His own life and still had so much life that He never even missed what He gave.

So is there nothing that God needs? *That's it.* That's what God needs: nothing. We can't bribe Him. We can't cajole Him. We can't obligate Him. We can't withhold from Him. We can't make a deal with Him. There's nothing we have that He needs anyway. We're completely at the mercy of His grace, and glory to God. He even has an overabundance of <u>that</u>, ready to pour out on us!

God cares for our needs because He has none of His own to care for.

7 God is love
would God really lay down his life for us?

"So we know and rely on the love God has for us. God is love. Whoever lives in love lives in God, and God in him."
1 John 4:16

God's love is a sure thing. There's nothing in all existence that comes close. It's God's love that enfolds us, wraps us in His grace and mercy, keeps us from permanent harm, and lifts us into His presence forever as the apple of His eye, His beloved children. His love is not doled out tiny bit by bit; it's a raging torrent.

Man's love is based on fragile feelings; God's love is based on an irrevocable choice to love. Man's love is inconsistent; God's is rock solid. Man's love runs out; God's love is inexhaustible. Man's love is based on an aspect of the recipient; God's love is based on an aspect of the donor. Man's love is based on necessity; God's love is based on a superabundance. Man's love possesses; God's love liberates. Man's love is self-aware; God's love is self-effacing. Man's love is the stuff of pop songs that eventually flame out; God's love is the stuff of never-ending angel choirs. Man's love turns heads; God's love turns the world around. Man's love responds; God's love initiates. Man's love is offered; God's love is lavished. Hello. I mean, holy Toledo. Can we get the difference? Is this too hard? Should we slow down?

Go ahead and do your Greek word studies on love. *Eros* (attraction), *Philia* (friendship) and *Agape* (self-sacrifice). Good. We should know the differences. Great sermons have come from that study. Undeniably, our English language doesn't begin to do justice to the complex ideas contained in the word "love." Yet the thing that separates God's love from all other loves is that God's love *transforms*. It reaches and delivers and protects and beautifies. God's love moves and animates and seeks and inspires. Other loves may reach this plateau periodically, but God's love *lives* there. His love changes absolutely everything.

Love is God's MO. He doesn't leave home without it. Even His righteous wrath is checked by His love. Wait, did I just say that love is how God operates? That's not quite right. Love is not what God *does*, it's who He *is*—love *defines* God. God *is* love. Love is seen unfiltered in the face of God. And the face of God is Jesus of Nazareth, through whom God plainly demonstrated His heart for all humankind.

There's ready proof that God loves us. There is irrefutable corroboration. Just look at what Jesus was willing to do to express His love for each one of us. Laying aside His splendor and glory, His authority and will, His nature and His dominion ... He became a frail baby. He lived in constant danger of disease, exposure, accidental death, and outright murder (Hebrews 5:7). From being Joy himself He became **"a man of sorrows"** says Isaiah 53:3. From unrestricted fellowship to agonizing abandonment by His heavenly Father (Mark 15:34), when He took on the sin of the world and drank from the vile cup of our sins. Standing silent before slanderers and false witnesses, making no reply to the trash and the taunts, resisting the temptation to come down from the cross and squash the scornful in their mockery of him (Mark 14:60 and Luke 23:35).

And then—unthinkably—to surrender His life. Life Himself gave up His life, abandoning His very essence, as reality careened on the edge of insanity. God *died*. Impossible. Unimaginable. Unthinkable. God died for us. Yes, He rose again, for how could He do otherwise? Should you ever wonder if God loves you, remember the cross and what Jesus said about what He thinks of you there.

Now we, recipients of the life-giving rays of God's love, have become satellites that scatter His signal. We, who have come down with a bad case of God's love, are contagious carriers. We, who are swimming in the joy of God's love, are pleading to those on shore to dive in. Calling to those on the ground to soar in the bracing air of God's life-giving love.

We're both the targets and the demo models of His love.

• CREATOR

if you construct the cosmos, do you own it?

"THROUGH HIM ALL THINGS WERE MADE; WITHOUT HIM NOTHING WAS MADE THAT HAS BEEN MADE."
JOHN 1:3

David in 1 Chronicles 16:26 put it this way: the people of the earth have made gods for themselves, but *our God made the people of the earth*. Nice.

Nothing has life unless God first lends it some of *His* life. We live because He decided we would. Do you see why God told Adam and Eve they wouldn't just be sorry, they would *die* if they choked off their lifeline through rebellion? God didn't have to kill Adam and Eve, it was a double suicide. Acts 17:28 says everything owes its very existence to God. Nothing could exist without His prior existence. From His BEING everything IS. It must amuse God when people wonder if He exists! As C.S. Lewis laughed, "As if the good Lord had nothing to do but exist!"

We've been misled. The theory of evolution may explain variation *within* a species; however, Darwin called his book *The ORIGIN of Species*. A much more lofty boast. Clearly the book falls woefully short of its title with a tautology for a mechanism: the fittest are defined as the ones who survive. A bankrupt dogma masquerading as intelligent thought. Reject the lie that your life is a happy spontaneous accident.

Follow me into some hip-deep waters. A "singularity" is a threshold. For instance, beyond our birth we don't know if we existed. There's no data that has made it across the portal to this side. The major singularity for our universe is thought to be the Big Bang. Present scientific thought can't formulate what the universe was before they claim it expanded into its present state. So if a scientist tells you you're an idiot for believing in creation, let them know their sawing off the branch everyone is standing on. No one has a cosmology that accounts for anything past their own initial singularity. Secular scientists have a mystery made out of nothingness even though they know that they don't know what they don't know. They think our sun spun out the planets by accident, but won't allow the possibility that our very existence was spun out of God's central, huge, bright-burning life.

Scientifically speaking, there's no explanation for space, time and matter to even be here except that Somebody *made* it be here. Write off the creation account as myth, but it's the only reasonable narrative we have. Don't try to sell me the one about exploding hydrogen gas or rocks in hot water. Those fairytales are oddly popular today among the hyper-educated class, laughable to everyone else. When we catalog the stunning design and complexity of the world we must conclude that it was unquestionably *fashioned* and that whoever did that is stunningly brilliant. Assuredly powerful. Unquestionably artistic and a lover of beauty. The designer of the operational laws of physics and morality. Without God, there can be no science, for science can only discover and catalog the laws set into place in the initial build-out of the space-time reality. Scientific laws can't *create* a single solitary molecule. They can only hope to partially *describe* what we see in the world around us.

The most important corollary to the fact of our creation is this: *God is the owner and master of His creation,* the whole enchilada. It belongs to Him, because He made it. Right along with that ownership is His self-assigned responsibility for *sustaining* it. Each spring we get new plants, new bugs, new horses. The trees inhale the oxygen-depleted air we exhale and re-oxygenate it, then we breathe the oxygen out and send it back to them for more. The moon continues to orbit the earth, never closer or farther away, causing tides which produce abundant plant and animal activity which renews the ecosystem. This continual renewal violates the scientific law of entropy: that systems left to themselves run down. Our system is not left to itself.

Our own bodies heal from wounds and viral infections and our emotional state can be rejuvenated because our Maker renews and renovates. He restores and replenishes, recycles and restocks. He didn't wind the universe up like a clock and walk away as Richard Dawkins the atheist lamely argues. He stays in touch moment by moment. Read Job 38 on and tell me God doesn't sustain His creation. God's not some kind of parent who never thinks about their kids. Instead, He's intimately, daily involved with His creation, causing the sun to rise and His creatures to find food, making sure that everything we need is provided for us, even to the extravagance of showering us with hope and joy and love.

Our Creator doesn't need sleep, or food or exercise! Our Creator doesn't need to learn. He doesn't need to grow. He doesn't need to explore. Our Creator doesn't need to be worshipped. He doesn't need to be served. Our Creator doesn't need our self-abasement or our subservience. Our Creator doesn't need our money. He doesn't need our love. Our Creator doesn't need our tears or our blood or our sacrifices. Romans 11:36 says it like this: ***"For from him and through him and to him are all things."*** That about covers it!

We cannot obligate God because all we have comes from Him.

1 Trinity and Unity

if we can't understand it, is it still true?

"HEAR, O ISRAEL: THE LORD OUR GOD, THE LORD IS ONE."
DEUTERONOMY 6:4

"THEREFORE GO AND MAKE DISCIPLES OF ALL NATIONS, BAPTIZING THEM IN THE NAME OF THE FATHER AND OF THE SON AND OF THE HOLY SPIRIT."
MATTHEW 28:19

Trinity is a word you won't find in the Bible. No matter. The theology of the triune God is standard orthodox doctrine. Just check out the two Christian creeds at the end of this book. Or look at the baptism of Jesus: the Son of God in the water, the Spirit descends, the Father God speaks from heaven. All three of them there at the River Jordan, all of them together God and each of them individually God. No one said it was easy to understand ... it's not. We only declare it. We can't even begin to comprehend it. Like a panorama that won't fit in our camera lens, no matter how far we back up.

The Trinity is in unity. There's no disagreement between the Father, Son and Spirit. They're all on the same page. One in purpose, one in character, one in identity. You cannot possibly divide the three natures of God. They're indivisible, like the number 1 itself. Consider the mathematical equations: $1 + 1 + 1 = 3$, and, equally true: $1 \times 1 \times 1 = 1$. The ones can be together as three *and* the ones can be together as one. If God explained it to us, we still wouldn't get it, so He never *has* explained it as far as I know. We don't worship the Son over the Father, nor the Spirit over the Son, nor the Father over the others. Christians are not polytheists!

God is one. Notice in Genesis 1:26 that when God creates people He says, **"Let us make man in our image."** Who's God talking to? The angels? No. They didn't make us; we're not made in *their* image. Is He talking to the other gods? Psych! There aren't any! So who IS He talking to? There's nobody else there but Him. He's *talking to Himself in the plural.* In <u>Lord of the Rings</u>, Gandalf was asked why he was muttering to himself, and he replied, "A habit of the old. They choose the wisest person present to speak to." Ouch!

Nature's full of echoes of the Trinity. Like water, which can be a solid, a liquid or a gas. Like an egg with a yolk, a white and a shell. Like a butterfly which also appears as a caterpillar and a chrysalis. Three *and* one. Three *in* one. Three. One. Whichever you pick, congratulations, you're absolutely totally partially right.

The Nicene Creed states that the Father is uncreated, that He *begot* the Son, and that the Holy Spirit *proceeds* from them both. Many heresies have arisen in the last two thousand years such as Gnosticism that specifically attack this truth. The enemy must think the doctrine of the Trinity is strategic somehow. He even has his own bizarre kind of trinity with the Dragon, the Beast and the False Prophet. Read Revelation 16:13. Imitation is the sincerest form of flattery. But don't study the unholy trinity; study the holy one! Both are mysteries.

Since we're made in God's image and God is three in one, we also have three parts to *our* being. Listen to the Apostle Paul in 1 Thessalonians 5:23, ***"May your whole spirit, soul and body be kept blameless at the coming of our Lord Jesus Christ."*** Paul is telling us the same thing that the She'ma says, ***"Love the Lord your God with all your heart, soul and strength."*** Our bodies are just temporary earth suits until we get eternal ones to once again house our heart (spirit) and soul (mind and personality).

Three. One. God calls Himself the *Father* and we get that. Even if our earthly fathers don't measure up, we still know deep inside what a father ought to be like. *God the Son* came to earth to teach us how to please the Father, then died in our place for the sins of the whole world, rose in victory from death to life, and now intercedes for us with the Father. When He rose, the Son sent us *God the Holy Spirit*, to comfort, guide, bring to mind, empower, and to live inside us. God is three. God is one.

The Father is *total otherness*. The Son is the *place where we touch God*. The Spirit is the *continual presence of the Living God*. And they all are all of them. There's only one of them. All of them are one of them, just as one of them is all of them.

The Trinity is the original relationship. All others come from His with Himself.

2 incomprehensible
would we even want a God who could fit in our brains?

"OH, THE DEPTH OF THE RICHES OF THE WISDOM AND KNOWLEDGE OF GOD! HOW UNSEARCHABLE HIS JUDGMENTS, AND HIS PATHS BEYOND TRACING OUT! WHO HAS KNOWN THE MIND OF THE LORD?"
ROMANS 11:33-34

We wouldn't even *want* a god we could understand. So good news—we don't have one of those. Instead, we get the real thing—a God who is beyond our figuring out —a God who does things we don't understand. It doesn't stop us from getting to know Him, but it sure puts a damper on our comprehension of why He acts the way He sometimes does.

Read about the early Christian martyrs and the people around the world going through horrific persecution. Does it make sense that God allows Christians to be tortured and killed? It's hard. I'd like to know why God allows His own dear family to be persecuted by the evil powers of this present darkness. Everyone's got some ideas, but the full explanation is over our heads. God tries to help us understand by saying that seeds must die to produce a harvest, that adversity is important to being an overcomer, but it still doesn't take away the painful questions or the tears when it happens to you or someone you know.

Have you ever seen pictures of starving, bloated children, flies buzzing around their sores and the bones clearly visible in their little bodies? Doesn't God care? Of course He does. Then why do children still starve? I don't have a satisfactory answer. I do know that He tells us to feed them, and in so doing we will be feeding *Him*, but it seems like an inefficient way of getting food where it's desperately needed, trusting to selfish people like you and me to provide for them when He could rain down food from heaven and feed them whenever He wanted.

Look up. Why does the earth continue to orbit the sun instead of slowly spiraling in through centripetal force to crash and burn? Or why aren't we slung into space by centrifugal force? Same thing for the moon and the earth, the Solar System and the Milky Way, and the electrons in our bodies. How does lightning figure out what to hit? How does a coil of wire and a magnet produce electricity? Where does light come from when you turn a light switch on? Where does it go when you turn the light switch off? Why is our planet the perfect temperature range for us to be able to survive? Why is water wet? Whatever clever demonstrations you've seen, nobody really knows. Nobody can really explain it. There are answers for some questions but even those answers only heighten the mysteries shrouding the world around us. Often, the best explanation we can come to is no more complicated than "God did it." We seek answers, but often only come away with more riddles.

Why is God good? Why does He even want us in His house? Why did He pick Abraham? David? Mary? What's in it for Him to befriend us whose intellect (compared to His) is equal to a box of hammers? Why does God love us? Why did Jesus die for us? What could He possibly see in us? As we've already said, God is incomprehensible. Explanations are partial, they fall short, they can mislead.

If God fed His thoughts into our brain undiluted, the sensory overload would explode our skulls long before we had downloaded even a trickle of them. That's the kind of God we really want. That's exactly the kind of God we have.

Don't feel badly about not being able to understand God. I think we should rejoice. It's actually a *comfort* to be as dumb as the sheep God loves to call us! I don't know if you're up to date on the intellectual capacity of the ruminant species *Ovis aries*, but I think we already talked about the box of hammers and we'll leave it at that. When God calls us knuckle-headed sheep, it's not the insult you might think. It's an honor to be *His* knuckle-headed sheep ... cared for, led to green pastures by quiet waters, carried in His arms and protected by His watchful strength. The sheep don't *understand* the shepherd, they follow Him, depend on Him, and belong to Him.

It's not vital that we understand God. The question is, do we love and trust Him? Will we follow Him?

3 the uncaused cause: ex nihilo
so ... question: who made God?

"I AM WHO I AM. THIS IS WHAT YOU ARE TO SAY TO THE ISRAELITES: I AM HAS SENT ME TO YOU. SAY TO THE ISRAELITES, THE LORD, THE GOD OF YOUR FATHERS, THE GOD OF ABRAHAM, THE GOD OF ISAAC AND THE GOD OF JACOB HAS SENT ME TO YOU. THIS IS MY NAME FOREVER, THE NAME BY WHICH I AM TO BE REMEMBERED FROM GENERATION TO GENERATION."
EXODUS 3:14-15

Modern materialists trace their heritage to the Greeks who, they claim, first threw off the superstitions of the surrounding cultures and began to describe nature as a series of operational formulas: scientific laws. The Greeks were the first, they say, to posit the idea that those laws created the universe by just doing what they naturally do. Gravity, repulsion, inertia, magnetic fields, electrical currents, orbital mechanics, yada yada, blah blah.

But centuries before the Greeks had a single thought, the Jews could have already told them that laws never *produce* anything, they can only *describe* something that's already been produced. The cultures around the Jews believed in gods that worked the forces of nature like a puppeteer, but in stark contrast, they claimed that God created the governing laws of nature along with nature itself. No self respecting Jew would buy materialism or naturalism; that was for the dimwitted and the superstitious. The Greeks didn't eliminate the gods; they just substituted impersonal laws for personal gods and never figured out the ultimate truth—there *must* exist at the core of everything a Causal Being, deep beyond the laws of science and yet the instigator and author and genesis of those very laws.

Moses heard God Himself announce His own name, **"I am who I am."** Other translations of the Hebrew have been "I am *that* I am," "I am *because* I am," "I will be *that* I will be," and "I will be *who* I will be." I don't know which is absolutely right, but they all say that God *is*. Nobody undergirds Him, overarches Him, or caused Him to be. Everlasting, infinite, immeasurable, boundless, never-ending, and that's not the half of it. His is-ness is ultimate.

I love what Dr. Shadrach Meshach Lockridge replied when asked where God came from: *"The reason God came from nowhere, was there was nowhere for Him to come from. And coming from nowhere, He stood on nothing for there was nowhere for Him to stand. And standing on nothing, He reached out where there was nowhere to reach and caught something where there was nothing to catch, and hung something on nothing, and told it to stay there."*

Everything else is everything else. God *made* all that. God is uncreated and self-existing, needing no one's help to begin or continue. The time-space continuum is His, to do with as He pleases. This isn't idle speculation. This is an inescapable fact about reality. God *is*. He just *is*. If that perplexes or confuses you, join the club.

This is why God does not exist *in* time. Time is His creation, His servant, His toy, His instrument, but He does not *exist* in time any more than you exist in a pie you make. Again, I'm not expecting any of us to understand, but it's absolutely true.

The Latin word *nihil* means "nothingness." It speaks of the state of the universe before God decided there would even be one. God made it "ex nihilo," out of nothing. There was nothing but God, then God made everything. The Apostle John says in his gospel that without Christ, nothing was made that has been made. Sure there are phrases like "man made material," and "whip up supper," and "conjure up a reason" and even the phrase "cough up some cash," but no one expects you to just magic-wand space and matter and energy out of *nothing*. Only God can do that.

Everyday we face people at work, in school, on TV, in the movies and even at church who say that everything in the universe came from an explosion of hydrogen gas. The typical response of most of us has been, "Well? Where did the gas come from, huh?" But that sort of misses the point. People who say the universe came from exploding gas are *bluffing*. It's not that they can't answer the question where the gas came from, they can't answer *any* question whatsoever about this mythical gas: What was it doing before it exploded? Why does gas explode? Why did THAT gas explode? What caused it to explode? What would we expect to happen from such an explosion? And the kicker, why gas? Those who speak of this hot gas are full of their subject.

It's like the people who get all excited when they discover the presence of water on Mars. They think it proves that life could have formed there because they believe life on earth happened due to the simple availability of water. Is there water somewhere? Oooh! The sun might bake rocks in that water and accidentally produce deoxyribonucleic acid which could become a giraffe! These people who get happy about water are thinking in the shallow end of the pool.

They don't know beans about where the universe came from; they just don't want to believe God did it. Why? I don't know,. Maybe because they'd have to bend their will to God's will and change their behavior to please Him instead of pleasing themselves. So they form societies of really smart people, people with four and five degrees in advanced something or other, and repeat to each other that the universe came from exploding gas. If they wanted, they could tell each other that the world came from a bean burrito in the freezer section of the gas station, but they think it sounds better to say it came from exploding gas. But what they believe is *stupid*. And to believe in something stupid isn't smart. Is it?

It takes less faith to believe God caused everything than to believe that the universe is an accident of something big-banging to make everything. Please. Give it up.

"Ex nihilo, nihil fit." That's Latin for, "nothing comes from nothing." Logically, the

inverse is true too: something could only come from Something. And all the someones in the world could only come from a Someone. Our minds can only come from a Mind. Our personhood can only come from a Person. Don't give me exploding gas. I'm not a nincompoop! Well, not a *complete* nincompoop. And I'd have to be a complete nincompoop to think the universe just magically happened.

Good news. There actually is <u>another</u> created world that will someday come, that's being put together as we speak (read John 14:2). And that world will also not be caused accidentally by exploding gas or anything else. It will be from the Uncaused Cause whose name starts with a "J" and ends with an "esus."

When God told Moses His name, He said it was "I am that I am." Another way to say that is "I am the uncaused Cause."

4 purposeful
does God really know what He's doing?

"I MAKE KNOWN THE END FROM THE BEGINNING, FROM ANCIENT TIMES, WHAT IS STILL TO COME. I SAY: MY PURPOSE WILL STAND, AND I WILL DO ALL THAT I PLEASE. WHAT I HAVE SAID, THAT WILL I BRING ABOUT; WHAT I HAVE PLANNED, THAT WILL I DO."
ISAIAH 46:10-11

You know, *it ain't braggin' if you kin do it.*

God is highly intentional. This is a hallmark of God's nature—that He's deliberate and full of purpose. He's never caught off guard or has to rethink His strategy. As it says in Ephesians 1:11: ***According to the plan of him who works out everything in conformity with the purpose of his will.*** Did you notice the noun "everything" in that verse? What part of "everything" leaves anything out? Nothing in the whole of space and time is haphazard from God's perspective.

God didn't create the world just to pass the time; He made the world and put us in it so He could be actively and purposefully involved. Does it sometimes seem to us like we have been forgotten by God? That He's got other stuff that's more important, stuff that takes priority and He can't be bothered with our little petty lives? Don't believe it. God has got plenty of attention span for every minor detail of a thousand universes. He can spin the stars and planets and know when your hamster is out of water and never skip a beat. He can be running a series of super nuclear reactors like the stars in Orion and be concerned that Miss Johnson's second grade class is out of construction paper without a perceptible power drop.

His plans reach from the first inkling He had to create the time-space continuum until the final curtain will come down on it, and beyond. "Row, row, row your boat" is a lie. Life is *not* a dream. It's not an accident either. We've been told that maybe God started everything, but then after He wound up the universe like a giant clock, He got bored or angry and walked away. That's nonsense. Everything in the cosmos is immersed in God's grand design. He's totally hands-on. Read Isaiah 49:15-16: ***"Can a mother forget the baby at her breast and have no compassion on the child she has borne? Though she may forget, I will not forget you! See, I have engraved you on the palms of my hands; your walls are ever before me."*** God <u>will</u> not forget us.

How could God, who invented the law of gravity, not have a purpose for it? Why did we ever fall for the joke that God gave us an appendix that has no function? How could God be haphazard, who made water to be uniquely *less* dense as a solid so ice floats to the top as water freezes, preserving life in ponds and rivers through the winter? How could God, who has placed the galaxies in perfect paths through the heavens, not have a trajectory plotted for our comings and goings? How could God, who made our lungs and eyes and heart in their precise complexity, not have a plan for our souls? How could God be flying by the seat of His pants when He decided He would die for us before He even created us? Revelation 13:8 says Jesus was on the cross at the inception of the world. Read it and see what you think. "Oh no!" has never been uttered by the mouth of God, nor has that idea even remotely entered the tiniest corner of His mind.

God *purposed* that He would work in and through us to share His love with the people He created, the ones He loves so much. We partner with Him in His mission to reach hearts and minds with the good news. Like getting to help your dad fix the car when you're six years old, you're not much help, but you get to know your dad and you learn a lot about cars. We get to know God and learn about the world around us as we get to share in His awesome work.

Ephesians 2:10 says, ***"For we are God's workmanship, created in Christ Jesus to do good works, which God prepared in advance for us to do."*** The false religions of the world seem to think that if we DO enough right things, God will love us, that if our good works outweigh our bad works, that we can enter into God's heaven. They've got the good works thing exactly backwards. We're not saved by *doing* good works on our own so as to earn God's approval. No! We're saved *in order* to do them ... do them alongside our Creator, in joyful relationship <u>with</u> <u>Him</u>. We can get in on what He's doing now and in the ages to come. Good works are an indication that our lives are under new management, heavenly ownership. The title of our life has been transferred from Sin, our old master, to God, our new master (Romans 6:13-14).

Jesus said to judge a tree by its fruit (Matthew 12:33). He's really not talking about trees; He's talking about people. "Fruit" is a word picture of good works—acts of love and kindness towards others. John 15:5 says, ***"If a man remains in me and I in him, he will bear much fruit,"*** and 15:16 says, ***"I chose you and appointed you to go and bear fruit."*** Matthew 5:16 says to let our light shine so others may see our good works and glorify God. More purposefulness.

We're not going to spend eternity playing harps on clouds. God designed and built us to share in doing His good works both in this world and the world that is to come—works He planned before time, works He always intended from the very beginning. Though some of us MIGHT be playing harps, how many harpists do you think we'll really need? Think about it: someone will have to bang on the drums.

This is ultimately God's purpose—to have us join Him in what He's doing. And what He's doing is beyond the most exciting stuff we can possibly imagine.

5 immutable
is God the same in the Old Testament as in the New Testament?

"I THE LORD DO NOT CHANGE."
MALACHI 3:6

God is immutable, unchanging. The upshot for us? This means that God is utterly dependable. He's not like the mercurial thermometer. He's not like the shifting sands. He's not like the changing weather. He's not like a fickle friend. He's the same, yesterday, today and forever. If you sample Him during Abraham's time and compare that to a sample of Him today, you'll find the exact same amazing God.

That's comforting. Think about it. How many times have we wished for the good old days? We go to our favorite restaurant and it's got a new chef who misses the whole point of our favorite dish. We go back to a theme park we loved as a kid and the magic is gone. We see a friend from high school who's changed for the worse. The weather changes, the scenery changes, the economy changes, our outlook changes. Well, one thing never changes. God. His purposes, His character, His values, His precepts, His righteousness, His promises, His goodness, His steadfast love. Rock solid.

We go to elementary school until we are kicked out to go to high school until we're kicked out for college and then they kick us out to look for a job that will one day kick us out to look for another job that will kick us out. Change. As we age, our noses and ears grow, while our eyes and mouths stay the same. Change. As we sleep, fire ants from somewhere south advance and build new fortress mounds in our sidewalks, yards and parks. Change. The balance of power in the world careens from east to west and back again. Old allies become enemies and old enemies become allies. Change. If you leave food out on the kitchen counter, it begins to turn furry blue as it's eaten by microscopic organisms you didn't realize were even *in* your kitchen and would rather not have known about. Totally-gag-me change.

Did you know that the orbit of the moon is decaying? It's racing around the earth at a velocity change of a centurial rate of +10 arcseconds (whatever THAT means)! Add into that the measurement that the earth's rotation is slowing, makes the moon appear to be speeding up as well. The gain in speed is due to a smaller orbital arc, which when combined with the velocity of the moon makes it accelerate in speed. Like taking a corner more tightly: you save time. But the moon's orbit is changing. One day, says the Bible, it will "turn to blood." Yucky change again.

It's expected that all things will change. Everything, without exception. Rivers find new channels, continually leaving behind old beds for new ones. Glaciers which covered continents in thousands of feet of ice are long gone, leaving lush green landscapes, warm as toast. Oceans dry up to form inland seas which turn into salt flats. Mountains are lifted up and then eventually worn down, then lifted again. It's hard to see, but it happens with absolute clockwork certainty. Life is born, grows up, matures, ages and dies ... and those same molecules become available for another life. Change is in the fabric of creation but not in the fabric of our Creator.

That's why God is so unique. There's no one remotely like Him. He stays the same. You wonder if you can have a relationship with Him like Moses, the friend of God? You can. He's immutable. You wonder if God will ever do miracles in your life? He will, because He's a miracle-working God and He's immutable. Do you wonder if God loves you the way they told you He did when you were in Sunday school? He does, because He's immutable. Do you worry that He might forget the promises that he gave you when he called you as a beloved member of his own family? He won't, he's immutable. Don't depend on anything or anyone else. I promise you they will change. Depend on God. He promises us that He will *never* change.

Unchanging, unvarying, timeless, static, fixed, permanent, constant, unchanged, consistent, uniform, undeviating; stable, steady, unchangeable, unalterable, invariable. Immutable.

Isn't that what we want from the One on whom we are building our lives?

6 imago dei

why do kids look like their parents?

"THEN GOD SAID, 'LET US MAKE MAN IN OUR IMAGE, IN OUR LIKENESS.'"
GENESIS 1:26

Unlike what the secular humanists would have us believe, we're not highly evolved members of the monkey family. You may need to throw open a window, lean out and scream, "I AM NOT AN ANIMAL!" Because you're not. You're made in the image of God. A gorilla is not made in the image of God. I hope you really get that.

The image of God includes the distinction of mind and spirit that we do not share with the plants and the animals. We are something *other*, akin in a far off way to the *other*-ness of God Himself. Like the rest of the universe we're created, and yet we should carefully note the differences in our manufacturing.

First, we were made *last*. This is not insignificant. God made a world and then put us in it. That says something about how He feels about us. I don't care about how huge the sun is ... it was made seemingly for us. Don't try to impress me with the vast extent of the known universe, we occupy the place of honor in the created order. Space was made on day one, and the heavenly bodies were made halfway through the week. And after everything else was in place, God said, "Now! For the final crowning display of my imagination and power, I'll make the most remarkable thing of all. I'll make people." We were made last, and that's good.

Second, everything else came into being via voice command. *"Let there be light! Let there be swarms of fish! Let the ground produce vegetation! Let there be tame and wild and creeping things!"* But that's not the way people came to be. He <u>formed</u> us. Genesis 1:26 says, **"Let us <u>make</u> man."** Genesis 2:7 says He fashioned us out of dust. This is amazing! The Hebrew verb the Holy Spirit employs here is also used to describe the throwing of pottery. God was uniquely involved in our making, in a very different way than the rest of creation. With us, He got down and got His fingers dirty. The animals were called into being by His voice, and we were brought into being by His hand.

And third, Genesis 2:7 also says that God did a unique and surprising thing with us —He *breathed* into us and we came alive. Can we say, "Wow"? This is a stupendous revelation. *We have God's own life breathed into us* who are made in His image. His essence, His calibre of being, His class of animation. A gift, freely given. Before we were created, He decided His life-giving breath would bring us life. How 'bout that?

Question: For what conceivable reason would God have made us in His image? Attempted answer: Being made in God's likeness gives us the capacity to *relate* to Him. We can't interact with bugs very well, but we can interact with horses and dogs much better. They have a kinship to us in mind and heart. Yet, much closer is our kinship to God's mind and heart. God made us like Him for relationship's sake. Cool, huh? More on that in the next section ... stay tuned and keep reading.

You might say that we don't appear to be made in God's image. We appear to be like the animals in our appetites and our passions. Far from looking like God, we look kind of sickly and off our meds. Romans 1 says people knew they should worship God but they wouldn't do it, and as a result they lost their minds. Humanity is caught in a downward vortex. Romans 3:10-12 says there's not a "good apple" in the whole barrel of us: **"As it is written: There is no one righteous, not even one; there is no one who understands, no one who seeks God. All have turned away, they** *have together become worthless; there is no one who does good, not even one."* We used the gift of free will to rebel against God and set up our own kingdoms where <u>we</u> were in charge … where everything happened the way <u>we</u> decided. How's that working for us down here these days? Good or not so good?

God's image is hard to see among us as we scratch and claw to protect our turf. Racial affinity separates us, based on the outside 4 millimeters of skin tissue. Cultural, linguistic, educational, religious, and socioeconomic differences separate us. Ideological differences, philosophical differences, x-chromosomal differences, and *especially* sports team differences divide us. But whatever divides us, we're all the family of man descended from Adam and Eve who were made in God's image; there are no exceptions. In each person on earth, we can recognize the image of God. This means that everyone is worthy of respect. Again, no exceptions allowed.

Being made in God's likeness means we have the capacity to grow in godliness. The more your dog hangs out with you, the more "human" he becomes. The more we hang out with Jesus, the more we begin to look, act, talk and even think like Him. 1 John 3:2 says, *"Dear friends, now we are children of God, and what we will be has not yet been made known. But we know that when he appears, we shall be like him, for we shall see him as he is."* The Imago Dei, the image of God, once marred beyond recognition by our sinfulness, is being restored; little by little, a step at a time.

God is three persons, and like Him, we have three parts: body, soul, and spirit, according to 1 Thessalonians 5:23. You think that's not huge? Think again! Our bodies will one day die, but our soul and spirit will be housed in a new body that will never die, never grow old, never experience pain or sorrow. Our souls house the intangibles unique to each of us, such things as our personalities, our sense of humor, propensities, giftings, wiring, memories, and preferences. And our spirit houses something far beyond, for Jesus Christ lives in the temple of our spirit when we are born again. Three parts: body soul and spirit. The picture of the Trinity is uniquely to be seen in us who bear the likeness of God.

Psalms 8:5 says that although God made human beings lower than the angels, we who surrender to God will someday be raised to even greater heights than they. God really does love us, as whacked out as we are; and somehow, He can see His image in us. Did I mention that He has *really* good eyesight? When He looks at us, He sees a bit of Himself. Not the fallen, sinful part. No, instead He sees the part of us that looks like Him: glorious and eternal. He sees us as He is making us to be. He sees us as His own, His beloved, His treasure (Malachi 3:17).

Did anyone ever tell you that you have your Father's smile?

7 relational

do you suspect God's trying to connect with us?

"Jesus replied, 'If anyone loves me, he will obey my teaching. My Father will love him, and we will come to him and make our home with him.'"
John 14:23

For God, it's *always* been about relationship.

Yes. Sure. God rained down fire on Sodom and Gomorrah, laid down the law on Mt. Sinai, wiped out nations, sent plagues, stopped the sun, and warns us that He will one day destroy the universe . . . but even in His wrath, God is redemptive. Even in His judgment He is reconciling us to Himself. He acts to turn us from wicked ways that will eventually kill us, like telling a dog to stop chasing cars. He wants us to turn back from deadly choices and return to Him. When we do, He establishes a covenant with us—a secure, well-defined, lavishly generous *relationship.*

He didn't make us so he could have servants! He wanted friends. He wanted confidants. He wanted brothers and sisters. He wanted kids. He wanted to share the wonder of His life and love, not for His sake, but for ours. Not for His enrichment, or fulfillment, or satisfaction, but for ours.

When a person returns to their Creator, the picture the Bible gives us is not of a captured slave who has to knuckle under or be punished. Instead the picture is that of a *bondservant*: voluntary obedience that's both honorable and personal. Exodus 21:5-6 says, *"But if the servant declares, I love my master and my wife and children and do not want to go free, then his master must take him before the judges. He shall take him to the door or the doorpost and pierce his ear . . . Then he will be his servant for life."*

Relationship. Closeness. Voluntary surrender. Offering our life back to the One who gave us both our life and our freedom. Plus, according to this Exodus 21 verse, you get a cool earring. Well, maybe that's only in the Old Testament.

You may have observed prayer from a Hindu or a Muslim or an American Indian. They're impressive as far as prayers go. They're confident. They're full of reverence and awe. But one thing they're *not* full of, and that's personal relationship. Judeo-Christian prayer is quite different from all other religions. The reason? While we approach God with the same fear and reverence, we also approach Him with joy and anticipation coming before a Father God who loves us and calls us His own. Our prayer is highly *relational.*

So when Christians pray, it's not an exercise in ritual, but more like a telephone call to the most powerful and wonderful friend we have. Always available. Bonus: He pays for the call. (Jesus did that on the cross; He paid for everything.)

Christians don't believe God must be appeased or placated. We don't have to make God happy. Jesus did that for us at the cross. Anyway, God has everything He needs already. There's nothing we can do to make Him love us more than He already does.

Speaking of relational, our new relationship with God transfers seamlessly to our whole world. Jesus is the initiator of a new way of interacting among us all. We were estranged from each other and from God Himself, but no longer. We're *reconciled* to God in Christ, and reconciled to each other in the same way.

Don't believe me? Look at the Royal Law that Jesus instituted. You thought Jesus ended the law, but He really fulfilled it. What is the Royal Law (the law of King Jesus)? It is simply this: "Love one another *in the same way that I have loved you*" (John 13:34). Because of His finished work on the cross and the empty tomb, Jesus has inaugurated a new era in personal relationships. This changes *everything*. Not just the relationships *among* us ... it changes US! Once *we* are changed, the relationships just fall into place! He gives us a new heart with the capacity to love as He loves.

God is all about relationship. He loves us, and not just sort of. Ever heard the term "Christophany?" This is a pre-incarnate appearance of Jesus, perhaps including Abraham's third angel (who stayed with Him when the other two went off to destroy Sodom and Gomorrah), the angel who wrestled with Jacob, Moses' Melchizedek, Joshua's Commander of Heaven's Armies, Shadrach, Meshach and Abednego's extra man in the fire. God couldn't wait for the Bethlehem stable to be with us. He came to be with us in the person of Jesus perhaps multiple times BC. It's really fun to wrap your brain around these "extraordinary" people who come out of nowhere to rescue and to reveal. Theologians disagree on which appearances are the Lord Jesus, but that doesn't stop us from wondering, does it?

Not content to have been with us BC, and during His earthly ministry, when Jesus ascended, He comes to us as the Holy Spirit. Jesus is not avoiding us up in heaven. He's not busy at the office. He doesn't hide from us. He's not far off. We're not an inconvenience to Him. He's not a dead-beat dad. He continually comes to us with all of His amazing self and gives us a chance to know Him better (since He already knows us perfectly).

The Tabernacle was called the tent of *"meeting."* Get it? God arranged a place where we could come into relationship together with Him—sanctified man and holy God. Same thing with the Temple of Solomon and later the Temple of Zerubbabel. The earthly tabernacle has disappeared. Both earthly temples are destroyed. But God still has a holy place to meet with us on earth: inside each born-again child of God. In John 14:23, He said He'd make His home *in us*. We are now the tabernacle where the Ancient of Days dwells. Each of us, and together as the body of Christ, we are the temple of the Living God.

He wants us for His friends. He calls us His children. He came to visit us long before Bethlehem. He tabernacles in us. He's the one who initiated the relationship. He's the one who made a way for us to know Him by what He did at the cross and the empty tomb. He must want to press into our lives and become more involved in our everyday deal. He must want to draw closer, heart to heart with us. He must mean it. He must be serious about this relationship thing.

We ought to be serious about our relationship with Him, too.

• JUDGMENT

do we really want what we deserve?

"FOR WE MUST ALL APPEAR BEFORE THE JUDGMENT SEAT OF CHRIST, THAT EACH ONE MAY RECEIVE WHAT IS DUE HIM FOR THE THINGS DONE WHILE IN THE BODY, WHETHER GOOD OR BAD."
2 CORINTHIANS 5:10

The Bible has some major points to make—understatement of the millennium. The biggest takeaway is the <u>good</u> news of Jesus. The *next* biggest revelation is the <u>bad</u> news that God cleans up wickedness by pronouncing and executing judgment.

The epochs of God's work among us can be roughly divided into *dispensations* which are the stages of His unfolding plan. Crucial point that must be made: dispensational theology doesn't limit God! The dispensations are a device for us, not a barrier for Him. They help us gather what we know about God's working among us into grand piles of generalized accomplishments. The dispensations are often fashioned to be seven in number: the Garden of Eden, the time of conscience (knowing good and evil), the time of God's covenant with Noah (God promises to never again destroy by water), the time of the Patriarchs (Abraham, Isaac and Jacob), the time of Moses and Israel (the Law and the Prophets), the time of the Church and of grace (we're in this right now), the thousand-year reign of Christ (coming as surely as the sun rose this morning).

At the end of each dispensation, God sends a judgment, a *cataclysm*. Cataclysm demarcates each generalized period of God's work. So how many do you think there are? Did you say seven? Sharp.

Check this out. The dispensation of innocence in the Garden of Eden ends in God's judgment called *The Fall*. The dispensation of conscience from the tree of the knowledge of good and evil ends in *The Flood*. The dispensation of the post-flood nation of Ham, Shem and Japheth ends in judgment: the confusion of man's single language at *The Tower of Babel*. The dispensation of the promises God gave the

Jewish patriarchs ends in judgment: *Egyptian slavery*. The dispensation of the Mosaic Law ends in judgment: the conquering *invasion of the kingdoms of Israel and Judah*. The dispensation of grace in which we now live will end in judgment: *the second coming of Christ*. The millennial reign of Christ will end in the final battle and the judgment of *the Lake of Fire*. I just find that fascinating. I love big picture stuff.

Judgment has nothing to do with any milquetoast, wimpy modern secular idea of *fairness*. That kind of fairness is different from each person's perspective. Sorry, but God doesn't care about our precious opinions on that. He cares about what's <u>right</u>. Justice is about *truth*. God's justice is black and white, cut and dried, plain as day and not up for discussion. With God, it's either right or it's wrong. 1 Corinthians 3:10 says God torches all of our works to see if they can take it. If they burn, they weren't built out of the right stuff. That's a severe test! We're very concerned with *intentions*. We say, "Sorry, but I *meant* well." God is more concerned with results, not what we intended to do, as a barometer of our hearts. You want to argue? Read the parable of the fruit tree in Luke 13:6. The status of the fruit saves or condemns the tree. Read the parable of the two sons in Matthew 21:28. One intended to and didn't, one refused and then did it anyway. Jesus prefers the ultimately obedient over the initially well-intentioned!

In the end, crime does *not* pay. No one "gets away with it." There's a reason that we don't celebrate scumbags and mass murderers, however innovative and charismatic they may be. It's the same reason we celebrate those who work hard, sacrifice and persevere. And, in the end, they will receive what they've labored so long to attain. We innately agree with God's values because He made us. In the DNA of the universe, we understand that evil must be judged and good rewarded.

Our crimes go way beyond admitting we've broken a few rules. Imagine if your home were invaded and the thugs began to throw the furniture around, shooting out the windows, battering your TV and computers and then brought their degenerate pals in to party in your home after kicking you out.

God made a perfect world and we, aided and egged on by the fallen angels, trashed the place and kicked Him out ... not the way the environmentalist religion claims. It's actually worse. We trashed the world spiritually, behaviorally, intellectually, morally, physically, intrinsically. All you have to do to see the extent of the damage is to browse a news website any day of the week. Horrible, gut wrenching stories of wickedness and outrage. Gross, hideous displays of arrogance against God.

What would *you* do if you were Him?

You'd deal with the problem. Once and for all. That's exactly what God's going to do. The last time He did it, He submerged the world under water in a cataclysmic flood, leaving only eight survivors. This next time, no one will survive except those who are in Jesus' boat, trusting Him to save them from the coming wrath of a righteous and personally insulted God. It might look right now as if the wicked are getting away with their evil, that Satan has a free hand, that the dark world is chewing up the naïve suckers who try to live for Jesus, but just wait a while and see what happens in the end. One day, Christ will stand up, roll up His sleeves and clean house. The naïve suckers will be looking good that day.

For more information, search for biblical references to "the day of the Lord," and hold on to your pants.

1 mercy
does God ever let anybody off the hook?

"LIKE THE REST, WE WERE BY NATURE OBJECTS OF WRATH. BUT BECAUSE OF HIS GREAT LOVE FOR US, GOD, WHO IS RICH IN MERCY, MADE US ALIVE WITH CHRIST EVEN WHEN WE WERE DEAD IN TRANSGRESSIONS ..."
EPHESIANS 2:3B-5

Pure undiluted justice would make carbonized toast of us all for repeatedly and willfully breaking God's rules. But God's mercy reaches out in forgiveness, and even more than that, restores us to fellowship with Him. His perfect justice hands down faultless punishment, and happily, if we will only turn to Him, His blessed mercy steps in to intercept that very punishment in the finished work of Christ on the cross. God's heart is revealed in James 2:13, *"Mercy triumphs over judgment."* We'd have no respect for a God who *wasn't* just, and we'd cower before a God who was *only* just, but we fall awestruck before a God who is *both* just *and* merciful. Here is a God worthy of our worship.

There's a wonderful story about a magistrate who finds the convicted man brought before him to be none other than his long-lost childhood friend. As a righteous judge, he passes the full sentence the crime deserves and requires. Then, taking off his robes and laying down his gavel, he comes down from his high seat of judgment, steps in front of his friend and takes upon himself the full judgment and consequence of his friend's sentence. This is a picture of God's mercy in Christ. Jesus Christ steps in front of the just punishment we earned and intercepts our death sentence.

When you stop and think about it, mercy makes no sense. Who expects mercy in this dog-eat-dog world? Mercy is for the dupes. Mercy is for the bleeding hearts, the do-gooders and dreamers, the saps who don't know the hard realities of life, right? In God's case, wrong. He's no wide-eyed idealist. Just try to pull a fast one on Him. Yet, He continually operates in mercy, not weakness by any stretch of the imagination, but rather God's overwhelming strength held in check by His own volition. God is secure in His power, therefore He's merciful.

If you read 1 Peter 1:20, you'll know that Jesus had already decided to go to the cross long before He made the world. How did He know that the cross would be necessary? Hey, He's God. We'll just have to settle for the fact that He knows it all: front to back and then back to front again.

But more than deciding to die for us before He ever made us, why give suckers like us a break? Why mercy? Why indeed? Would we worship an unmerciful God? Many would. Many wish God would rush in right now and start handing out absolute justice. Especially to so-and-so who did such-and-such to us. We want God to work them over, to rise up like some Norse god and hurl fire and lightning on them from above. Read about this very thing in Luke 9:54. The disciples were tossed out of a city and wanted to know if they could call down fire on the people like Elijah did. Jesus rebuked them and said (paraphrasing), "Our family doesn't do that."

Truth be told, we want justice for everyone else and *mercy* for ourselves. Destroy them. Save me. Yet God, the offended one, has issued a blank check of forgiveness and grace. The one with the power to pardon has spoken up for all of us on execution row.

Read what's written *after* John 3:16, that God sent Jesus not to condemn, but to save the world. That's mercy. This world has earned annihilation. If we could see some of the things evil people have done to kids we'd be wanting God to eradicate the universe. But God, who weeps for the lost according to Luke 19:41, in His mercy gives each of us every chance to turn back to Him. He doesn't deal with us as we deserve for our transgressions and our trampling of His Son and our mockery of His love. His heart is like the father of the prodigal who waits at the window for the returning son, running to meet him in acceptance and mercy.

Have you ever wondered why Jesus split His coming to us into two visits? It's gut-wrenchingly beautiful when we see it. The second time He'll come to judge, which is what we all expected Him to do when He came. But God does not desire the death of anyone. He does not wish to enter into judgment with the people He loves so much. So, instead of coming to condemn, He came the first time to rescue, to offer an escape route; He came on a mission of mercy to lead us out of the coming destruction. He loves the whole world so much that He came the first time to this planet to die on a cross so that whoever turned back to Him could receive His mercy and life eternal. Many focus on God's awful judgment as reason to reject Him, but if we could ever realize the price He paid on His first visit so that we could escape the due penalty of our rebellion, we would fall on our knees in awe before him. We would shout our praises as we lay prostrate on our faces in His presence.

How can we not love such a God?

2 the fear of the LORD
can we be scared of God in a good way?

"I TELL YOU, MY FRIENDS, DO NOT BE AFRAID OF THOSE WHO KILL THE BODY AND AFTER THAT CAN DO NO MORE. BUT I WILL SHOW YOU WHOM YOU SHOULD FEAR: FEAR HIM WHO, AFTER THE KILLING OF THE BODY, HAS POWER TO THROW YOU INTO HELL. YES, I TELL YOU, FEAR HIM."
LUKE 12:4-5

Really, someone might say, the fear of the Lord simply means that we should have a healthy respect for God. Nuh uh. Not even close. Anyone who tries to sell that soap has never read about people in the Bible who meet heavenly beings like Gabriel, let alone seraphim with eye-covered wings and living gyroscopes for transportation! When we meet real angels, we can't see, we can't move, we can't think, we fall down like we had been struck and lie there hoping to die. That's not a description of healthy *respect*. These are all the symptoms of abject *terror*. We should have healthy respect for poisonous snakes, submerged wall sockets, and lightning. Yet God . . . well, He's in His own category as far as respect goes.

Jesus said in Mark 12:17 that we should give government the respect it deserves and give God the respect *He* deserves. These are two different leagues in the game of respect. The government can only arrest you and your family for no cause, confiscate all your assets, torture and starve you in a windowless pit with no trial, and then put you to a messy death. That's it. No more. But God can do that and *then* throw you into hell! Our fear meter for God should be way past pegging. It should be spinning like a propeller.

If our mothers went with us wherever we went, we wouldn't do half of the stuff that we do. We don't want our mothers to see us behaving the way we often do. This is a clue to why the fear of the Lord is "pure," according to Psalms 19:9. Follow this. When we were born again, what happened? God came to live inside us. This means that there is now no place or time when we're not in the presence of God; after all, He's right inside us every moment of every day.

So forget about your mother seeing you do stuff. We have to worry about God watching every move we make! He's not looking down from heaven with His vision blocked by a planet or a group of angels now and then. He's with us when we told that lie, when we passed that hurting person without a second thought, when we laughed at that freak, when we snuck a little more for ourselves. The fear of the Lord, when we realize that He's always with us, as He promised in Matthew 28:20, will keep our feet on the narrow road, never *wanting* to wander off. Fear of God is a clean motive.

When the teacher leaves her class for a while, the students begin to look around to see what happens next. Perhaps someone will make a bathroom noise that gets timid chuckles. The rebellion grows from there and who knows how far it escalates. God sometimes seems like that teacher: Jesus ascended into heaven and left us behind on the earth and we don't know when He's coming back.

In the meantime, it seems like the bad guys are running the show. Periodically, God sends calamity like an earthquake or a disease or a tsunami or some kind of attack, and for a time, our hearts turn back to Him in repentance. Then evil goes unpunished and the cycle starts again. But, unlike Eastern religions which see the universe as a Möbius strip, God has an itinerary. The seasons will stop, the world will grind to a halt, the moon will turn dark red, the stars will fall from the sky, the sun will no longer rise.

One day, the cycle will end, and Jesus will return not as the Lamb, but as the Revelation 19 conqueror whose eyes blaze like fire, whose robes are dipped in blood, who rides a white horse, treading the winepress of the furious wrath of God. On that day, the Bible says there will be standing pools of human blood 5.5 feet deep. With a word, this Rider will strike the combined armies of the entire world and chop them to pieces with the sword of his mouth.

"Healthy respect" my eye.

The fear of the LORD is the beginning of wisdom, says both Psalms 111:10 and Proverbs 9:10. If we would be wise, we must learn what it means to fear the LORD as we ought to fear Him. 2 Peter 3:11 asks, since the whole universe will one day be incinerated into smoking non-existence, what kind of people should we be?

It only makes sense to fear the overwhelmingly terrifying God whose fiery presence will one day incinerate the sun.

3 the Great Flood

can you tread water for a year?

"Long ago by God's word the heavens existed and the earth was formed out of water and by water. By these waters also the world of that time was deluged and destroyed."
2 Peter 3:5-6

The Great Flood has been inarguable history for all but the last 150 years of civilization. But since the ascendance of the quasi-scientific dogma of Neo-Darwinian evolution, our intelligentsia no longer believe in the Great Flood. They claim the world is governed by a principal they label *Uniformity*. Uniformity states that whatever processes are at work today explain what happened in the past. As you can easily see, this principle is untestable, and therefore an article of faith. Why the great "brains" of recent times should substitute their article of faith for faith in biblical revelation is the real question. But let's look at the amazing usefulness of uniformity in making definitive statements about things of which we can know nothing.

If we measure the quantity of sediment at the Mississippi Delta and then measure how much sediment was deposited last year, we can calculate precisely how old the Mississippi River is! Brilliant! And happily, unverifiable! It works beautifully as long as God doesn't do anything to muck up our calculations with a catastrophic event. Like a local flood which happens constantly somewhere on the fourth longest river in the world. Like a levee break, as in the one that happened in 1927. Like a drought, such as the one in 1988. Like an earthquake that causes the water to flow *backwards*, as it did in 1811. If you want to apply the Principle of Uniformity to the age of the Mississippi River, *none of these events did happen or could happen.* You see the problem with introducing a secular dogma into empirical science: you hamstring the science with your lamebrain assumption.

That's why, for the modern scientist, the Great Flood *can't* have happened. It messes with all our beautifully illustrated charts and graphs.

Modern science is riddled with perverse naturalist ideas. Naturalism is the unprovable belief that what we see is all there is. Since you can't see God, according to Naturalism, he doesn't exist. The visible world is the limit of what's going on, say the naturalists. If it won't move a thermometer or show up on a camera, forget it. These days, we're told that if you believe the Bible you are obviously anti-science. But you see, modern science was begun by Roger Bacon and developed by others, most of whom were Bible-believing Christians. Yet, according to our naturalist criteria, the ones who pioneered modern science also must be anti-science! You see how it works when you carry utter nonsense out to it's logical conclusion.

Peter was told by the Holy Spirit that in the last days, people would do something never done before: deny the Great Flood. 2 Peter 3:3-6, ***"In the last days scoffers will come ... They will say, 'Where is this coming he promised? Ever since our fathers died, everything goes on as it has since the beginning of creation.' But they deliberately forget that long ago by God's word the heavens existed and the earth was formed out of water and by water. By these waters also the world of that time was deluged and destroyed."*** This verse proclaims that the patently unthinkable will happen in the last days of the earth. Proud people will deliberately forget what has been known to everyone for thousands of years: the watery destruction of the ancient world. Not believing in the Great Flood was so perverse that it would be a *sign of the last days* when we saw it happening! These same people will talk all day long of the mythical city of Atlantis disappearing beneath the waves, not realizing they are describing Noah's Flood.

And did you notice what the scoffers in that verse said? According to those who think God is never coming back, everything goes on "just like it always has." Voilà, the principal of Uniformity! *"Move along citizens, there's nothing to see. No miracles, no catastrophes, no God to interfere with our graphs and charts. The present is the key to the past. What Flood? It couldn't happen."*

The lie of Uniformity supports the farce of Darwinian evolution. Pull that theory out and there is no Darwin. Uniformity also props up the theory of the Big Bang which says the universe is a glorified clock. Time is god. Time is creator. And the bonus of believing in Time as the creator? Time is impersonal. It will not condemn anyone for depraved behavior. Time will not toss you into hell for your rebellion against the King of Heaven. We can do as we darn well please with no worries about judgment if Time is god. Time becomes the mindless force that brought about the cosmos and all living things. These people will tell you, "It doesn't matter how. We're here, aren't we? Time *must* have accidentally created everything, since everything is here or else everything wouldn't be here, um ... right?" Just tell them you don't believe time did it. Your theory is that cornstarch was responsible. Makes just as much sense.

The Great Flood destroyed the ancient world. Why would God have done such a thing? What does the Great Flood teach us? It teaches us that God is in complete charge no matter how much people try to tell themselves and others that He doesn't exist. It teaches us that there's a limit to God's forbearance. It teaches us God will destroy what cannot be redeemed. It teaches us that we need to fear God, obey His commands and find out what pleases Him. It teaches us that God is merciful even in His wrath. It teaches us that when God judges a planet whose time has run out, He will provide a way of escape for those He loves.

Our scripture above about the Great Flood continues in 2 Peter 3:9 to say that God is going to destroy the earth a second time not by flood but by fire. It warns, **"The Lord is not slow in keeping his promise, as some understand slowness. He is patient with you, not wanting anyone to perish, but everyone to come to repentance."**

The Great Flood is a stern warning and a great hope: God brings wickedness to utter destruction and still is forever able to bring fierce deliverance to those who are his own.

4 the judgment of God's children
are parents who spank their kids trying to kill them?

"WHEN WE ARE JUDGED BY THE LORD, WE ARE BEING DISCIPLINED SO WE WILL NOT BE CONDEMNED WITH THE WORLD."
1 CORINTHIANS 11:32

How faithful do we really have to be once our ticket for heaven is punched? Can't we just sort of slide through the pearly gates with minimal effort? I mean, we're in.

Why go for holiness? Why would we want to be like Jesus? That's hard. Really hard. Too hard. (*It's actually impossible ... which is why we need Jesus!*)

1 Corinthians 9:24 says we run the race of life to win the prize. God does not want us limping through the gates poor, penniless and defeated. We should know that there'll be a final test, not of our belonging in the family of God, but of our stewardship of His gifts and responsibilities. God is like any investor, wanting to see a return on His investment. What will we have to show Him?

God's discipline of His children is *pain with a purpose*. He wants to make us stronger. Palm 84:5-6 says we walk through times of discipline so that we may grow in strength. That makes all the difference. His discipline is a course correction, not a disqualification. It's the difference between walking a tightrope over a pool of sharks or over a pool of sharks with a safety net to catch us. His constant care is the safety net over which we make our awkward way across the tightrope of life. Tough times are a blessing. There's a reason we're going through whatever He's allowed to come our way. I like what Mark Heard wrote, "Out in the eye of the storm, the friends of God suffer no <u>permanent</u> harm."

God not only disciplines those of us whom He loves, He disciplines entire nations to bring them to repentance. Hurricanes, famines, earthquakes, enemy attacks ... God could stop them but He allows them to happen. Could He be entering into discipline with nations, to turn the people's hearts to Him and to His will? Don't ever rule that possibility out. There are preachers who pipe up with this after many "natural" disasters, and the standard reaction is to roll our eyes. Next time, it would be better, I think, to check and see if it could be true. The old-fashioned word is "chasten," a word we need to rediscover and incorporate into our thinking.

In these modern times of permissive parenting, God's discipline may seem old school and harsh. We coddle our children and tell them they're wonderful and perfect. We paste stars and smiley faces on their homework, even when it stinks. God's not like that. He's more proactive. I'm guessing He probably knows what He's doing.

God's children are not exempted from judgment, just the judgment of condemnation. We will still be judged, but it will be as an inspector judges a builder's house. 1 Corinthians 3:14-15 reads, ***"If what he has built survives, he will receive his reward. If it is burned up, he will suffer loss; he himself will be saved, but only as one escaping through the flames."*** The Bible is clear about the children of God being judged, not for their sins, but for their deeds. When Jesus talked in Matthew 6:20 about laying up treasures in heaven, He was speaking to God's family, the ones who have an eternal bank account in the ages to come. God's judgment of His children is for their good, and for their growth.

This testing is sort of like homework assignments at school: Did you do the paper the teacher assigned, or did you turn in whatever you felt like? If you turned in whatever you felt like, how did your teacher react? How do we expect God to react if we come before Him with whatever we felt like or didn't feel like doing?

Like all analogies, it breaks down at some point, because God's children can't flunk or be kicked out of the family. But they can arrive in heaven without the stored-up treasures Jesus speaks about in Matthew 6:20. Earthly treasures can be stolen or devalued or lost, but heavenly treasures will be waiting for us there. God loves us all exactly the same, but that doesn't mean our behavior on earth is inconsequential. It matters how we build our lives.

Discipline is redemptive. So why do we complain so loudly about undergoing it?

5 the judgment of the dead
is there a final reckoning of the unbelieving?

"THEN I SAW A GREAT WHITE THRONE AND HIM WHO WAS SEATED ON IT. EARTH AND SKY FLED FROM HIS PRESENCE, AND THERE WAS NO PLACE FOR THEM. AND I SAW THE DEAD, GREAT AND SMALL, STANDING BEFORE THE THRONE, AND BOOKS WERE OPENED … THE DEAD WERE JUDGED ACCORDING TO WHAT THEY HAD DONE AS RECORDED IN THE BOOKS."
REVELATION 20:11-12

Frightened? We should be. The Bible gives us a raw picture of the absolute terror that is coming upon the dead. Yes, *the dead.* There is no hiding place from God, though people will ask the very earth to shield them from His righteous anger, says Revelation 6:16-17: *"They called to the mountains and the rocks, 'Fall on us and hide us from the face of him who sits on the throne and from the wrath of the Lamb!' For the great day of their wrath has come, and who can stand?"*

We don't have to be the objects of God's wrath. We can choose to let Jesus' finished work at the cross protect and defend us in that day. If not, there's no other Savior. We're on our own. Some people want nothing to do with God. They want to be left alone to live and die their own way. Well, anyone can live as they like, but when they die, they have an unbreakable appointment with God's throne of judgment.

We cannot easily turn a blind eye to God. God is the King, the Creator, the Master, the Owner of the world. Those who return to Him He will welcome in compassion and love. As for those who remain rebellious, flaunting His laws and spitting in His face, He will bend their knees *for* them, against their will. Jesus prayed, "Thy Kingdom come, *thy will be done.*" Do you think His prayer has gone unanswered? God's will is the only will that prevails in the end. Jesus prayed that into reality and instructed His disciples to continue that prayer.

In Romans 14:7, Paul says that none of us lives or dies to himself but to God. God is not optional viewing. He's not someone who just goes away. Ask anyone who's dying, whose mind is still clear. We all know that God is who He is. C.S. Lewis writes in _The Great Divorce_, "There are only two kinds of people in the end: those who say to God, 'Thy will be done,' and those to whom God says, in the end, 'Thy will be done.'" Textbook definition of irony.

Because God made us with a free will, we have the capacity to stiff-arm Him and end up separated from Him. Permanently. At some point (a point that God only knows), the door will close and the judgment of the dead will arrive with terror and precision. Revelation 20:14 says that death will be thrown into the Lake of Fire. Does anyone think they can _hide_ from God in death? Then, why would they think they can hide from Him in life? Hebrews 4:13 says, **"Everything is uncovered and laid bare before the eyes of him to whom we must give account."**

There are books in heaven that keep a deadly accurate account of every person who's ever lived. Every one of us is running a tab, so to speak. There's a record kept of each rejected chance, each shabby deed and each wicked thought. We may have hoped that nobody saw, or heard, or guessed, but the plain truth will be right there in the books. The "books will be opened" at the judgment of the dead, according to Daniel 7:10 and Revelation 20:12. Those books contain the evidence to convict each person of willful rebellion against the King of Kings. Those books and the record they contain will testify against us. Don't like it? It doesn't matter if you do or don't.

There's only one plea that carries any weight with The Judge: the blood of Jesus. Every other defense will fail. Every other excuse will fall on deaf ears. This Judge cannot be gulled or hoodwinked. He cannot be bought off or gotten around. We all know John 3:16, **"God so loved the world ..."** and so on. That same section of John says, three verses later in John 3:19: **"This is the verdict: Light has come into the world, but men loved darkness ..."** The verdict pronounced on our sinfulness is eternal separation from God. Separation from life is death. The _judgment of the dead_ will send the unrepentant to the Lake of Fire. You've heard of the Good News? This is what's known as the bad news.

The bad news helps us really "get" the astounding amazingness of the good news.

6 hell

if people don't want to be with God, where do they go?

"[HELL:]WHERE THEIR WORM DOES NOT DIE, AND THE FIRE IS NOT QUENCHED."
MARK 9:48

Expletives are made from the weightiest words: God, Jesus Christ, damnation, hell. Nobody yells "Buddha!" or "Allah!" or "Nirvana!" or "Valhalla!" when they hit their thumb with a hammer. Other nouns just don't fit the requirements needed to qualify as profanity. Why is that? Feel free to come up with your own reason, but I think that Satan wants to trivialize certain proper names, including hell, so he prompts us to feel big when we blaspheme God or trivialize hell. The devil wants us to think hell's not so bad; it's a kind of cool place where you can get away from all those hypocritical church people and live eternity on your own terms. Cartoonists make jokes about the symphony conductor locked for eternity in a room filled with banjo players. Actually, that's *funny*. But then the full force of the finality of separation from God brings us back to knowing that hell's no laughing matter.

Hell, contrary to popular opinion, is not the empire of the devil, nor will it be his final, ultimate address. The devil is not in charge of hell. Who is? Not sure, probably a really large and high ranking heavenly angel. Jesus has the key, not Satan, if that tells you anything! Revelation 1:18. The Bible describes hell as a temporary holding cell for the most undesirable denizens of the universe: a fiery, violently destructive prison where wicked men and fallen angels are kept in flaming agony until the judgment. It's no joke. Hell is a horrific place of lasting torment. And even though hell is a moral necessity of a just and holy God, He wishes that nobody would ever have to go there. He wants everybody to be saved, according to 1 Timothy 2:4.

Hell is nothing to idolize. This seems remarkably self-evident, but much of our culture today casually *toys* with the darkness and the demonic as if hell were the more "exciting" place than heaven. Wrong, wrong, <u>wrong</u>! Hell's the last place you'd want to be if you had an ounce of brains. There's nothing exciting or alluring about it. Movies have romanticized it, but they romanticize a lot of disgusting trash. Never think of hell as anything but the second worst place in the universe. FYI, the number one worst place to end up belongs to the Lake of Fire, our next topic.

Is hell everlasting? Ironically, no. It gets burned up in the Lake of Fire. There may be existence in the Lake of Fire that continues, but it's no kind of life we can imagine, so let's not. Is hell the opposite of heaven? Definitely not. Hell is the opposite of what some Christians call purgatory and the Jews called Paradise. One is a death row of the unrighteous, the other the green room of the righteous. Sometime, google "Clarence Larkin" and find his wonderful charts from 1918, especially the one called "The Underworld", though they're all brilliant. Maybe they will offend your theology, but that's okay, right? Yours probably offends his! It's all good.

Did Jesus descend all the way into hell to pay for our sins? That's a sticky wicket. Some, I'm one of them, say yes, according to 1 Peter 3:19 and the early renditions of the Apostles Creed; but Christian doctrine is not adamant about this. Don't worry about it. Know that Jesus did *everything He had to*. When He won our salvation there was nothing He left undone. If He had to go into hell to secure our rescue, He went, and if He didn't, it doesn't matter. If He *did* go, it was so you and I wouldn't have to.

We might think street preachers who rave about hellfire and brimstone embarrass God. Nothing could be further from the truth. God's love will go to the limit to turn us away from hell, which includes scaring that very place out of us.

7 the Lake of Fire
what finally happens to what cannot be salvaged?

"AND THE DEVIL, WHO DECEIVED THEM, WAS THROWN INTO THE LAKE OF BURNING SULFUR, WHERE THE BEAST AND THE FALSE PROPHET HAD BEEN THROWN. THEY WILL BE TORMENTED DAY AND NIGHT FOR EVER AND EVER . . . THEN DEATH AND HADES WERE THROWN INTO THE LAKE OF FIRE . . . IF ANYONE'S NAME WAS NOT FOUND WRITTEN IN THE BOOK OF LIFE, HE WAS THROWN INTO THE LAKE OF FIRE."
REVELATION 20:10, 14 AND 15

All who are born will also die. Those who have the second *birth* will miss out on the second *death*. Those who will not obey the command of Jesus to undergo the second birth will undergo the second death—eternal separation from God Himself.

The *first* death is something that everyone will experience with some notable exceptions: Enoch, Melchizedek, Elijah and those left alive until the coming of Jesus. The *second* death is the Lake of Fire. The Lake of Fire is the final fiery destination of evildoers, as well as the devil and the demons, death and hell. Per our scripture above, the only escape is to have your name written in the Book of Life.

This is one of the most heart-wrenching things we will ever have to study. At some point, God will quit holding the door open for those who refuse to come in. His patience is inexhaustible, but He knows when the time will come that all of us who are coming will have responded. Jesus said in Matthew 24:14 that the gospel will be preached to the ends of the earth and then the final curtain will drop. When the earth is finished, it will be destroyed, not scattered like blocks that might be collected and rebuilt, but made to be nothing. 2 Peter 3:12 says that the elements, the building blocks of all matter, will be *undone*, disappearing in intense heat.

When you redact a document, it can still be partially read. When you shred a document, it can conceivably be pieced together. When you burn a document to fine ash, *it ceases to be a document*. Nothing comes out of the fiery lake of burning sulfur. Death itself will be thrown in along with all the demons and Satan himself. The Lake of Fire is eternal, not only in duration but finality. Termination. Nothingness. The Lake of Fire is not a holding tank for anything. Not even the incinerated trash. In this Lake, things are not simply held like in the Abyss and hell. In that place, things are disassembled and returned to nothingness—burned up as if they'd never been. From that death there is no resurrection. There's no way out.

In what form does this fire appear? John in Revelation says it's a lake. Don't ask me how fire can be a lake, I don't know. But I do know a lake has a finite capacity. Heaven is boundless, but evil will end up within precisely delineated limits.

How do we tell our friends and family that if they will not follow Jesus they might burn forever in the Lake of Fire? I don't have a good answer to that, we're dealing with some of the most difficult matters of Christian doctrine. I can only say that if we don't warn them, perhaps we're not loving them in the most clear-sighted way. Knowing what we know about the Lake of Fire gives us a responsibility of letting others know. I'm not talking about scaring people, but we shouldn't sugarcoat anything either. God told us about this place for a reason: *He doesn't want anyone to go there.* The fact is, one day God will judge everything and what will not be part of the Kingdom will remain part of the Burning Nothing. If they won't surrender to God there's a price to be paid. God is not going to have a trashy house.

We see a forest fire and we know that the brush and dead wood that burn are gone. The fire makes room for new growth of the trees in the forest, renewing the soil and jumpstarting the process of releasing vital nutrients for the remaining plants. The Lake of Fire is redemptive too, in the total destruction of the wickedness of this world, and in ways that we cannot process now. God's ways are always good, always right, always for the best.

For us who follow Christ, the next age will begin with the devil's works gone for good, burned up without a trace. Are you hearing me? 2 Peter 3:13 says we're looking forward to a new creation—the home of righteousness. The new creation will be something we can't imagine—a world without evil. Not a trace of it. No wonder there are no tears in heaven except tears of joy. Darkness may rule the headlines for now, but when the new world comes, we won't give it a second thought.

Part of making room for newness is getting rid of oldness altogether.

How would you like it to find yourself sailing on an unsinkable luxury liner in April of 1912 and the captain announces, "I've got good news and bad news! The good news is that we're opening up the kitchen, so come eat whatever you want, as much as you want, then throw the rest of it on the floor and dance! The bad news? Let's just say you'd better eat fast . . ." That's what the Law is like. The Law is very good, but in the end, the Law is an iceberg that will sink a ship full of scofflaws.

. . . .

¬chapter three
LAW: THE IMPOSSIBLE STANDARD
who told God He could make the rules?

"NOW WE KNOW THAT WHATEVER THE LAW SAYS, IT SAYS TO THOSE WHO ARE UNDER THE LAW, SO THAT EVERY MOUTH MAY BE SILENCED AND THE WHOLE WORLD HELD ACCOUNTABLE TO GOD. NO ONE WILL BE DECLARED RIGHTEOUS IN HIS SIGHT BY OBSERVING THE LAW; RATHER, THROUGH THE LAW WE BECOME CONSCIOUS OF SIN."
ROMANS 3:19 AND 20

God did not give us the Law to make us good. God's not naive. The Law doesn't make *anyone* good, it simply reveals the goodness, or in our case the wickedness, inside us already. You don't give your children laws about playing with tigers or lighted sticks of dynamite in order to make them good. The great irony of world religions is that they're all an attempt to make people good by obeying man-made regulations. If we can't be made good by observing *God's* rules, how will it help to make up our own? Apparently, it still doesn't stop us trying. We're idiots.

Truth be told, one reason He gave us the Law was to demonstrate exactly how perfect we have to be to make it into heaven on our own. Would you let your preschool football squad play an NFL pro team full of 300-pound maulers? Would God give us false hope that we might be good enough, only to arrive at the gate with absolutely no shot? No. The Bible never says that if we obey *most* of the Law, we can live forever. It plainly says that if we mess up just once, we might as well have broken *all* of God's laws for all the good it'll do us on Judgment Day.

This is the tyranny of the Law. Juan Carlos Ortiz says we used to belong to Mr. Law, a righteous taskmaster we could NEVER please. He was always condemning us, and he was perfectly right to do so. The situation was desperate. One of us had to die, and since Mr. Law could not be killed, *we* must die. In Christ, we died at the cross and are now free to belong to a new Master: Jesus, who loves us. Mr. Law is still chugging along though, in perfect health. He never grows a day older. Mister Perfect. He is in fact holier-than-thou, and the sooner we realize it, the sooner we can plead the blood of Jesus. Until then, we're under the brutal system of the Law.

So why does God get to make the People Rules? Easy. He made the people.

• COVENANT

will God set limits on Himself for our benefit?

"I WILL ESTABLISH MY COVENANT AS AN EVERLASTING COVENANT BETWEEN ME AND YOU AND YOUR DESCENDANTS FOR THE GENERATIONS TO COME, TO BE YOUR GOD AND THE GOD OF YOUR DESCENDANTS."
GENESIS 17:7

We don't use the word "covenant" anymore, perhaps because we don't keep promises anymore, but the word covenant is a highbrow theological term that the Bible is riddled with. It just means "an agreement." Actually, it's an *ongoing* agreement, not a piece of paper backed by a court order, but a living pledge taking place moment by moment. It's an adventure, not a monument.

King David, a man after God's own heart, does not consider his covenant with his great friend Jonathan to be completed even after Jonathan has been dead for years. In 2 Samuel 9:3, David puts forth every effort to find a remaining relative of Jonathan with whom he can continue to honor their covenant. This is a picture of God's promise-making style. God's promises are never in default. They never expire. They never go bad on the shelf. They're never *over*.

God makes binding agreements and calls them covenants. He keeps them without blinking. He makes covenants with nations (Exodus 19:5). He makes covenants with individuals (Genesis 6:18). He even makes covenants with Himself (Genesis 22:16). In the Old Covenant, agreements He made with people were contingent on whether people kept up their end of the bargain. In the New Covenant, He keeps *both sides* of the agreement. This is the "good" part of the good news! If the gospel of the Kingdom of Christ were just another agreement we couldn't keep, the news wouldn't be that great. The new covenant is complete amnesty, total provision, and God holds up both sides of the deal. *In Christ*, of course.

His covenants are as famous as the rainbow, and as amazing as the new birth. His covenants are as exacting as the one He made with the children of Israel and as loaded with assurances as the one He makes with His blood-bought adopted children. His covenants are binding, closely monitored, and everlasting because He is a covenant-keeping God. The small "g" gods of the ancient heathen nations were capricious. Those gods were more likely to change their minds than to keep their word. But God is not like those small "g" gods. He forgets none of His promises. He is not mercurial.

If God weren't God, the covenants He makes would be outrageously impossible to perform, so, good thing God *is* God. One of the covenants was the promise that He would send us a Savior to rescue us from The Fall. He told Satan (Genesis 3:15), Abraham (Genesis 49:10), Moses (Deuteronomy 18:18), and David (2 Samuel 7:12). He bound Himself with this promise that the Messiah was coming. Physicists for years have looked for the principle that will tie all the actions of the universe into one nice package. They call it the theory of "everything." Well? This is that. Jesus is the unifying principle of all the actions of the universe. Sending Jesus to us has always been the one and only action plan God is working and ties everything together in one neat package.

The lineage of the Messiah is unthinkably miraculous. Satan made it his most desperate ambition in life to destroy it. From Cain murdering Abel, to the enslavement of the Israelites in Egypt, to the destruction and captivity of the people of Judea, to the slaughter of the innocents under Herod, Satan has done the Revelation 12 thing and tried to abort the Messiah's birth. But God's covenant triumphs over the dark powers of hell. He keeps His promises without fail.

God's covenants give us hope. His covenants are more binding than legal documents because they're a reflection of His heart. A contract has escape clauses and default clauses and buyout clauses and clauses that no one knows what they do. God's covenants have none of those.

God has no use for an escape clause where He can legally stop loving us. God will never default in His promise to bring us to heaven. 2 Corinthians 1:22 says He's sealed the deal with His own Spirit as a deposit that guarantees our inheritance! If

God should default, *we get to keep His Spirit!* Astounding. The only buyout clause in God's covenant is that Jesus, with His lifeblood, came to buy out all our bad debts. And there's no lawyerly gobbledygook in God's covenant. A child can understand it.

What kind of God are we dealing with? A covenant-making, covenant-keeping God who makes clearly understood promises and guarantees to anyone who wants to sign up to follow Jesus Christ.

There is a flavor of theology called *covenantal theology*. Covenantal theology is wonderfully inclusive: if you're part of the family, you're part of the family's covenant with God with all the perks. A wonderful concept of covenantal theology is the term *commonwealth*: Israel has a collective inheritance in the promises of God that are shared throughout the members of that nation. In Christ, we are part of that commonwealth, according to Ephesians 2:12-13. ***"At that time ye were without Christ, being aliens from the commonwealth of Israel, and strangers from the covenants of promise, having no hope, and without God in the world: But now in Christ Jesus ye who sometimes were far off are made nigh by the blood of Christ."*** (KJV)

Covenant is God's idea of how to deal with us human beings. We worship a faithful God who makes and keeps covenants.

1 the promises of God
can we count on anything in this world?

"HIS DIVINE POWER HAS GIVEN US EVERYTHING WE NEED FOR LIFE AND GODLINESS THROUGH OUR KNOWLEDGE OF HIM WHO CALLED US BY HIS OWN GLORY AND GOODNESS. THROUGH THESE HE HAS GIVEN US HIS VERY GREAT AND PRECIOUS PROMISES …"
2 PETER 1:3-4

If you know a kid, or if you've ever been one, you know the first question you get when you put a child in your back seat: "Where are we *going?*" It's not a question to which they really expect an answer. They just can't help themselves. If you're able to tell them ahead of time, you can relieve their anxiety about being in the car. It has something to do with a sense of purpose, one of our greatest needs.

God likes us to know what He's about to do. So He puts it in writing, ahead of time. Don't tell me you've never said to someone you were taking a walk with, "Hey watch while I hit that tree over there with this rock!" God is a father. God loves showing off for His kids. So, in the Bible, we find promises. Guarantees of shots God is going to take and make. He points to a spot in the future and says, "See that? I'm going to hit that with this promise."

For example: God told the Israelites that He would lead them out of slavery. He called the shot before He made it ... generations before. Read Genesis 15:12-13 where God tells Abraham, ***"Your descendants will be strangers in a country not their own, and they will be enslaved and mistreated four hundred years. But I will punish the nation they serve as slaves, and afterward they will come out with great possessions."*** Read Genesis 50:24-25 where Joseph says to the Israelites years before they were enslaved by the Egyptians (my paraphrase), "The time will come when you'll be slaves to the Egyptians, so trust God and He will lead you out. Oh, and when you go, *take my bones with you.*" It wasn't about his bones. Joseph was saying that God had called a shot. Joseph was prophesying that his descendants would one day be in bondage and after that they'd be set free, taking the riches of the most wealthy nation on earth with them. Joseph was so confident in God's promise that he told them to take him with them when it happened. It took 400 years from promise to fulfillment, but it happened just like God said it would! God points to a spot. God calls the shot. God comes through like a champ. All day, baby. All day.

There's a wonderful book called <u>The Jesus Person Pocket Promise Book</u>. What do you guess is in that book? Right. All the amazing promises of Jesus to His disciples, covering every conceivable circumstance and trial. Too numerous to list in one place, the promises of God are merely roughed in by this wonderful book. Are you lonely? Confused? Weighed down by guilt? Scared? Knocked around? Bullied? Ashamed of the same old sins? Wanting to share your faith? Whatever the need, Jesus has a promise to meet it. Of course, we shouldn't take His promises out of *context*, but it's just as important not to take His promises out of *the Bible!*

It may take awhile for God's promises to come true. That's not important (even if it FEELS like it is). We just said the promise of freedom from Egyptian slavery took 400 years to happen. According to Genesis 3:15, it took 4,000 years for the promised defeat of Satan by the Messiah, and that defeat still hasn't been fully realized 2,000 years after it happened. But it will, as sure as the sun rises. Those who *rest their hope* upon the LORD get stronger and stronger says Isaiah 40:31.

Some say Christians shouldn't hijack the promises of the Old Testament. It's true that we should guard against presuming on those promises, but we can also take Ephesians 2:11-13 to heart and walk in our birthright. In that passage, it says that we were "formerly" separated from Christ, and "formerly" implies that something has changed. We were "formerly" excluded from the citizenship and the commonwealth of Israel. We were "formerly" foreigners to the covenants and promises. That was "formerly." But now in Christ Jesus, we who were far away have been brought near.

I love 2 Corinthians 1:20, ***"For no matter how many promises God has made, they are Yes in Christ."*** In Jesus, every promise of God is ours.

We are God's family by adoption through Christ, through His grace and mercy. What a God. He's not hiding in heaven, marking us down on His blacklist for our bad behavior. Instead, He's intimately involved with our everyday lives, promising us His own glory and goodness. His promises are like signed and certified checks drawn on His own bank account.

We ought to cash in on God's promises like quadruple coupon day where the store pays you to take their merchandise.

2 free will
is God's covenant with Adam still in effect?

"THE LORD GOD TOOK THE MAN AND PUT HIM IN THE GARDEN OF EDEN TO WORK IT AND TAKE CARE OF IT. AND THE LORD GOD COMMANDED THE MAN, YOU ARE FREE TO EAT FROM ANY TREE IN THE GARDEN; BUT YOU MUST NOT EAT FROM THE TREE OF THE KNOWLEDGE OF GOOD AND EVIL, FOR WHEN YOU EAT OF IT YOU WILL SURELY DIE."
GENESIS 2:15-17

Pretend you have a dog. Maybe you actually do. Consider your dog the object of your affection. Do you want him to come when you call? Of course you do. However! Do you want to implant a mind-control device in his brain so you can MAKE him come? So he can't refuse? Not unless you're one sick puppy! Why would we think God might want us to be His mind slaves? God wants the object of *His* affection to be *free* to come to Him as well. It's a mystery, but we don't love our dogs more than God loves us! Are you with me?

God gave His people creatures the gift of free will. Along with that gift came the possibility to obey or disobey or ignore. To want what God wants or to prefer what we want. To bow our knee or to rebel. God's love cannot be returned by creatures who don't have, intrinsic in their very nature, some semblance of a choice in the matter. We're not robots or automatons. *Automaton* is a cool word—it sounds so '50s. A droid or a cyborg might possibly have their own will, but not so with automatons. Rabbit trail! Sorry. Back to free will.

From our perspective, free will is an incredible gift. From God's perspective, it's an incalculable risk. Never wonder if God is secure in His own God-ness! It's very revealing that God would make creatures who could tell Him to take a hike, who could tell Him to get lost.

But the reason should be obvious. He desires creatures who can honestly give Him back the love He gives them. Not because He needs us to tell Him how wonderful He is. The small 'g' gods of the heathens demand that kind of sacrifice and adulation. God needs nothing: neither our worship nor our sacrifice. He made the only needed sacrifice Himself, on the cross, and created creatures who can, after their own fashion, create and love and plan and exercise their will. Our secure, unlike-any-other-god God let's His creatures have a lot of free rein!

God began His free will experiment in the Garden of Eden by giving His newly made people a choice: to obey or to eat from the forbidden tree. Later He told Abraham to leave Ur, but didn't force Him to do anything. God allowed Boaz to decide to redeem Ruth and, unknown to Boaz, to become King David's great grandfather as part of the line of the Messiah. He laid choices before the fishermen, before the diminutive guy in the tree—Zacchaeus. Those who say that there's no such thing as free will must ignore large tracts of biblical real estate.

We're free to disobey and also free to turn back to God. Some say we don't have the capacity to repent. This is labeled the doctrine of *total depravity*. Perhaps they're right, but maybe there's more to it than that. Consider Jesus' call to us: repent and believe. Is He asking us to do something that we can't possibly do? Is He taunting us, pushing our noses in our inability to repent? That's not His style, is it?

It's more likely that as we begin to repent, to turn back to Him, His love runs to meet us like the prodigal son's father, and His love supplies the power for us to make the whole turn. If first we decide to repent, God will give us what we need to follow through. Power steering works the same way: as we make the slightest twist of the steering wheel, the engine does the job of making the four wheels below conform to our every wish. If you've ever tried to parallel park without power steering, you realize how nice it is to have the muscle of the engine working on your side. When we make a move towards God, He meets us with His awesome resources and helps us complete the turn. His strength is made available to us as we make up our minds to align with His will.

Does the doctrine of free will seem to conflict with the doctrine of predestination? Well yes, of course it does. But we will never apologize for the Bible! We'll just have to wait to understand the full counsel of God on this matter. Our minds aren't able to grasp two true, yet apparently opposite, ideas. God's teaching is more vast than our minds can understand, so we can embrace and believe this mystery, this conundrum, along with all the other things we don't yet understand. Let the heathen howl about the "contradictions" in the Bible. *They're* the nuts who think the cosmos came from exploding gas and that life came from rocks in hot water! Really, they're wrong about so much that it's hard to take them seriously. Free will and predestination might be two sides of the same coin. Or, as I like to think about it, we're dealing with a truth so large that the handles we pick it up with look too far apart to be connected. Truth is happily bigger than our tiny brains.

Just know this: God wanted us to experience the joy of choosing to love Him BACK.

3 faith
what was the trademark of the Abrahamic covenant?

"ABRAHAM BELIEVED GOD, AND IT WAS CREDITED TO HIM AS RIGHTEOUSNESS. UNDERSTAND, THEN, THAT THOSE WHO BELIEVE ARE CHILDREN OF ABRAHAM. THE SCRIPTURE FORESAW THAT GOD WOULD JUSTIFY THE GENTILES BY FAITH ... SO THOSE WHO HAVE FAITH ARE BLESSED ALONG WITH ABRAHAM, THE MAN OF FAITH."
GALATIANS 3:6-9

Note that this passage doesn't say Abraham believed _in_ God. The Devil believes _in_ God; that is, he is fully convinced that God exists. No, it says Abraham _believed_ God. Huge difference, if you stop and think about it. To believe God is to invest our lives in Him, to trust His leadership, to do whatever He says. Faith is more than mere acknowledgment of a particular truth; it's a sold-out mindset that can't help but show up in our words and our actions.

Nothing you will meet with in your life with Christ will be as simple to understand and, at the same time, as hard to understand and access as faith. Everybody knows exactly what it is, and yet it remains the most difficult skill to master. It's impossibly easy and easily impossible to live a life of faith.

Faith affects how we think and how we live our lives. The notion of faith is difficult to comprehend these days, since we use that same word as a synonym for mind-over-matter. But it has nothing to do with mental toughness or psyching ourselves up. We're not saying, "If you'll only believe, your dreams will come true," which is the theme of every Disney movie ever made. That kind of "faith" may sound more believable with music, but it's just another lie. _Biblical_ faith is more than a way to manipulate your world or even manipulate God. Faith doesn't produce whatever _we_ desire, but whatever _God_ desires. Does that makes sense? Faith is not a headlock we get on God but an entry point to His divine plan. Yes, faith moves mountains, but really, they were the ones God wanted out of the way to begin with.

Faith isn't dependent on _our_ ability or performance, but on God's. It has more to do with _His_ character than with ours. People who live by faith think of God as utterly reliable. They do amazing things because God, who rewards faith, is amazing.

Faith is a word that should have a verb form as well as being a noun, for it means to take hold of the power of God by submitting our will to His. Why did Jesus' faith always and unfailingly produce healed people, walked-on water, and the most amazing wine? Because He never _"faithed"_ outside of God's will, which He plainly said in John 5:19, 5:30, and 8:28. Jesus' faith was not in Himself, but in the faithfulness of His Father.

Two wrong teachings on faith. First, the one we call 'name it and claim it.' The promise in John 16:23, **"My Father will give you whatever you ask in my name,"** is not a blank check. The "in my name" part means "in keeping with my character," or "if it's what I would do if I were there." His name is not a magic incantation; asking in His name means *for His sake,* for the honor of His name and the advancement of His kingdom. God is not a vending machine or a sugar daddy. He is purposeful and powerful and He answers prayers that have in mind the glory of the Gospel.

Second wrong teaching: we don't have to end all of our requests with, "If it's your will," as in, "I'd love a Cessna 310, if it's your will." "If it's your will" is not a mindless catch phrase; *it's a requisite heart attitude.* We should always earnestly desire God's will, diligently seek it, and boldly pray for it, in the glorious certainty of surrendered faith. I love the prayer that goes roughly like this: "God grant my prayer, unless you have something better in mind, then I ask for THAT."

Faith isn't blind, weak, or emotion-based. According to Hebrews 11:1, faith is being sure, completely convinced, unconditionally persuaded by evidence. Evidence of what? Of that which we cannot see. If we could see it, we wouldn't need faith!

How do we become sure of what we cannot see? We listen for God to speak, and when He does, we simply *faith in Him.* We trust him. We stand down upon Him. We download His strength, access His ability, walk in His will. Faith is how a Christian lives life. It's the way a Christian approaches every situation. Faith is the means by which a Christian overcomes within each circumstance while waiting to either be delivered from it or to die in it.

Faith is the modus operandi of the Kingdom of God. It <u>was</u> the way the Kingdom works, <u>is</u> the way it works, and <u>will</u> be the way it works. There's not another method waiting to be revealed. We can harness the lifestyle of the future, faith, right now.

Romans 1:17 plainly and definitively states, ***"The righteous shall live by faith."*** *The words "shall live"* convey a sense of *ongoing* faith, a sense of *continual, constant* faith, faith that doesn't turn off and on, but becomes a moment by moment way of life.

Faith is the secret to living for Christ. There never was another way of doing it.

4 the Ten Commandments

wish God would write His expectations in stone?

"WHEN THE LORD FINISHED SPEAKING TO MOSES ON MOUNT SINAI, . HE GAVE HIM THE TWO TABLETS OF THE TESTIMONY, THE TABLETS OF STONE INSCRIBED BY THE FINGER OF GOD."
EXODUS 31:18

Love God first. Love God only. Love God's name. Love God's day. Honor your parents. Don't murder. Don't break your vows. Don't steal. Don't lie. Don't want what belongs to somebody else.

Count 'em: ten. The whole world has heard of them. They're a great clue to God's character. A tiny part of who He is gets represented in these commands.

There's nothing wrong with the Ten Commandments. They're good. (They're actually perfect says Romans 7:12.) The problem is that _we_ aren't good, and the Law demonstrates it for the world to see. The Law shows us the standard we fall short of.

The average student in America would be stunned to find out that our legal system has been influenced more by the Ten Commandments and Jewish instructions than all other influences put together. Stunned, because no one mentions the Ten Commandments in school. Plenty of talk about laws and rights and fairness, but no talk about the basis for those in our country. No reference to the underpinnings of our entire legal system being found in the Pentateuch.

On top of that, you can't even post the Ten Commandments without triggering a crippling lawsuit that will drain your life of substance and joy. That lawsuit will be brought based on the laws given to Moses, by people who deny those very laws.

In 1963 Madeline Murray O'Hare and the United States Supreme Court, with the apparent blessing of most of the rest of us, removed prayer and the Bible from classrooms, and took the Ten Commandments off the walls. Ever since then our schools have done a progressively poorer job of educating. This is a demonstrable fact. The schools have experienced an undeniable slide into sub-mediocrity. From 1963, SAT test scores declined for 17 straight years. Why would taking a 3500 year old set of Jewish rules off the wall possibly affect the quality of test scores?

It's not because of what the commandments magically do to the school walls. It's what they do inside a human heart. You can't put a Bible under your pillow and be a better person when you wake up, nor can you put an inscription on the wall and come up with a better society. But taking them down from the walls included diminishing them as foundational to turning out successful scholars.

You can't graduate wise students with foolish education. And it is the fool who has said in his heart, "There is no God." Fools don't just want there to be no God, but no _mention_ of Him is allowed. They welcome every small "g" god in the universe, every perverse humanistic abomination, every laughable enlightenment idiocy before they will allow Jews or Christians to speak the name of Yahweh or Jesus in public. They will celebrate Kwanzaa and Ramadan and Halloween (for crying out loud!) then turn around and ban the celebration of Chanukah, Thanksgiving, Christmas, and (gasp!) the worst of them all: Easter.

All because of that Supreme Court decision from Hell itself that ripped the Ten Commandments off the school walls. What a price has been paid by our country in abandoning our fear of God, and substituting a fear of offending someone. The founders' rejection of a state church has been twisted from the freedom OF religion to the freedom FROM religion, especially if the religion is Judaism and Christianity.

Why this hatred toward God? John 3:19 gives us the answer: ***"Light has come into the world, but men loved darkness instead of light because their deeds were evil."*** When you're lying, talking behind people's backs, cheating, stealing and carousing, you do it in the dark. The Ten Commandments are a spotlight that exposes evil, like roaches scurrying from the switched-on kitchen light.

In God's eyes, are the Ten Commandments still in force? Absolutely. Nothing man decrees can cancel God's decree. Are the Ten in effect for Christians? Good question. Jesus said not a punctuation mark of the law would pass away until it was fulfilled, but He Himself did the fulfilling (Matthew 5:18 and Romans 10:4).

So the Ten are no longer applicable for Christians, right? Wrong and right! Both. For those who place themselves under the jurisdiction of the Law of the Spirit of Life in Christ (Romans 8:2), the Ten are changed from an impossible standard to nothing more than routine behavior. We are God's kids indwelled by God's Spirit and we're growing up to look more and more like our older brother, Jesus. He kept every one of the 10 Commandments, and with Him living in us, we can do the same. You can't seriously claim that having Jesus *in* us leaves us unable to live the life He expects! Who says we can't keep the Ten Commandments anymore? Of *course* we can. Why else would Jesus have put His Holy Spirit in us? As 2 Peter 1:3 says, ***"His divine power has given us everything we need for life and godliness!"***

Keeping the Ten Commandments doesn't make us better, doesn't make God love us more, and doesn't get us any reward. We don't keep the Ten Commandments to get into heaven; we keep them because that's just what our heavenly family *does*. The Ten are no longer our downfall, they've become our heritage. They're the identifying feature that let's everyone know we belong in God's family. Some families have red hair, ours has a healthy respect for the Ten Commandments.

We can now keep them, not in our own effort, but in the new way of the Law of the Spirit of life in Christ! So we who belong to Jesus Christ will never be *judged* by the Ten Commandments. No, now we have the power to obey them because of being born from above by the Spirit of God who lives in us. Can I get a "Glory to God!" out there? Yes! I see that hand.

The Ten Commandments are the impossible standard we now exceed ... in Christ.

5 righteousness
any hope that we'll be able to stand before a holy God?

"BUT NOW A RIGHTEOUSNESS FROM GOD, APART FROM LAW, HAS BEEN MADE KNOWN, TO WHICH THE LAW AND THE PROPHETS TESTIFY. THIS RIGHTEOUSNESS FROM GOD COMES THROUGH FAITH IN JESUS CHRIST TO ALL WHO BELIEVE."
ROMANS 3:21-22

Righteousness is a churchified word. We're not sure what it means anymore. It can be simply shortened to "right in God's sight." Oops, that wasn't shorter. But it *is* clearer. To be right in the sight of God, we have to be without sin. Like THAT'S going to happen! Righteousness is beyond our ability as human beings, but God has *given* righteousness to us in Christ. The Bible calls our own goodness "revolting rags soaked in disgusting bodily fluids" in Isaiah 64:6!

What we couldn't achieve by our own feeble efforts, has been gifted to us in the most one-sided exchange on record. 2 Corinthians 5:21 documents this lopsided swap: ***"God made him who had no sin to be sin for us, so that in him we might become the righteousness of God."*** How could this possibly benefit God? It doesn't. And not only does He not care that there's nothing in it for Him, He's actually happy about it being all for our good. We who simply repented and turned to Jesus have won the lottery and are awarded full pardon for every one of our sins—past, present and future—plus a never ending supply of life with the promise of more to come!

Rightness with God is something everyone knows they need, deep down. That's why there are so many religions. God has, of course, told us the things He expects of us, what we must do to be right with Him. But everybody thinks they're so smart. *We tell God* why He should pardon us. We go on impossible journeys. We make great sacrifices. We accomplish heroic deeds. Never mind if God doesn't really want any of that. The mindset of every world religion is to make a valiant effort to please God using our own ideas. Everybody knows better than God. Everybody has a better plan than the cross of Christ and His blood atonement.

What if I brought you a big plate of liver and onions and wanted you to thank me? What if you told me you don't like liver and onions, you like steak and potatoes with butter, cheese, sour cream and pepper, but I keep bringing you liver and onions? I promise you'd start avoiding me.

Well? God doesn't like liver and onions either. Humankind can bring God whatever we wish, but we can't demand that God has to thank us for it. Righteousness isn't something we pronounce on ourselves. There are only two religions in the world that man did not invent: Judaism and Christianity. All other religions of the world are helpless when it comes to making us right with God. I'm not being crass, just looking at it God's way.

We need to ask God to reveal to us what *He* wants, and then ask Him to help us bring Him *whatever that is*. Does God want us to cut ourselves with bloody knives like the priests of Baal in Elijah's time? Does He want us to choke out our natural desires like Buddhist monks? Does He want us to deceive and murder infidels like Mohammed told His followers? Does He need our money, our cleverness, our approval, our event attendance or our professional production value? Isaiah 66:3 says, ***"They have chosen their own ways, and their souls delight in their abominations."***

What is it that God wants? We have only one thing to offer. He wants a heart that beats for Him, a heart that burns for Him, a humble and contrite heart (Isaiah 66:2). God gives His righteousness to those who come with nothing but a surrendered life. He gives His approval to those who abandon themselves and kneel before Him.

Imagine having the valedictorian's grades handed to you, though you could only manage an "F" on your best day. Imagine having the wealth of the richest man in the world, though you only pull minimum wage. Imagine having the world at your feet, instead of on your shoulders. This is the gift of righteousness: God takes our humbled and surrendered hearts and offers us the perfect righteousness of Christ.

Jesus' righteousness in exchange for our complete failure is a straight-up swap. We'd be dumb to turn it down.

6 stewardship
what's the difference between hoarding and investing?

"WHO IS THE FAITHFUL AND WISE MANAGER, WHOM THE MASTER PUTS IN CHARGE OF HIS SERVANTS TO GIVE THEM THEIR FOOD ALLOWANCE AT THE PROPER TIME? IT WILL BE GOOD FOR THAT SERVANT WHOM THE MASTER FINDS DOING SO WHEN HE RETURNS. I TELL YOU THE TRUTH, HE WILL PUT HIM IN CHARGE OF ALL HIS POSSESSIONS."
LUKE 12:42-44

Stewardship is the duty of man concerning the gifts of God. To each of us He has granted resources. In Matthew 25 the servants were judged or approved according to their management of entrusted talents. Their master was pleased with the industrious and diligent servants and put them in charge of even more. But He was angry with the servant who did nothing with His one talent and punished that servant severely.

The fourth commandment defines our work week—Six days, not four or even our standard of five. Work is a big deal to God. The Scriptures emphasize the *work ethic*, as in 2 Thessalonians 3:12. If we're biblical, we'll work as hard as we can for as long as it takes. *Give it everything we've got.* Laziness is not excused for any reason in any scripture I know. In addition, work that's not done *cheerfully* and with *excellence* is of no value (2 Corinthians 9:7).

There is perhaps no shame as great as being able-bodied but continually living off someone else's hard work. Nothing robs a people of their dignity so quickly as a dependence mindset. There's no political system that leaves a people more conquered and controlled than a welfare state. The Bible issues a warning against idleness throughout the book of Proverbs. In 2 Thessalonians 3:10, Paul tells the church that laziness is a poison that will kill a culture. Hard work is the true path of healthy self-esteem. A job well done with a smile and willing heart is a joy to God.

Stewardship is easy to quantify in matters of money. A tithe is a tenth. Yet a tenth of our money given back to God is just the bare beginning of a life committed to stewarding God's gifts. *Every piece of us should be pre-surrendered to God.* Nothing is ours to stockpile. When we came to Christ, we gave Him everything, right? Let's not renege. Everything we have and everything we are belong to the Lord who gave them to us first. Our checkbooks, our yards, our refrigerators, our houses, our cars and our worldly stuff are all His, to be used in any way that He sees fit.

Think. God doesn't need our stuff! What would He do with a million dollars? Why would He need a car?! Why would He conceivably need anything we have? Maybe when we take up the offering, it isn't for God's sake. It's for OUR sake.

He knows we need to be open-handed in possessing our possessions. God doesn't need our stuff, but we sure need to let go of it. Oh HOW we need to let go! Listen. We have a pressing need to have our clutches pried loose from our possessions *lest they possess us.* Money's not the root of all evil—the *love* of it is. God gives us stuff so we can use what we need and pass the rest on. It's not good for us to be attached to our stuff, so God makes a way to separate us from it and calls it stewardship.

We work out of joyful obedience to God's command to work. We work because He said we ought to. Wages are a way to *value* work, but it's not the *purpose* of work. We need money, but it's not our motivation. We cash our checks, but we don't live for them. A man once prayed, "God, if you'll let me win the lottery, I'll give it all to you for your Kingdom." God replied, "If money was what was needed to build my Kingdom, why would I have sent my Son to the cross?"

Stewardship is the diligent management of our time, our talent, and our treasure. When we put these to work for Christ and His Kingdom, they produce a profit. (The Bible calls it a *harvest,* but we don't know that term as well.) Jesus has given us so much, including the gift of life. How we invest our lives is crucial to whether we get the Master's praise or His rebuke. Stewardship is nothing less than worship, a great way to say thanks' to God.

One glorious day, we will thrill to hear our beloved King Jesus say, "Well done, good and faithful servant. You have been faithful in little, I will put you in charge of much. Enter into the joy of your Master!"

7 the law of the Spirit of life in Christ
there's actually a restriction that sets people free?

"THROUGH CHRIST JESUS, THE LAW OF THE SPIRIT OF LIFE SET ME FREE FROM THE LAW OF SIN AND DEATH."
ROMANS 8:2

There is a new law in place that supersedes the law of sin and death. Under the terms of the law of sin and death, you and I who transgressed the law were justly condemned to die by that law. Not a lot going for THAT system. But under the law of the Spirit of life in Christ, we can opt into obedience to God and skip death. You can see where this is headed.

The law of the Spirit of life, it won't shock you to learn, is different from the law of sin and death. The law of the Spirit of life is the default operating software for those who are "in Christ." It has nothing to do with the old world system of sin and death, which is the default operating software for this world, but it gives us the possibility of pleasing God outside of our own miserable failed attempts. The key to pleasing God is obedience to the Spirit's law of life using faith. As we obey the Spirit of God, we walk in newness of life. As we say yes to the commands of Jesus, we drink deeply of refreshing renewal and restoration. As we come under the authority of our new Master, we can turn our backs on sin and self, taking up our cross daily and following Jesus.

Everyone is under law, no exceptions. Faith in Christ does not take us out from under law. It gives us a new law to be under. Since we're now citizens of the Kingdom of God, we're under the law of that Kingdom, and no longer under the law of this world. The law of the world's kingdom brings death; the law of God's Kingdom brings life. The reward of the old law was eternal condemnation; the reward of the new law is life and peace and joy forevermore.

This is stupendous. We have got to get this. The Law of the Spirit of life in Christ is freedom ... not freedom from obeying, but freedom from sin and death. One more time ... not freedom *from* law, but freedom *under* law. We used to have a desire to sin, a predisposition to sin. We had a sin nature. But if we're in Christ, we are brand new recreated beings according to 2 Corinthians 5:13.

Are you in Christ? Yes? Then you no longer *want* to sin. You may still sin, but your "want to" has been realigned. And if we <u>do</u> sin, we aren't "sinners," we're children of God who've done something our family just doesn't do. Sin for us is not a violation of the law of sin and death, it is a violation of the Law of the Spirit of life in Christ.

When we break the law of sin and death, we die. When we break the Law of the Spirit of life in Christ, we let the family down because we didn't *have to.*

Sin is not our master. Life in the Spirit is. That life includes a <u>love</u> for God's ways.

Please hear me in this. I'm not saying that Christians don't sin, but I *am* saying that Christians don't *want* to sin and Christians don't *have* to sin. Yes we're in the flesh, but, ***"If he who raised Christ Jesus from the dead lives in you, he will give life to your mortal bodies."*** We're no longer under the old legal system of sin and death, but under the new legal system of the Spirit of life in Christ. We're saints who occasionally sin, not sinners who occasionally saint.

The old law of death is in place for two reasons: to either bring us under the new law of life or to deal with those who simply will not come. The old law brings condemnation; the new law brings justification. The old law is a tyrant; the new law is a teacher. The old law is a prison; the new law is an open door. The old law reveals how low we have fallen; the new law is the mechanism for how high we will soar.

We won't progress by becoming more enlightened, the naturalist lie, but by becoming more dependent on the power of the risen Christ. We won't progress by believing in ourselves, the humanist lie, but believing in Christ. We won't progress by the balance of the yin yang, the lie of the pantheists, but of the balance paid at the cross by Christ. We won't progress in amassing and disposing earthly riches, the lie of the materialists, but in accessing by faith the true riches of Christ. There's a new sheriff in town: the law of the Spirit of life in Christ. In Christ. <u>*In Christ.*</u>

The old law brought us death without end. The new law brings us everlasting life.

• SIN AND DEATH

what happens when you're cut off from Life?

"ONCE I WAS ALIVE APART FROM LAW; BUT WHEN THE COMMANDMENT CAME, SIN SPRANG TO LIFE AND I DIED. I FOUND THAT THE VERY COMMANDMENT THAT WAS INTENDED TO BRING LIFE ACTUALLY BROUGHT DEATH. FOR SIN, SEIZING THE OPPORTUNITY AFFORDED BY THE COMMANDMENT, DECEIVED ME, AND THROUGH THE COMMANDMENT PUT ME TO DEATH."
ROMANS 7:9-11

God's Law is good. God's Law is perfect, faultless, just, and right altogether. There is nothing wrong with God's Law. So, since we defy and defile His Law, there must be something wrong with us.

In the Garden of Eden, there was just one law: don't eat from the tree that will kill you. How hard could that be? "Honey, what did God say?" "Don't eat from the tree that will kill you." That's it. Boom. Nobody had to go to law school to figure it out. As simple as that was, it took no time at all before we had broken that law and suffered the penalty—death—spiritual and physical death.

Cain had a law under which he operated: his conscience. His dad and mom had eaten from the tree of the knowledge of good and evil. (Yes, I think it was a real tree. What do you think ... it was a metaphor?!) So the guy knew what God expected him to do. He didn't wonder if it was okay to dust his brother, yet knowing it was wrong, he still did it. Result? Death again. Do you see a pattern?

No one's ever had to wonder how God wants us to behave. And oddly, no one's ever lived up to what they knew were God's lawful expectations. The law is a harsh master. It cuts no slack. It gives no grace. It makes right demands and doesn't back off. To break the law is to seal your fate. God thought He would teach the Israelites about His law. He let them know that He would give them blessings if they obeyed and curses if they rebelled. Inexplicably, but I guess predictably, they rebelled.

So God taught them that death was the consequence for broken law. They had to slaughter innocent animals and sprinkle their blood on an altar to pay for breaking the Law. This is the nature of the law of sin and death: transgressors are condemned to severe penalties with no mercy. The Law is a righteous tyrant. There's absolutely nothing wrong with the Law. But just try to comply with it! Only one ever *has*. Only one ever *could*. The Law of sin and death is unfeeling, uncompromising, unforgiving, and always infuriatingly right.

God didn't tell the Israelites to sacrifice animals to fix the problem of sin. It's not the blood of animals that does that job. Only the blood of Jesus can forgive sin. But God wanted the Israelites to see that death was the consequence of sin. And God wanted to see the obedient repentance of their hearts. It's the godly sorrow of the contrite that touches God's heart of grace. That grace is seen in the cross and the sacrificial death that paid for the sin of the world.

There can be no good news without bad news. The bad news is that God is holy and righteous and has let us know in specific terms what He will and won't put up with from us. We've laughed in His face with our behavior. We know what to do. We don't do it. We're under the law of sin and death until we turn to Christ.

Eventually, the law of sin and death hunts everyone down and kills them. There's only one escape—Jesus.

1 Satan
is there a world-champion Liar of all liars?

"[SATAN] WAS A MURDERER FROM THE BEGINNING, NOT HOLDING TO THE TRUTH, FOR THERE IS NO TRUTH IN HIM. WHEN HE LIES, HE SPEAKS HIS NATIVE LANGUAGE, FOR HE IS A LIAR AND THE FATHER OF LIES."
JOHN 8:44

The name "Satan" means accuser, slanderer. He's a snake according to Moses. He is our adversary, according to Peter. He's the accuser of the believers and the great dragon according to John. He was created good but wanted to swap places with God, causing him to become distorted, perverted and evil.

The devil is not God's opposite! There IS no one opposite God! You're thinking of a philosophy called dualism, not Christian doctrine. If there's an opposite of the devil, it's the great archangel Michael, says Revelation 12:7.

The devil is our "accuser" according to Revelation 12:10. He's basically a tattletale. I don't know how dangerous he is to Christians, but Peter says he *impersonates* a lion. Created an angelic being, he's now fallen. Jesus called him "the ruler of this world." He's become nothing more than a tool that God is using in His master plan.

Called by many names: the devil, Lucifer, Satan, the dragon. My favorite is Beelzebub, which means "lord of the flies", an apt description as he is annoying and seems to enjoy dead and decaying things. Lucifer means light bearer. Some say he was God's worship leader. He bears the light no more, having fallen from his high position in foolish self-exaltation. Satan has always had his heart set on ascending to God's throne and being worshipped. The truth is not in him. God's will is not in him. C.S. Lewis in *Perelandra* depicts him as a massive intellect with nobody home inside—an empty shell of a bratty child with great powers of mind and body.

Is Satan responsible for all the bad things that have ever happened? Are you kidding me? No! But he's a major player. If the same hijinks go on for generations, it's probably his work. Since the devil is *not* omnipresent, it's a little prideful to think he is tempting us. You and I are probably not that important. I'll bet he sends one of his low level demons to do the job. Jesus rated Satan's personal appearance when He was tempted in the wilderness at the beginning of His ministry. Jesus' unbeaten streak remained unblemished with the best the devil could throw at Him.

Who does the Bible say is the one to blame when we *fall* for temptation? Our own selfish self (James 1:14). *We* are the ones responsible for turning away from God. Still, 2 Corinthians 2:11 says that we shouldn't be naive. Satan has schemes to wreck our lives, he's working them as we speak. We should be wise and be warned.

Satan is not omnipresent nor is he omnipotent. Never believe he can't be pushed back. James 4:7 says that if we humble ourselves before God and *resist* the devil, he'll run away. So he's not irresistible. Just say no and mean it. Always remember that we can fight temptation in the power of the Holy Spirit and win. There are some temptations that we must run from, according to 1 Corinthians 6:18. These are the temptations coming from the lusts of the flesh. When we're up against sexual temptation, scoot. Other than that, we should never give an inch. Remember Tommy Lee Jones and Will Smith in <u>Men In Black</u> standing to watch as the giant spaceship they just shot down plummets towards them, not even flinching as it plows up tons of earth and comes to a smoking stop right at their feet? That's us standing and resisting Satan just like it says in Ephesians 6.

Satan is not omnipresent, not omnipotent and he's *not* omniscient. He probably can't read minds according to 1 Corinthians 2:11, and he definitely doesn't know half of what he ought to know. For one thing, he doesn't know he's already defeated and that he did it to himself (1 Corinthians 2:8), **"None of the rulers of this age understood [God's secret wisdom], for if they had, they would not have crucified the Lord of glory."** Satan sealed his own doom when he thought he was orchestrating Jesus' death on the cross. That was dumb. The cross was the only way Satan could ever have lost possession of the world, and he unwittingly helped God accomplish it. Not Satan, nor Pilate, nor the Jews put Jesus up on the cross, according to John 10:18 and John 14:30. It was Jesus Himself, the Lamb of God who freely offered Himself up. Satan, clueless, played along with the whole thing, imagining he was finally winning, when he was being played for a fool.

Fear God. Don't be afraid of Satan. The devil may be bigger and badder and smarter than you, but he's not bigger or badder or smarter than Jesus. And Jesus lives in we who believe. Together with Jesus, we're bigger and badder and …

Give Satan the respect of a crazed giant cockroach in a shot-down spaceship, rising from the wreckage only to be splattered again.

2 temptation

is looking at an open door the same as going through it?

"No temptation has seized you except what is common to man. And God is faithful; he will not let you be tempted beyond what you can bear. When you are tempted, he will also provide a way out so that you can stand up under it."
1 Corinthians 10:13

Some say that temptation is sin, so Jesus could not have been tempted because that would mean He sinned. Wrong! Read Hebrews 4:15. Temptation is *not* sin, and

Jesus was tempted in every way just as we are, never sinning. This is crucial to know about temptation. Jesus experienced the full force of it and never once gave in.

Our understanding of temptation begins with the fact that God tempts no one (James 1:13). We are tempted when we allow our own evil desires to grow and bear fruit. Temptation is not from God. However! God DID give each of us a free will, starting in the Garden of Eden. We can choose a way other than God's way. We have freedom and with that comes responsibility. We must choose rightly.

Understanding temptation also includes facing the fact that temptation is our own evil desires festering inside us (James 1:14). We lead ourselves away from God by coddling temptation instead of standing against it. Free will allows us to choose to stand or fall under temptation. We can choose to obey sin, making it our master, or we can choose to obey God, making *Him* our Master.

You don't believe that? God told Cain in Genesis 4:7, ***"If you do what is right, will you not be accepted? But if you do not do what is right, sin is crouching at your door; it desires to have you, but you must master it."*** Paul in Romans 6:14-18 says we who are now under God's grace have been set free from sin. Our new inclination is not falling for temptation, but choosing holiness and godliness! Amazing!

Every time temptation comes, God promises us a way out. There will never be a temptation where we will be on our own with no choice but to give in. Our verse for this section tells us that temptation is beatable if we will let God into the situation. As soon as we spot what's going on, we need to look around for the escape God has provided. In the moment we are aware of the temptation, we can overcome it using God's exit. But if we play around and see how close to the edge we can get, chances are we'll fall in. Mess with temptation and it will mess with us.

Once again, *temptation itself* is not sin. Temptation is the *doorway* to sin. Corey Ten Boom, survivor of the Holocaust, said that sin is like birds. You can't keep them from landing in your tree, but you can sure keep them from building a nest!

Who's immune from temptation? No one alive. Wait! "No one alive" is a clue. Romans 6:11, ***"Count yourselves dead to sin but alive to God in Christ Jesus."*** Here's the key to fighting temptation—death. Didn't see THAT one coming, did you? This verse isn't talking about physical death, but rather a death of our will, a death of having things our way. Death to expecting to get everything we want, when we want it and how we want it. Dying to ourselves. Dead people don't sin!

This verse is elemental bookkeeping. To count yourself dead is to figure yourself that way, to mark yourself down that way, to let the sum of your life be death to self. Didn't Jesus say that whoever would follow Him should die daily? He said we should pick up our cross and that's what a cross is—death. Again, not a physical death, but killing the *I-want-it-and-I-have-to-have-it-'cause-I-deserve-it* nerve.

Satan is called the tempter, setting up traps and stumbling blocks to catch us and drag us down. But even when he wins, we can make sure he still loses. As soon as we mess up, we should 'fess up. Let God convict us and draw us back to Himself as we confess our sin. "Agree with your accuser quickly," as Jesus says in Matthew 5:25.

Temptation isn't game over. It's a chance to trot out our Holy Spirit victory dance.

3 spiritual warfare
what happens when angels and demons meet up?

"FOR OUR STRUGGLE IS NOT AGAINST FLESH AND BLOOD, BUT AGAINST THE RULERS, AGAINST THE AUTHORITIES, AGAINST THE POWERS OF THIS DARK WORLD AND AGAINST THE SPIRITUAL FORCES OF EVIL IN THE HEAVENLY REALMS. THEREFORE PUT ON THE FULL ARMOR OF GOD, SO THAT WHEN THE DAY OF EVIL COMES, YOU MAY BE ABLE TO STAND YOUR GROUND, AND AFTER YOU HAVE DONE EVERYTHING, TO STAND."
EPHESIANS 6:12-13

People really stink. Bad. It's not even arguable. They say and do things that nobody ought to say or do to their trashcan. They can come up with the most hurtful and destructive ways of trying to make life miserable for others. But whatever they do, our problem is never exclusively with them. Jesus taught His disciples to see both the visible and the invisible world around them.

In our Western minds, demons and angels are the subjects of fairytales; we're too sophisticated to fall for shining figures and boogeymen. Jesus *does* believe in them. He often addresses demons as part of the process of fixing people. The Bible records lots of times where the angels are sent to strengthen and encourage and rescue people, sometimes to push back the demons.

Invisible does *not* mean nonexistent. The unseen world was created right along with the one we see, says Colossians 1:16. What does the unseen world look like? Trick question! We can't see it so we don't know much about it other than it's very real and very much part of the whole of creation.

In Matthew 18:10, Jesus says children have angels who stand continually in God's presence. In Luke 10:20 he says that we should be happier about belonging to God than being able to order demons around. And in Mark 8:33, Jesus looks straight at Peter and says, "Out of my way, Satan." Don't ask me to explain that one. But just maybe we're not as smart and clever as we think we are if we ignore angels and demons. Believe in them or don't believe, they're still part of our daily lives.

What are the angels and demons primarily doing when they're not doing something *to* people or *for* people? The Bible gives us a hint: they're fighting each other for the domination of planet earth. Daniel 10, Revelation 12, Luke 10, Ephesians 6—check those scriptures out. See what *you* think. There's spiritual mayhem going on all around us at this very moment.

Remember when Jesus said all Satan wants to do is kill, steal, and destroy? John 10:10? Even though it seems as if he can do what he wants, he's restrained. God has him on a leash. That restraint is provided by God's mighty angels, who are constantly and tirelessly contesting the forces of evil all around us. ***"He will command his angels concerning you to guard you in all your ways,"*** Psalms 91:11.

2 Thessalonians 2:7 talks about the *mystery of lawlessness*. It reveals that there is a man of lawlessness, probably the Antichrist, held in check, unable to do what he wants until God's power no longer holds him back. Revelation 9:14-15 says that there are four angels bound "at the Euphrates river," who will, when God releases them, kill one third of all people on the earth. Revelation 20:2 says that one of God's angels will grab Satan by the scruff of his neck and bind him for a thousand years.

Something is holding evil back. Here in this world, things are bad, but we'd better not complain. It really should be worse! If wickedness weren't being constrained by the armies of the Kingdom of Light, our lives wouldn't be worth a plug nickel.

Some people believe that since we can tell demons what to do, we can tell angels what to do. Wrong. We're not in charge of the forces of light. Those angels work for God and obey His orders (Psalms 103:20). We don't pray to angels and we don't command them either. We just pray to the Father in Jesus' name and He may choose to rescue us using His angels. It's His call.

Our job is not to rush in and start swinging, but to stand by faith in the doctrine we know (2 Corinthians 2:15). Patiently waiting for the coming of Christ and His Kingdom we stand (James 5:8). Protected within His armor, we stand (Ephesians 6:11-14). Against the powers of wicked darkness we stand (1 Peter 5:9). For our family and friends, we stand (Exodus 14:13). When our Commander tells us to take down an enemy stronghold, we march onto that ground and stand (Joshua 3:8).

Some of the best fighting we'll ever do is to simply *not back down*. Stand.

4 The Fall

why does it seem that everything is all messed up?

"SIN ENTERED THE WORLD THROUGH ONE MAN, AND DEATH THROUGH SIN, AND IN THIS WAY DEATH CAME TO ALL MEN, BECAUSE ALL SINNED."

ROMANS 5:12

Can we imagine a world without sin? I submit that we cannot. We've never lived in anything but a fallen world, a world under God's curse.

When Eve listened to the snake and Adam listened to Eve, they were still okay. You can't stop somebody from talking. But when Eve *acted* on the snake's tempting advice and when Adam *disobeyed* what God had clearly and specifically told him to do, for the very first time ever, sin entered the world. Hence the term "original."

Original sin is something that's *never* taken into account when explaining the world around us, and it's like forgetting the sun when predicting earth's surface temperatures. To talk about the world in any meaningful way while ignoring original sin is like asking someone to play center on your basketball team and neglecting to check how tall or how old they are. It's like having your clothes washer loaded with clothes and soap and remembering the water to your house has been disconnected.

It's not a simple oversight. The world is the way it is due in large part to original sin. Paul spends a lot of time in Romans 5 talking about all of this. Christians believe that Christ died "once for all." When we sin, Jesus doesn't have to die on the cross again. And as the cross was a once-for-all event, Paul is saying original sin is the once-for-all reason for the cross. If The Fall never happened, there would be no need for the cross. As the cross is not merely a literary device, neither is The Fall. As the cross is the focal point of hope, The Fall is the focal point of despair. When we talk of sin and the cross of Christ, if we don't include original sin, we're missing a huge chunk of what's really going on.

The right relationship God wants to have with us has been cut off by our sinful rebellion, specifically through Adam's Fall. Our own present rebellion against God's ownership of us didn't help either. Each of us wants to do things our way. We want what we want, we want it when we want it, and as much as we can get of it. In children, this is called throwing a fit, but in adults, it's eulogized as being a maverick. The rebel is a popular figure to us, because we ourselves are rebels and wish to inoculate ourselves against God's disapproval of our sin.

For reasons that God only knows, sin is woven into the fabric of this world, and we're being trained in the presence of that sin to be fit to live in the ages to come. There's a strange passage in Hebrews 5:8 which says that Jesus ***"learned obedience from what he suffered."*** I'm not sure what to make of Jesus needing to learn from suffering in a fallen world, but if *He* had to learn in that way, it's easy to figure out that you and I need to learn the same way He did.

Temptation was one of the things Jesus suffered, and victory is what He learned from it. *Sin exists, in part, so that we can experience victory over it.* God has given us every advantage: a new nature inside (2 Corinthians 5:17), a direct help line (John 14:12-14) and, unimaginably, His Holy Spirit (Romans 8:11). In other words, God has given us Himself, without limit, powerfully available to us in our battle with temptation. We get to share in the victory Christ has over sin. We get to not only be called holy, but to *be* holy in our words and our behavior. Make no mistake, our God has reached down to us in our fallen state and lifted us up again in Christ.

If you want to summarize the first section of all of history, try this: The Creation, The Fall, and The Flood. The Fall is one of the major themes of the account of man on earth. Leaving it out of your theology is like leaving out a third of the foundation of your house. Good luck building anything sturdy on top of *that!*

Because of original sin, our world is fallen, the people around us are fallen, and the times in which we live are perverse and fallen. If we forget this, we'll be constantly surprised and ambushed by the world and often defeated by it. We ought to wear God's Ephesian 6 armor and stay vigilant in the battle around us. Jesus has rescued us from The Fall. Now our job is to press toward His upward call (Philippians 3:14).

We live in a world that's fallen from original perfection. Explains a lot, doesn't it?

5 all have sinned

is there any such thing as a "good person?"

"ALL HAVE SINNED."
ROMANS 3:23

In our society, it's fashionable to not even believe in sin. Darwinism substitutes survival for morality. Materialism dulls our sense of guilt with the euphoria of accumulating stuff. Situational Ethics preaches that what's wrong in one scenario is perfectly alright in another. Rationalism says we're more advanced than our inferior religious forbears. And our culture says that if it feels right, looks good, and "doesn't hurt anybody else," go ahead and do it. What a crock!

Because you know what? At one time, it was fashionable to believe that sickness was the result of having too much blood, so the "cure" was to drain out your blood! A belief can be more than wrong—it can be deadly. Believing wrongly about sin can kill you. We should get our perspective from _Script_ure, not _cult_ure.

The thing about sin is that it's easy to understand. The Bible often uses the illustration of indebtedness to paint the picture of sin. That's why the Lord's Prayer in the KJV reads, **"Forgive us our debts as we forgive our debtors."** It's a matter of bookkeeping. There's a ledger that God keeps on each one of us. One column is what's owed and another is what's been paid against our account. Since innocent blood is the only thing that pays for sin (Hebrews 10), Jesus is the only one who can put anything in the credit column for our account.

The Bible uses lots of words to describe sin: *godlessness* (unrestrained evil), *unrighteousness* (being on the wrong side), *guilt* (a feeling of condemnation), *lawlessness* (substituting our rules for God's), *transgression* (overstepping God's boundaries), *ignorance* (not caring to know), *going astray* (wandering), *falling away* (joining God then rejecting Him), *hypocrisy* (being two-faced), *wickedness* (embracing evil), *errancy* (being off target), *falling short* (not measuring up), and *rebellion* (rejection of authority).

"Missing the mark" is often given as the literal meaning of the Greek word *hamartia* used in Romans 3:23, but *hamartia* also means to miss out, to be mistaken, to wander from the path of righteousness, to do wrong, and/or to violate the law of God. More than just a bad shot! We <u>meant</u> to miss. We deliberately <u>intended</u> to sin. In that sense, we didn't *miss*. We absolutely hit what we were aiming at. Sin is not an accident but a decision.

Sin brings death. If you had a nest of poisonous snakes in your living room, would you ignore it? If you lived on the edge of a thousand foot cliff, would you bother to put up a fence? If you left a ticking time bomb in your car, would you get back in? Since sin results in death, why in the world would we try to pretend there is no such thing? In <u>Pilgrim's Progress</u>, the protagonist goes nearly out of his mind as he contemplates his sinful life. This is a healthy attitude to have. At least until we surrender to Jesus and He washes away our sin.

Sin is described in Romans 3:23 as "falling short." Short of what? God's glory! Maybe *that's* why nobody can be perfect! The benchmark is the glory of God, for crying out loud! If we can't measure up to that, forget it. Humankind is utterly vile and hopelessly degenerate, compared not to each other, but compared to the glorious, unstained, white-hot holiness of God. It's not, are you better than me, or better than anyone else; it's are you better than God? Read it and weep. We can't measure up. We don't have a chance. With an impossibly impossible standard, we're sunk.

Small wonder people don't think we should even use the word "sin" anymore.

6 demons
if we can't see evil spirits, are they still there?

"AND THERE WAS WAR IN HEAVEN. MICHAEL AND HIS ANGELS FOUGHT AGAINST THE DRAGON, AND THE DRAGON AND HIS ANGELS FOUGHT BACK. BUT HE WAS NOT STRONG ENOUGH, AND THEY LOST THEIR PLACE IN HEAVEN. THE GREAT DRAGON WAS HURLED DOWN, THAT ANCIENT SERPENT CALLED THE DEVIL, OR SATAN, WHO LEADS THE WHOLE WORLD ASTRAY. HE WAS HURLED TO THE EARTH, AND HIS ANGELS WITH HIM."
REVELATION 12:7-9

Demons are simply fallen angels. Created good then gone bad, like milk left out on the countertop. The angels who joined the rebellion of the dragon in Revelation 12 were kicked out of heaven, falling to earth. They could not prevail in heaven, they will not ultimately prevail on earth. For a time, they're permitted to infest our planet, but in the final reckoning, the demons are toast.

Are they stronger than we are? Probably. However, if we have Jesus inside, if we're wearing His armor, acting on His instructions and standing in faith, we can make the *demons* fear *us*. There's danger if we're careless, like mishandling venomous snakes, but the demons cannot *ultimately* harm us. God keeps His kids safe.

If you care to know, there's a way to tell the difference between the good guys and the bad guys in the spirit world. Demons want to be worshipped. It's a dead giveaway. The head of the demonic world, Satan, originally fell because he wanted to ascend to God's throne and be the object of heaven's worship (Isaiah 14:12). God's angels will *not* receive worship (see verses like Revelation 19:10).

Demons can possess people just as people living in a house possess that house. You can imagine the problems they cause. No doctor today would ever cast a demon out of a patient, but that's because we're so *sophisticated*. I'd rather go with Jesus' diagnosis and He, the Great Physician, casts out demons all the time. With His success rate solid at 100 percent, He probably knew what He was doing.

Ephesians 6:12 tells us there are spiritual forces of wickedness in heavenly places: demons. Often, the conflicts we have with people or the violence between nations and cultures are the product of demonic activity.

Jesus said Satan wants to kill and steal and destroy (John 10:10). The demons want to kill relationships, destroy friendships, steal a sense of unity among people. When we're fighting each other, they're happiest. And of all people, Christians can be the worst at falling for demonic tricks! The demons often concentrate on pastors, elders, church boards and congregations with little resistance from us.

But word up. We have God's spiritual weapons to fight our spiritual enemies says

2 Corinthians 10:4 and Ephesians 6. Weapons of offense and defense. Powerful weapons that are ultimately effective every time. That is, if we think to *use* them.

Demons are more responsible for history than gets reported. Ever noticed how evil continues undeterred after any sort of setback? It doesn't seem to ever go away. That's because wickedness is directed by the deathless enemies of mankind, the demons. For example, look at the hatred for Abraham's children, the Jews. Why does it continue unabated through history? It's because the demons hate Israel, the apple of God's eye, and through the ages they've found plenty of people willing to help them in their plan to destroy the Jews. But it's been their idea all along.

It's critical to remember that *demons cannot do whatever they wish*. They're mad dogs, frothing at the mouth and barking ferociously, but God has them on a leash. They snarl and they slaver, but they seldom are permitted to bite. Read the first part of the book of Job and see Satan have to get permission from God to touch Job. He is only allowed to do a specifically restricted amount of damage in Job's life.

We've all wondered: if God is good and all powerful, how come the demons are not already defeated? Think about the famous phrase, "Why do bad things happen to good people?" Well, first off, there aren't any good people, and second, how do you know the demons are NOT defeated already? Turn the question around? If demons are so strong, and so bent on our destruction, how come they haven't *accomplished* our destruction? The answer to both questions is the same: God is allowing them to rampage for a time, but they are restrained. God is all powerful AND good, and the time will come when the demons will be let loose to do horrible things. After that, they'll be gathered up, rolled into a ball, and tossed into the Lake of Fire.

Bon voyage, demons. You're eternity has a different mailing address than the children of God.

7 the world system
does peer pressure come in a giant-size?

"THE DEVIL LED JESUS UP TO A HIGH PLACE AND SHOWED HIM IN AN INSTANT ALL THE KINGDOMS OF THE WORLD. AND HE SAID TO HIM, 'I WILL GIVE YOU ALL THEIR AUTHORITY AND SPLENDOR, FOR IT HAS BEEN GIVEN TO ME, AND I CAN GIVE IT TO ANYONE I WANT TO. SO IF YOU WORSHIP ME, IT WILL ALL BE YOURS.'"
LUKE 4:5-7

Is this "my Father's world" as the hymn says? Yes. And yet something's seriously wrong with this place. People lie, cheat, steal and stomp all over each other. The powerless are abused, wickedness seems triumphant, emptiness abounds.

If the Kingdom of God doesn't run on money, and it doesn't, why is money so important? If external beauty is not what God primarily prizes, and it isn't, why do the beautiful people have all the open doors? If God hates pride, and He does, why do the arrogant among us seem to get everything they want—no change that—why do they seem to get everything *we* want? Why do we open up the newspaper and see people behaving badly and getting away with it? Why does it seem like every government, especially ours, is peopled by absolute idiots? Why does it seem like the most empty-headed chumps are elevated to rock star status in our culture?

This, my friends, is the world. The world *system*.

The best description I've ever heard of the world system is in 1 John 2:16. The world system is the ***"lust of the flesh, the lust of the eye, and the pride of life."*** A paraphrase would be something like: the arrogance of mankind in trying to eternally possess immediate gratification. Now do you recognize the world system? It's all around us. You can't possibly miss it now you know what to look for.

Cain and Abel lived in two different kingdoms. Abel did what God wanted. He brought the offering God told him to bring. Cain, however, brought the offering he *presumed* God would like. Cain made up his own rules. There it is. The Kingdom of God is governed by God's royal Law, and the kingdom of the world has a roomful of small "k" kings trying to make everyone else bow to them and the rules they invent.

Scripture is full of major players in the world system: Cain, Nimrod, Og, Goliath, Sennacherib, Nebuchadnezzar, Herod, Pilate, Judas. It's also full of those opposed to the world system who lived for the Kingdom of God: Noah, Abraham, Joseph, Samuel, David, Isaiah, Peter, Paul. During their lives, the kingdom-of-the-world guys had it good, and the Kingdom-of-God guys had it rough. But we can easily see which kingdom is worthy of our allegiance. Clue: it's *not* the kingdom of the world.

Revelation paints a clear picture of what happens to the world system. It calls the world symbolically "Babylon." In the end times, the Antichrist will be the head honcho of the world government. Babylon will appear to be triumphant, but the triumph will be short lived. The world system may be attractive for now, but as in the case of a beautiful woman, time is not always kind. The world's beauty is passing, the glamour is fading, the luster is tarnishing. Moth and rust and thief will steal it away. The future of this world is that it will be history.

If everyone speaks well of something, it's usually part of the world system. If people ignore it or are made uncomfortable by it, it often belongs to the Kingdom of God. The difference *can* be that easy. Ever wonder why awards seldom go to PG movies, why corrupt politicians rise quickly, why bad news is all the news there is, why we're seemingly fascinated by pathetically stupid screw-ups and why people who do selfless things for others are boring to read about? Now you know.

The kingdom of this world—opposed to every worthwhile thing. We live in it.

• ISRAEL

can you wrestle with God and live to tell the tale?

"YOUR NAME WILL NO LONGER BE JACOB, BUT ISRAEL, BECAUSE YOU HAVE STRUGGLED WITH GOD AND WITH MEN AND HAVE OVERCOME."
GENESIS 32:28

Israel, Yishra-el or Y'srael. Some say the name means: *Prince of God* in Egyptian. Others say it means *God rules* or *God persists* or *God struggles*, or perhaps *he who contends with God*, or even, *he who prevails with God*. There's a possible meaning that might be prophetic: *triumphant over the false gods*. Names are complex things and Hebrew scholars have many opinions on this matter.

But we don't have to wonder why God changed Jacob's name to Israel because the reason is right there in the verse: the Holy Spirit says that Israel struggles with both God and men and overcomes. How about that? God didn't choose Abraham, Isaac and Jacob because they were pushovers. God doesn't need flatterers or yes men, nor does He use people who are cupcakes. He doesn't mind a little attitude. Moses had murdered a man. David killed lions, bears, Philistines and a giant. Elijah faced down 450 demon-worshiping priests. Peter could curse a blue streak. James and John were "sons of thunder." Paul was persecuting Christians when God found him. God likes feisty, fiery people. If you haven't noticed, He's a little fiery Himself.

Abraham, the patriarch of Israel, follows God's leading by faith, willing to leave his home and follow God to a place he'd never seen. God always intended that His people would live by faith, trusting in Him. Sure He gave Moses the Law. And the Ten Commandments are the most influential statutes in the history of the world, but the Ten do not *define* Israel. Israel is defined by Abraham's faith, cited 450 years before the Law was given. Genesis 12:1-4, **'The LORD had said to Abram, 'Leave your country … and go to the land I will show you. I will make you into a great nation' … So Abram left, as the LORD had told him."**

Most countries have a ruling bloodline, a succession that clearly indicates royal status descending from a past king. It's not like that with Israel. Their bloodline is to establish the authenticity of the coming King of kings, the Messiah.

In a single people, God preserved the ancestry of the Messiah. While scholars have questions about the ancestral names in the Gospels, it appears that in Luke we have the lineage of the Messiah's mother, and in Matthew, that of His father. If that is indeed the case, the lineage of Mary would be Jesus' *chromosomal* ancestry, and the lineage of Joseph in middle eastern culture would be His *legal* ancestry. Joseph took Mary and her son into his lineage through marriage, which makes it amazing that *both* of Jesus' parents, the one with whom Christ shares blood and the one who "adopted" Him and married His mother, were meticulously in the Messianic line.

God took a nation, called them to obedience and faith, taught them holy from unholy, and revealed His written Word to them. As God did with the Messianic bloodline, He produced and preserved within Israel the Scriptures. God proclaimed to Abraham that all the nations in the world would be blessed by his descendants, and that has happened in myriad ways, especially through the Anointed One: Yeshua HaMashiach.

Israel is the apple of God's eye. The Jews have a very close and unique place in God's heart, due to people like Abraham (the father of our faith), Moses (the friend of God) and King David (a man after God's own heart) ... all dear to God and people of great faith. Is God done with the Jews? No way. The book of Revelation is almost exclusively about the last days, and which nation is the most important? You guessed it, and it's not America!

Although Jesus has been rejected by the overwhelming majority of Abraham's *descendants*, He's believed on by untold numbers of Abraham's *family of faith* (Romans 9:6-8). If you are trusting in Jesus, you are a descendant of Abraham through Christ, even though you weren't born a Jew. What a glorious thing to be a gentile adopted into God's own family, the Jews! What an even more glorious thing to be a Jew who puts their faith in the promised Savior Messiah of Israel and returns home like a prodigal son.

Did you know that Jesus is not a Christian? Not even remotely. He's 100 percent orthodox Israelite. Jesus never became a Christian because a Christian is someone who follows Christ and Jesus didn't follow Himself! Anyway, Christianity didn't begin until Pentecost, 50 days after the crucifixion and Jesus' return to heaven. Amazing, huh?

The beloved Founder of Christianity is, to this day, the most kosher Jew to ever wear a yarmulke. Oy vey.

1 the obedience that comes from faith
is it smart to say no to God for any conceivable reason?

"THROUGH HIM AND FOR HIS NAME'S SAKE, WE RECEIVED GRACE AND APOSTLESHIP TO CALL PEOPLE FROM AMONG ALL THE GENTILES TO THE OBEDIENCE THAT COMES FROM FAITH."
ROMANS 1:5

Abraham is the father of our faith. He was not a perfect man of course. There's only been one of those. But he *faithfully* obeyed God. He did whatever God asked him to do, when he was asked and in the manner God asked him to do it. We understand from Abraham's life that faith and obedience are the same thing when it comes to our relationship with God. Faith and obedience are theologically inseparable.

Because of Abraham's faith, God blessed him and honored him and made amazing promises to him. Hebrews 11:6 says it is *impossible to please God without faith*. Abraham definitely pleased God. He's heralded as "the man of faith" (Galatians 3:9). God even put Abraham's name into His own name, as He instructed the Israelites, "I AM the God of Abraham, Isaac and Jacob."

Jesus, God in a human body, operated in the obedience of faith throughout His first coming. As God, He has unlimited authority and might, but He did not use it. Instead, He chose to relinquish His will and His power and to live His life in faithful dependence upon His heavenly Father. Philippians 2:5: ***"Your attitude should be the same as that of Christ Jesus: who, being in very nature God, did not consider equality with God something to be grasped, but made himself nothing ..."***

He did nothing but what He saw His Father doing. He said nothing but what the Father told Him to say. Before the great events of His life, He spent the night in prayer, alone with His Father, seeking grace to help in time of need (Hebrews 4:16). Abraham may be the "father" of our faith, but Jesus is the perfect example of *living* by faith.

If we want the faith that Jesus has, He is the author and the perfecter of that faith in us (Hebrews 12:2). In other words, Jesus is the starter and the finisher of faith in us. What we're saying is that the exact same faith that Jesus used in His life is available for use in ours. Have you ever wanted to keep something that one of your sports heroes used? To use the same cookware that the TV show does? To wear the same sunglasses that a particular pop culture icon wears? Forget about that. Jesus offers us the same faith He used when He lived a perfect life on this earth and raised Him from the dead. Exactly the same faith. We can have it. And we can *use* it.

You may say, "Oh sure, it was easy for Jesus because He's *God*. I could live by faith if I were God." Yada yada, what*ever*. Jesus demonstrated a life of faith by relying completely on His Father for everything. He moved His foot forward, but trusted the Father to direct His steps. He opened His mouth, but counted on the Father to speak through Him. He surrendered His life as a sacrifice, but depended on the Father to raise Him up (Colossians 2:12).

Did you get that? Jesus had the power and the right to raise Himself from the dead (John 10:18) and didn't use it! He waited by faith on His heavenly Father. Man, oh man, *that's* faith for you.

The opposite of faith is said to be doubt, but more specifically, the opposite of faith is self-dependence. Because depending on God is what faith is. To use faith is more than giving mental assent, more than tricking ourselves into positive thoughts, and much more than Forrest-Gump-like naiveté. It is to empty ourselves of our own will and to live for God.

A good synonym for faith is "trust." And a picture of faith is a bridge over a great chasm. We trust the bridge. We step onto the bridge trusting in its ability to help us arrive where we could not go on our own.

Some say we must *grow* our faith, but Jesus simply said we just had to *have* it. If faith is at work, it doesn't take much; an amount the size of a mustard seed is all that is necessary according to Matthew 17:20. Faith does not depend on the strength of the one using it. Samson was in all likelihood a 115 pound shrimp with really long hair! God doesn't share the credit on stuff like that.

Many mighty men of faith have been truth-challenged (Abraham said his wife was only his sister to save his own life), conviction-challenged (Gideon required a whole bunch of miracles before he would obey), courage-challenged (Saul was finally found hiding when called to be king), and compunction-challenged (David murdered Uriah to get his wife).

Faith can heal a sick person because it accesses the One who created that person whole. Faith can move mountains, because faith depends on the One who raised up those mountains. Faith can stop the sun, because it accesses the One who moves the sun and the earth and all the heavens.

The obedience of faith is key to accessing God's promises. Until a mustard seed is "invested" in the ground, it can't become a tree. We would never say that if a seed tries hard enough or thinks positive thoughts or says the right things it can become a tree. We would figuratively say that a mustard seed can become a mustard tree when it surrenders its will to be buried in order that it can be raised up at the right time. By faith. A mustard seed is tiny, just a speck. But Jesus says it's the perfect measure of faith needed to start throwing mountains around with. He's saying it's not how much we have, it's whether or not we have any of it at all.

My old pastor Ron Ferguson says faith isn't so much a matter of how much we have, but rather *who it's in*. I like that.

2 the elect
is it okay if God makes some choices in advance?

"HE CHOSE US IN HIM BEFORE THE CREATION OF THE WORLD ... IN LOVE, HE PREDESTINED US TO ADOPTION."
EPHESIANS 1:4-5

God selected His Jewish and Gentile children before He even thought about making the world and before we had done anything right or wrong. If you have a problem with this doctrine, it's not my fault! It's in the Bible. I'm just reporting.

Is it fair? Well, no. It's not fair. You'll want to take that up with God, not me. You can't possibly think God is unjust, but if you want to say He violates our cherished ideas of fairness, go ahead, I agree. For all the good that does, go ahead and say it. Maybe our cherished ideas of fairness are hogwash.

Have you observed that life itself isn't fair? Solomon, in Ecclesiastes 9:11, observes that the race is not always to the swift or the battle to the strong. Fairness gets whomped upside the head quite often in life. If we simply read the Scriptures, we might conclude that God doesn't give a flip about our ideas of fairness. Why should He? What's so great about our ideas of fairness? Still, don't try to tell me that God's not just. Perhaps the words "just" and "fair" are not synonymous. They may sometimes even be incompatible.

God makes His choice of who He's going to save on the front end, according to the Bible. We have a hard time dealing with this. It seems hard on the unchosen. Is it possible that our minds can't grasp why God does some things?

For some, the problem is this: Does predestination preclude free will? In other words, if God chooses us in advance, where do *our* choices come in? Does it matter what we do if the outcome's already decided?

This conundrum has split churches and confounded theologians ever since the Holy Spirit revealed it. Can we be both free to make our own choices *and* already bound by God's decisions?

Absolutely. Yes. If the only truth we will accept is the truth we have the ability to understand, we'll never travel very far into the landscape of reality. How small would God have to be to fit into our tiny brains? Do we *want* a God that small? Why should the truth simplify itself for our convenience and pride? Why should actuality be something we can reduce to a formula or a bumper sticker?

God is beyond us, and there's no better illustration of this than the seeming contradiction between the doctrines of predestination and free will. We should simply embrace all the truth God has revealed, and if we can understand it, hooray for us. But if we will only believe what we can grasp with our puny intellects, we will impoverish the Christian faith. Embrace the mystery of our faith. Truth is huge because God is huge.

Are we really saying that some people will not be saved no matter what they do? Wow. I guess we are, but I can't say that any of us like saying it. Because saying that doesn't adequately describe the process of God's salvation, only a portion of it.

We lean on the fact that God is good and everything He does is right. Let's say it again: not everyone will be saved. Ouch! We don't want to say it, but if we're going to value the Scriptures, we have no choice. Matthew 7:13-14 is one example of a hard truth: ***"Enter through the narrow gate. For wide is the gate and broad is the road that leads to destruction, and many enter through it. But small is the gate and narrow the road that leads to life, and only a few find it."***

The truth is often beyond our ability to comprehend, which is exactly why a comprehensive theology is beyond our ability to produce. Can we not just leave it that the Bible is all true, that God predestines people who also have free will? Do we have to circumscribe the limits of grace, or can we just be respectfully scriptural?

I think most of us have enough fear of God that we don't want to tell Him how He has to run His own universe. If you feel like arguing this apparent conundrum, fine, but you're going to be teaching a half truth by selecting one side or the other. If we want to discredit election *or* predestination, we'll get no help from the Bible.

We'd better just throw it all in the doctrinal mix and live with the uncomfortableness of God choosing who gets saved. But we shouldn't get past the uncomfortable feeling all the way to a cocky self-assured dogma! We'll be forgetting the other half of the mystery.

Life in Jesus is a dance, not a math problem.

3 the feast of the Passover
does anyone love a good party more than God?

"WHEN YOU ENTER THE LAND THAT THE LORD WILL GIVE YOU AS HE PROMISED, OBSERVE THIS CEREMONY. AND WHEN YOUR CHILDREN ASK YOU, 'WHAT DOES THIS CEREMONY MEAN TO YOU?' THEN TELL THEM, 'IT IS THE PASSOVER SACRIFICE TO THE LORD, WHO PASSED OVER THE HOUSES OF THE ISRAELITES IN EGYPT AND SPARED OUR HOMES WHEN HE STRUCK DOWN THE EGYPTIANS.'"
EXODUS 12:25-27

There is nothing like meeting someone new and finding that you've always been friends. Like remembering a place you've never been. Like hearing a song for the first time and yet trying to think of where you've heard it before. This is the delight that a Christian has the first time they participate in the Jewish festival of Passover.

The Passover is celebrated as the Seder today. As we go through this ancient Hebrew ceremony for the first time, we continually recognize the roots of our faith in the declarations and prescribed actions of the feast. In the upper room, Jesus had a final meal with His disciples. Every person in that room was steeped in Jewish tradition. There was no Christian faith because Pentecost was 53 days away.

And still, those 13 men were having *church*. They sang, they washed feet, they had a sermon, they even kicked someone out of the church (Judas), and believe it or not, they shared the Eucharist: communion. That's not what Jesus called it, but He told them that He had eagerly awaited this meal, probably ever since He thought about creating the universe. If Jesus looked forward to it so much, we need to know more about it. We need to apply ourselves and study it.

It was instituted the night the Angel of the Lord killed the firstborn sons of Egypt and passed over the Hebrew homes marked with the blood of a perfect lamb. That final act of *changing the inheritance* of two nations, rejecting the one and selecting the other, was the raw power of God, acted out, on one amazing night. This is the night the nation of Israel was *born*—brought into being.

The Hebrew slaves then left the land of their captivity, free, laden with the riches of that vanquished nation, having done nothing to secure their freedom but obey the command of God through His servant Moses. What was the command? Celebrate the first passover and sprinkle blood on their door. God wanted the Israelites to never forget this night, and He made it a yearly feast. Those who say the God of the Old Testament is severe and bloodthirsty are missing something. As the Passover feast proclaims, God does love to *celebrate*.

God gave the children of Abraham these instructions: select a spotless lamb as a holy offering, and bring it alive into your house. Rid your house of all leaven (which symbolizes our puffed-up pride). Then kill the lamb in a prescribed way and sprinkle its blood on the door. Roast and eat the lamb with unleavened bread, and be ready to go wherever God may lead. Celebrate this feast every year as a remembrance of the time when God spared His people from the Angel of Death, the time when God led your ancestors out of bondage into freedom, from being an enslaved subculture into a mighty nation. Most importantly, teach all of this to your *kids*. They'll tell their children the story ...

Passover is all about the lamb. He's perfect, faultless. He lives in the house all week and becomes a dear friend. But He is destined to be slaughtered. His blood will protect, His body will nourish, His sacrifice will bring liberty and life. Along with the lamb is the fruit of the vine, poured into four cups: the cup of sanctification (preparation and thanks), the cup of wrath (plagues and judgment—Jesus drank it in our place), the cup of redemption (salvation and victory), and the cup of praise (the return of Messiah—this cup is not drunk because Messiah is "yet to return" according to Jewish tradition, one of the only things Jews get wrong).

The foreshadowing is rich, for this happens 1,500 years before Jesus goes to the cross as the sinless, perfect Lamb of God to offer up His body and to sprinkle His blood for our sanctification, to intercept God's wrath against us, to redeem us and to promise His presence with us forever.

If you've never celebrated a real Jewish Seder, don't wait another year. Information about the Passover Seder is available all over the internet. Worth a look.

Typical Jewish humor (most of the great comedians the world has ever seen are Jewish) in characterizing their struggles with other nations throughout history and their feasts is: *They tried to wipe us out. They couldn't do it. So ... let's EAT!*

4 blood atonement
what does God require to pay our sin debt?

"IN FACT, THE LAW REQUIRES THAT NEARLY EVERYTHING BE CLEANSED WITH BLOOD, AND WITHOUT THE SHEDDING OF BLOOD THERE IS NO FORGIVENESS."
HEBREWS 9:22

Nothing can pay a sin debt except innocent blood. Reread that last sentence as many times as it takes to sink in. Don't blow past this. Inherent in this doctrine is the reason Jesus says no one can come to the Father except through Him. He's not being exclusive or snobbish, he has the only innocent blood available. As the old saying goes, *"Life is short, death is sure; sin the cause, Christ the cure."*

In ancient Egypt, God declared it was time for the Hebrews to leave their slavery and start up their own nation. But Pharaoh would not let the Hebrews go. Therefore, in a series of escalating judgments, God shook the foundations of the world system embodied in the Egyptian nation. Finally, God told Moses that He was going to kill every firstborn son in the land of Egypt. Killing the firstborn was what the Egyptians did to the Jews when Moses was born. It was meant to demonstrate total supremacy, domination, mastery. But as a final judgment, God reminded the Egyptians who the big dog really is. The Angel of Death killed every male child in the land in one grisly night.

Yet the Hebrews, in their slave quarters which we call the land of Goshen, were given a command that would protect them from this horrific judgment. God said to take a spotless lamb, slaughter it and sprinkle the blood over the doorpost of the house, so that when the Angel of Death comes to the house and sees the blood, he would pass over. Foreshadowing the *Lamb* of God. Blood atonement. For salvation. There's nothing else that can avail.

A lamb is the picture of innocence. What has a lamb ever done wrong? In the Passover ceremony, the lamb is to be without a physical fault or blemish—a perfect lamb. No doubt these were uniquely hard to come by and expensive, therefore it was a true act of worship to slaughter the best of the stock in obedience to God instead of using it to produce a more vigorous herd. Jesus is the perfect Lamb of God, costly and precious to the Father (1 Peter 2:4). Even His judge and executioner, Pontius Pilate, said Jesus had done nothing wrong.

Jesus was faultless, like a sacrificial lamb. Jesus stood before Pilate without opening His mouth in His own defense, like a sacrificial lamb. Jesus was handed over to death by the Jewish priests, like a sacrificial lamb. And Jesus died for the sins of the people, like a sacrificial lamb. As the Chief Priest unwittingly prophesied about Jesus in John 11:50, It is better ***that one man die for the people than that the whole nation perish.***

Just as the sacrificial lambs "cleansed" ancient Israel, so the Lamb of God has become the atoning sacrifice for the sin of the whole world. God painstakingly instructed the priests of the Jewish nation in the way to carry out these sacrifices: what was an acceptable animal to use, how to prepare themselves as priests to offer the sacrifice, how and where to kill the animal, what do with the blood and the rest of the body, what to sprinkle, what to burn. Jesus fulfilled every requirement for a kosher blood sacrifice. The Mosaic sacrificial system is a pre-enactment of the atonement Jesus paid with His lifeblood on a Judean hilltop in AD 33.

The payment has been made in full. There's nothing more needed to square the sin debt. Once and for all, says 1 Peter 3:18. A single, one-time payment, not one continually offered (Hebrews 10:12). It's over. If someone rebuilds and reuses the Jewish Temple, it will be an outrageous, scandalous sacrilege. The sacrifice has been made by Christ Jesus and there will never be need of another.

Atonement reunites the rebels with their King, abolishing the crimes of the treasonous and assuaging their sin guilt. Re-pronounce "atonement" and you have "at-ONE-ment" for now God and man are made to be at one, reconciled by the blood of Jesus Christ (Colossians 1:22).

Jesus is described as the Lamb sacrificed before the world was made (1 Peter 1:19). Here is illustrated the love and the wisdom and the faithfulness of God. Knowing He would be rejected by the very people He was creating, He loved them anyway and had already made a way for them to come back before He had even made them to exist. In the history of heaven, Jesus had been crucified on a hill called Golgotha before the hills were ever put in place.

There is only one man who ever had innocent blood flowing through His veins. Only one man *could* be the Savior of the World.

5 sanctification
what's better than being useful to God?

"IN A LARGE HOUSE THERE ARE ARTICLES NOT ONLY OF GOLD AND SILVER, BUT ALSO OF WOOD AND CLAY; SOME ARE FOR NOBLE PURPOSES AND SOME FOR IGNOBLE. IF A MAN CLEANSES HIMSELF FROM THE LATTER, HE WILL BE AN INSTRUMENT FOR NOBLE PURPOSES, MADE HOLY, USEFUL TO THE MASTER AND PREPARED TO DO ANY GOOD WORK."
2 TIMOTHY 2:20-21

Why are nursing homes such a downer? The mess, the smell, the atmosphere is no worse than a hospital. But a nursing home has an extra factor: the people there are no longer *useful* or productive. There's a sense of hopelessness brought on by no longer being necessary to anyone. What's the point anymore? What do some of our under-appreciated old have waiting for them each day that's worth waking up for? It's horribly sad.

God knows we all have a need to be needed. This is what sanctification is all about. When we're sanctified, God takes us through a process that makes us fit to be *used* by Him. I know, I know. Nobody's going to make you do anything you don't want to do and yada yada. The truth is you're going to serve *someone*: serve yourself (narcissist), serve the world (materialist), serve fairness (utopianist), serve the devil (nihilist), serve mother Earth (naturalist), or serve God (Jew or Christian). It's transcendently satisfying to be useful to God. Period.

Being made useful is invariably a process. To get iron ready for use, it's hacked out of wherever it was, separated from its native rock, broken to bits, sent through fire, melted, poured out, molded, hammered, formed together with other metals and sent through the fire again. To prepare a Christian for eternal life, the Christian is called out from the world, separated from their old ways, surrendered to God's will, shaped by discipline and the Word of God, broken to become more obedient to the leading of the Holy Spirit, sent through fiery trials and suffering, molded to become useful to God in spreading the news of the Kingdom, and thrown together with others in ways that produce elemental changes.

To prepare a soldier for service, they're enlisted, made part of a team, robbed of individual will, degraded, broken, built up, trained and armed for battle. An athlete goes through rigorous hardship and privation getting their body in shape for whatever it will be called upon to do. Sanctification is going on all around us wherever we turn.

In the days of Moses and Joshua, the people were made ready so they could meet with God. Not just the crucible of the desert wanderings and the battle for the promised land, but individual priests went through a detailed process of sanctification. Exodus 29 is an exhaustive manual for precisely what to do and how to do it in order to stay alive while performing your priestly duties in God's presence.

Jeremiah 18:3-6 speaks of our sanctification from God's point of view, something we should consider more often. ***"So I went down to the potter's house, and I saw him working at the wheel. But the pot he was shaping from the clay was marred in his hands; so the potter formed it into another pot, shaping it as seemed best to him. Then the word of the LORD came to me: 'O house of Israel, can I not do with you as this potter does?' declares the LORD. 'Like clay in the hand of the potter, so are you in my hand, O house of Israel.'"***

When the Israelites were sanctified, they were ready to experience the presence of the Lord. Want to experience more of God? Get sanctified. Israel had priests who were made ready to help others get right with God. Want to help others get right with God? Get sanctified. Revelation 1:6 and 5:10 says you and I are priests to serve God! That, my friends, is a purpose worth living for.

Sanctification is a lengthy, difficult and painful procedure. Yet, the very fact that God is willing to sanctify us is great news: he must have plans to use us. In the new creation, we won't be lounging around on clouds with nothing to do, for crying out loud! We'll have been made ready by our present lives to help God in our future lives. This world is preparation for the next. This is the time God is sanctifying you and me. This is when we are being formed into useful vessels.

Maybe God deserves a little more cooperation from us?

6 priest

why do we have bridges?

"Every high priest is selected from among men and is appointed to represent them in matters related to God ..."
Hebrews 5:1

An earthly priest is a liaison between humankind and God. After rigorous preparation, he approaches God on behalf of his fellows, who cannot approach a holy God in their sinful condition. The priest must continually be sanctified—set apart for the job—so that he can continue to speak to God for the people and to the people on God's behalf. It's a distant and awkward arrangement, but it's better than getting fried to a smoking pile of ashes, right?

Moses' brother Aaron was Israel's priest, hence the *Aaronic* priesthood. Aaron was a descendant of Levi, thus the—you guessed it —*Levitical* priesthood. The clan of Levi was set apart for the priesthood by their act of devotion that involved striking down their clansmen who had sinned against God while Moses was getting the stone tablets on Mt. Sinai. You can read about it in Exodus 32. It will offend your modern sense of morality. We have *got* to be okay with the Bible disagreeing with how we think God ought to behave!

The ritual requirements and duties of the Levitical priesthood were painfully exacting. No slipshod preparation for service or fulfilling of duty allowed. The priests were to teach the instructions of God, offer the sacrifices, maintain the Tabernacle (later the Temple), settle disputes among the people, and collect the tithe. A giant job description.

The Temple was destroyed in 70 AD, and with the destruction of the Temple, the *Levitical* priesthood was ended. We still have Rabbis today, but they are NOT the same thing at all. But you may be interested to know that there is a priesthood that is still in effect. And you won't be surprised to learn that it's Jesus, and because of His commissioning, the members of His Kingdom.

Hebrews 7:11-17 says that Jesus is not in the Levitical priesthood. He's descended from Judah. Rather it says that Jesus is a *new kind* of priest, heralding *a change in the Law*. The Law of the Spirit of life in Christ has replaced the Law of sin and death (Romans 8). Hebrews 6:20 says that Jesus will never die. That means we'll never ever need another priest. Jesus is a priest *forever* "in the order of Melchizedek." *Melchizedek*! Who's Melchizedek?

Glad you asked. Melchizedek is found in Genesis 14, Psalms 110, and Hebrews 5 and 7. Perhaps he's a Christophany—a pre-incarnate appearance of Christ. Who knows! No family, no recorded death. Oh, and we're told that Abraham *tithes* to him, and I hope your spiritual antennae are up on that one. Abraham's descendent Moses was instructed to give a tithe to *God*, just as Abraham had done to Melchizedek. Melchizedek is the King of *Salem* ("peace") and a priest of the Most High God. Salem later becomes Jerusalem, another point to consider in this remarkable man's dossier. God had planned a new priesthood for Jesus all along. Five hundred years before God institutes the priesthood, God has a priest called Melchizedek. A thousand years before His birth, Psalms 110:4 calls Jesus **"a priest in the order of Melchizedek."** Since Jesus brought in the new law (hence, the New Covenant), He also had to bring in a new priesthood (Hebrews 7:12). New deal, new reps.

Jesus, our high priest, is our advocate. He pleads for us before His Father's throne of grace. He didn't offer the blood of animals, but rather His own blood for our sins. He didn't sprinkle His blood on an earthly copy of the heavenly altar, but rather on the real thing in the heavens (Hebrews 9:24). Only His blood can atone for our transgressions, His sacrificial payment for our sins is the only one possible.

Jesus as our High Priest is absolutely unique. Apologies to all the other faiths with their big name people! There is only one priest who can speak to God on our behalf and it's none of those guys who sometimes get listed with Him. ***"For there is one Mediator between God and man, the man Jesus Christ,"*** 1 Timothy 2:5.

While we don't have priests per se, we do have offices in the church. Sometimes we call them priests, but they do not offer sacrifices; in fact, if they did, we would kick them out of the church! But the leaders of our churches do the other functions of a priest: maintain the stuff, settle disputes, and collect the tithe.

There's also the "priesthood of the believer" pictured by all the "one another" passages in the Bible. When we pray for each other, serve each other, keep an eye out for each other, stand in the gap for each other, and encourage each other, we're performing our duties as priests in the Kingdom of Jesus.

Fathers are also priests and are called to be the heads of their households, to lead their families in spiritual matters (Ephesians 5:25 and 6:4).

And yet, in a very crucial way, the office of priest is absolutely ended in this way. We no longer are required to use a representative to approach the throne of grace. There is no buffer anymore. When the Temple curtain dividing the holy place from the holy of holies was miraculously torn when Christ died, it signaled a new era in our relations with our holy God. The office of a fellow sinner who would approach God on our behalf ended among the human race. We can each come to God in repentance and humility and confidently expect Him to receive us, according to Hebrews 4:16.

It's a mystery. The priesthood has been both abolished and extended into the church. There used to be one family on the earth who could intercede for mankind, the family of Levi, and now all families can be conduits of God's grace to each other. There used to be a specific ceremony of sanctification that could be performed only by a priest, but now that has been done once for all at the cross. The old has gone; the new has come.

Called by the grace of the Father, sanctified by the blood of Christ, and used powerfully by the Holy Spirit ... that's us. The priests!

7 the Sabbath
was God tired, and so He invented a day of rest?

"IF YOU KEEP YOUR FEET FROM BREAKING THE SABBATH AND FROM DOING AS YOU PLEASE ON MY HOLY DAY, IF YOU CALL THE SABBATH A DELIGHT AND THE LORD's HOLY DAY HONORABLE, AND IF YOU HONOR IT BY NOT GOING YOUR OWN WAY AND NOT DOING AS YOU PLEASE OR SPEAKING IDLE WORDS, THEN YOU WILL FIND YOUR JOY IN THE LORD, AND I WILL CAUSE YOU TO RIDE ON THE HEIGHTS OF THE LAND AND TO FEAST ON THE INHERITANCE OF YOUR FATHER JACOB. THE MOUTH OF THE LORD HAS SPOKEN."
ISAIAH 58:13-14

Soil produces more crops when allowed to lie fallow. You can't milk a cow all day long and expect increased yield. Have you ever been talking with someone for a long time and they hold up their hands and say, "Why don't you give it a rest!" This is the Sabbath principle.

On the seventh day of creation, God rested. Was He tired? No. Look at me. *God never gets tired.* So why in the world did God decide to take a break? Because He wanted to set a *pattern* for us to follow. We need to work ... actually we're commanded to work. But along with work, hard work, work in which we give all that we have, we should also rest.

And way beyond simply stopping what we're doing the rest of the time, God calls his children to <u>delight</u> in the Sabbath—not just endure it, but to put our affection upon Jesus throughout it. The Sabbath was made for *us*, for our sake, not as a burden, but as a source of joy and healing and re-<u>creation</u> (hence the word, "recreation"). Restocking, restoring, replenishing. Preparing for the work of the week, rejoicing in the blessings, the provision and deliverance of the week past. Honoring God out of a motivation of love for Him and His command to "keep" the Sabbath. There's a lot packed into that one word "keep!"

Sabbath rest gives us a chance to acknowledge God's sovereignty over our busy schedule. It lets our batteries recharge, and gives the secular humanists fits. Don't even get me started on soccer and how it's inarguably from the devil since they schedule kids' games on Sunday morning. I'm only *sort of* kidding!

It doesn't take a genius to figure out that the Sabbath was originally Saturday, the *seventh* day of the week. When Christianity began, the disciples did not abolish the Sabbath, but merely relocated it to the *first* day of the week. Some say it's because the Temple where they met was used on Saturday. Some say it was to honor the Resurrection. I don't know which is true, neither or both, but it's common now for Sunday to be *called* the Sabbath. Still, the Sabbath is more than a day ... it's a heart principle.

When I was growing up, there was no alcohol sold on Sunday. Neighbors watched each other to make sure everyone went to church. I realize that was raw legalism, but the societal pressure to go to church wasn't all bad, was it? Sunday was time with the family, time to gather around the table with a special meal (the Bible says it has to be fried chicken, not really) and give thanks.

America used to stop every Sunday and acknowledge what we now acknowledge perhaps only at Thanksgiving and Christmas—in God we trust. God is the One we worship. He's the one we must ultimately please, whose blessing we seek. America is a Christian nation built on worship. Presidents close all their remarks with the phrase, "And God bless the United States of America," which I like to hear whether they mean it or not! Remember Balaam in Numbers 22 who couldn't help but pronounce God's blessings on a nation!

Google George Washington's Thanksgiving proclamation of 1789 and Abraham Lincoln's Thanksgiving proclamation of 1863. Powerful statements both. They seem to think God deserves national recognition and both in their own way inaugurated days of unique thanksgiving to Him. We are a nation whose leaders have always had the sense to stop and bow our heads to the gracious providence of God Almighty.

When we stop doing whatever we want on the Sabbath and take *deep joy* in the Lord according to His will, we get more than a pleasant interruption of our crazed schedules. We get closer to God. Our families build a foundation of faith to carry them through the storms of life. We experience God's blessing.

As well as physical rest, there is also the principle of ceasing from our own efforts to be good enough to earn God's approval and love, and accessing instead the power of the risen Christ. This too is the Sabbath principle, that we cannot produce the crop of mature fruit of the Holy Spirit: love, joy, peace, patience, kindness, goodness, faithfulness, gentleness and self-control. These things will never come out of our good intentions or the sweat of our brow, but only as we surrender our will to God's. This is what it means to *rest in the Lord*. This is true Sabbath rest.

What did we do to earn God's graciousness? Nothing. It was God's decision before He created the universe that He'd love us no matter what we did. What did we do to earn our salvation from sin? Nothing. It was Jesus' finished work on the cross and His victory at the empty tomb that accomplished our forgiveness. What did we do to earn adoption into God's family? Nothing. It was God who sent His only Son to redeem us. Our only plea is the blood of Jesus. Our battle cry is the glory of God. Our banner is the grace of God.

We have given up our striving to be good enough and have taken Sabbath rest in the mercy and provision of God, through Christ Jesus and His finished work.

Now if we can just *remember* that we already did that.

We were out of control. We'd gone over the edge and couldn't save ourselves. We were helpless, hopeless, hapless; hurting each other and ourselves; falling in a dead-end spiral down through the dregs of behavior and through the rock bottom of perversity. And then ... miracle of miracles! Someone stepped in. Someone huge and powerful, Someone compassionate and wise - the only Someone anywhere who could have stepped in. And He <u>did</u>.

....

¬chapter four
GRACE: THE UNEARNED INTERVENTION

how can we ignore so great a Gift?

"FROM THE FULNESS OF HIS GRACE WE HAVE ALL RECEIVED ONE BLESSING AFTER ANOTHER."
JOHN 1:16

Grace is undeserved favor, unmerited approval that bestows righteousness, clothing us with the very same approval the Father has for His perfect Son, Jesus Christ. How do we earn this approval? We can't. So then, how do we get it? It's already given. We just have to recognize that fact and embrace it.

Can I be more specific? Glad you asked. Here's how to find ourselves walking in the grace of God Almighty. We must humble ourselves before Jesus Christ, come to Him with a teachable heart and a surrendered will. That's it. No magic prayer, no long journey with obstacles to overcome, no self deprivation or flagellation that will get God's attention. Humility of heart and mind.

No more telling God how He ought to act, what He can and can't do, how the world ought to be be run. No more telling God what we will and won't do. Now we look to Him for our provision. We depend on Him for our everyday needs. We talk with Him about the things that bother us and the things that delight us. We live our lives in constant acknowledgment of His presence as He generously gives us His favor. Above all, we thank Him for His daily *grace* which sustains us.

Grace sticks in the unbeliever's pipe more than anything else. Until we experience it, it seems wildly unfair. Well? It *is* unfair. Grace is God being unfair but only unfair to Himself. Are you telling me that if Hitler repented two seconds before he died, God would accept him as a sinless child? Man says no. Grace says yes. And God acts through the filter of His unbounded grace.

Grace cannot possibly be justified; yet, it will take upon itself flesh and die on a cross to justify you and me. Go figure.

• INCARNATION

can a writer bodily step into their own story?

"SINCE THE CHILDREN HAVE FLESH AND BLOOD, HE TOO SHARED IN THEIR HUMANITY SO THAT BY HIS DEATH HE MIGHT DESTROY HIM WHO HOLDS THE POWER OF DEATH, THAT IS, THE DEVIL."
HEBREWS 2:14

Some things just can't be done. Blood can't come from a turnip. Words spoken cannot be unspoken. No one can reach down, grab their own ankles, lift and hold themselves upside down. A camel can't go through the "eye of a needle."

And ... the Creator *cannot* become one of His creatures. There's just no possible mechanism by which this might be accomplished. The problem is easily described: God is God and everything else isn't. We can make bread out of flour, because that's what bread is. We can grow oak trees from acorns, because that's where oak trees come from. But God's *composition* is foreign to ours. His makeup is totally *other*. Between the Maker and the made, the distance is too great to bridge, the chasm too deep to span. Good thing for us: God does the impossible for breakfast.

We can't imagine God before the incarnation. Sketchy passages of His presence make our knees knock together and our hair stand up. Before you even get close, you have to go through creatures filled with light, hovering with six wings, gyroscopes, unnervingly beautiful voices, crushing power and covered with ... um, *eyes*. God's throne is blindingly glorious, wildly colorful and unimaginably terrifying. We have a minimalist description of Him as shining brighter than the sun, with a voice like thunder and a paralyzing presence.

Truly *awesome*. Great and terrible. Unapproachable. And it is this God who has invaded our world. As a *baby*. You read that right, a baby.

Philippians 2:8, ***"Being found in appearance as a man, he humbled himself and became obedient to death."*** When Christ took on flesh, He left His surpassing glory behind (Isaiah 53:2). Jesus was not handsome in any sense of the word. If you passed Jesus on the street, you wouldn't have given Him a second thought. No giveaways that He's God. Isaiah 53:1b, ***"He had no beauty or majesty to attract us to him, nothing in his appearance that we should desire him."***

And further, at the cross, His face was beaten beyond recognition by the horrific abuse He received from the Roman guards. Isaiah 52:14b, ***"His appearance was so disfigured beyond that of any man and his form marred beyond human likeness."*** How do you go from having the most beautiful face that ever smiled to having a brutalized face that is unrecognizable, bloodied and horrifying? Easy. Start out as God and then take on human flesh. How great is the heart of God. How vast His love for us. Thank you, Jesus.

What is the incarnation? It is the most amazing thing anyone ever did. Making the universe out of nothing was easy. Rising from the dead wasn't all that hard. Singlehandedly beating Satan and the rebellion was easy as pie for Jesus. But how did He come to be born in a stable and need His diaper changed? That's outlandishly beyond outrageously inconceivable. It's just something we'll have to take by faith.

It's ditzy that the world chokes on creation and the resurrection, but blandly accepts and celebrates baby Jesus! Which is harder, for God to make the world, rise from the dead, or become one of us? My money is on that third option all day long.

The *essence* of God in Christ took on flesh and was made to be like us in every way, yet without sin. Now God Himself lives in a human body. Check the verb tense in Colossians 2:9. Read Revelation 1 and see Jesus still in human form. For eternity God in Christ has become a human being. Great for us. But how is that possibly better for Him? It's not. He must REALLY love us.

1 John and 2 John give us a hint of the power of this reality: the demons cannot bring themselves to admit it. If you want to find out if a spirit is sent from God or not, ask it the telling question: did God truly become a baby in a manger? The demons choke on this, and curse the day; the angels rejoice in heavenly hosts, singing, "Glory to God in the highest, and on earth, peace to those of good will!" The cross finished what the manger started. Yet from the moment Christ touched

down on earth as a babe in swaddling clothes, it was OVER. Satan was faced. Golgotha was the crucial battle, but the armament of the Kingdom of Light received an unconquerable weapon in the form of a tiny child that only His parents and a bunch of smelly shepherds witnessed.

If you ever wonder whether God values us all dearly, think about the incarnation and see if you can arrive at any other answer: "Considering what He gave up for us, He *must*."

1 the gospel of the Kingdom
did you know Jesus has opened the doors of His Kingdom to us?

"BUT THE ANGEL SAID TO THEM, 'DO NOT BE AFRAID. I BRING YOU GOOD NEWS OF GREAT JOY THAT WILL BE FOR ALL THE PEOPLE. TODAY IN THE TOWN OF DAVID A SAVIOR HAS BEEN BORN TO YOU; HE IS CHRIST THE LORD.'"
LUKE 2:10-11

God is the capital "K" King of all small "k" kings by right of creation. But some of His miserable creature/subjects spit in His face. Revelation 12 describes the great rebellion in heaven, echoed in Genesis 2 and Psalms 2. The mutiny has become entrenched in our self-image, represented well but childishly in our playground snark, "You're not the boss of me."

If I were God (and you should be *really* glad I'm not), I'd have fried the world into a hot steaming puddle. Happily, God is God, and He's made a way back to Himself for all the rebels who wish to return. The way back is the gospel of the Kingdom—the good news.

Before Jesus came, the world was in darkness, careening madly through space on a collision course with ultimate destruction, spinning further and further from God's light and love. But when God landed on the planet as a baby, the angels announced the mystery of the ages: *"Behold, I bring you good tidings of great joy which shall be for all the people! For unto you is born this day in the city of David a Savior, who is Christ the LORD!"* Good tidings indeed.

The bad news? The King will not allow evil to continue to fester and infect the whole creation. At some future point, He'll crush all wickedness and rebellion, wiping out those who oppose His will. But for now, the door is still open for those who wish to be reconciled, amnestied, brought back home.

The word *"gospel"* is transliterated from *"godspel"* from the Latin *"bona annuntiatio"*. *"Evangelist"*, which we use to mean gospel preacher, comes from the Greek *"eu"* meaning good, and *"angel"* meaning message. "Evangel" means the good message, the good news. So many ways to say the same thing—Jesus saves! God forgives!

We're no longer doomed to be forever shut out from the this-is-why-I-was-created-so-that-I-could-be-in-God's-presence presence of God. He has come into our midst to reclaim His own beloved people. Ephesians 2:12-13 says it: ***"Remember that at that time you were separate from Christ, excluded from citizenship in Israel and foreigners to the covenants of the promise, without hope and without God in the world. But now in Christ Jesus you who once were far away have been brought near."*** That word "citizenship" is translated in the King James as "commonwealth." What a jam-packed word! Commonwealth means the shared benefits of being part of the whole: the wealth held in common. In the case of the gospel, "the whole" is the Kingdom of Jesus Christ the Righteous. Yowza!

The commonwealth of the Kingdom of God was lost to us when we rebelled in the Garden of Eden. That Kingdom was what we fell *from*, what we could never again find. It was impossibly beyond recovery. Before Jesus was born in Bethlehem, the Kingdom of God was far distant from us, beyond the farthest star, according to Psalms 8:1b: ***"You have set your glory above the heavens."***

Romans 3:23 gives us the sad truth, ***"All have sinned and fall short of the glory of God."*** Our chance to experience God's kingdom had experienced a *shortfall.*

But when Christ arrived, He announced the good news of the nearness of the Kingdom. Mark 1:15 records His very words: ***"The time has come. The kingdom of God is near. Repent and believe the good news!"***

This is an astounding statement. Here is God's Son, walking the earth, proclaiming the gospel of the Kingdom and telling us that it's *near*, it's at hand. Not out there somewhere, it's now among us. The Kingdom of God has come to live in the midst of us in Christ Jesus. Oh wow!

The gospel of the Kingdom is a message of grace. The old system was effective only for those who kept the law of God ... which was no one. The new system is effective to those who accept the free grace of God ... which can be you and me.

The difference is night and day, or better put, death and life. In the gospel of the Kingdom, God's forgiveness is a gift, accepted in surrender and humility. While it is free to us, this gift cost God everything. The price He paid is beyond all the riches of the universe. There's no one else who could've underwritten our debt, no one else could have shouldered the weight of the sin of the world. Nobody else with the ability to win our forgiveness with the substitutionary sacrifice of His sinless life. Nobody but Jesus, who is God in the flesh.

The gospel of the Kingdom begins with the bad news of our sentence of death for the crime of rebellion against the King. It joyfully announces that for every rebel who will bow their knee, the King will issue a full pardon, erase the record of transgressions, bestow complete rights of citizenship in the Kingdom. All this for those who return to the King, Jesus Christ. We who were under the just penalty of breaking the King's law have now been pardoned and restored to an honored place within the realm of God's royal family.

Repent, for God, who was once impossibly far away, is now *at hand*. This is the gospel of the Kingdom.

2 the virgin birth of Christ
are we alright with God doing incomprehensible stuff?

"'HOW WILL THIS BE,' MARY ASKED THE ANGEL, 'SINCE I AM A VIRGIN?' THE ANGEL ANSWERED, 'THE HOLY SPIRIT WILL COME UPON YOU, AND THE POWER OF THE MOST HIGH WILL OVERSHADOW YOU. SO THE HOLY ONE TO BE BORN WILL BE CALLED THE SON OF GOD.'"
LUKE 1:34-35

It's not possible to have a zygote without both a sperm and an egg uniting.

And yet, we have Jesus Christ, born of a *virgin*.

Some translators have argued that the Isaiah passage that Luke quotes could simply mean "young girl." Perhaps. But I don't think so. For the Bible leaves us no doubt that Mary herself knew Gabriel was announcing that she was now pregnant never having gone through the only process by which pregnancy *can* occur. "How can this be since I have never been with a man?" Mary asks. Mary was a virgin in both senses of the Hebrew word: a young girl who'd never done what has to be done for a baby to be conceived.

Therefore, *there could be no baby.*

And yet, Jesus was born from Mary's womb, and Gabriel simply says that the Holy Spirit *overshadowed* Mary. Don't ask me how; I don't know, nor does anyone else. We can't even explain *natural* birth. How could we possibly explain this one-of-a-kind *super*natural birth?

The uncreated Creator becoming one of His creatures is the miracle to top all miracles. Splitting apart a sea was nothing, creating the universe out of imagination was nothing, rising from death was nothing in comparison to the incarnation. It is simply un*think*able. It cannot be done, and yet Jesus did it. It stands rationality on it's head. It dwarfs all the theoretical sciences in sheer mind-numbing complex perplexity. God *became* a human being.

Do you now understand why the main identifying mark of the antichrist is to deny that God has come in the flesh? (2 John 1:7) Once we allow for God in the flesh, *nothing's* impossible, *nothing's* too miraculous, too incredible. Once we let this truth into our hearts, we know that God can indeed do anything at all. This is the lynchpin of God's master plan to reclaim rebel Earth, and so of course Satan cannot let this go unchallenged and still have a chance in hades of winning. Now that Satan can't stop it, he can only try to discredit and deny it.

The amazing uniqueness of Jesus is tied up with His virgin birth. Jesus doesn't belong in the sinful line of Adam's family tree. We do. He doesn't. Our genetic heritage goes straight back to The Fall in the garden of Eden. We can trace the history of our sinful rebellion with precision.

Not so with Jesus. He's a brand new thing altogether—conceived in a virgin womb with no transfer of the old genetic sin.   He is both 100 percent God AND 100 percent man, with no lineage of sinfulness. Innocent. Spotless. Perfect.

I'm not even sure the Bible tells us that Mary contributed an egg. Maybe it does, but don't worry, it's all a miracle. The stark fact remains that Jesus is a completely new kind of human. Exactly like us. With one gigantic difference. When Jesus became one of us, He was made exactly like us in every respect except one.

He was without sin. 2 Corinthians 5:21, ***"God made him who had no sin to be sin for us, so that in him we might become the righteousness of God."***

By "him who had no sin," the Bible means Jesus and it means *no sin whatsoever at all.* Not just that Jesus was a really good man. He is the *impossible* man—the only one who has ever walked the earth and not broken the law of God. Not even once. Never. Think about that.

This is the overwhelming reason why Jesus is the only Savior, why He is the only way to the Father, why there is salvation in no other name but the name of Jesus Christ. No one else has ever been "without sin." Mohammed? Buddha? Gandhi? Confucius? Karl Marx? Charles Darwin? Joseph Smith? George Washington? Martin Luther or Martin Luther King? Gurus, shamans, witch doctors, medicine men? Rabbis? Popes? Scientists? Preachers? Disciples? Apostles? Saint Paul? You? Me?

No soap! *All* have sinned and fallen short of the glory of God (Romans 3:23). But NOT Jesus Christ of Nazareth. He never once sinned. Never-ever. Tempted? Sure. Enticed and sweet talked? Yes. Gave in to sin? Not a single solitary time.

This virgin birth doctrine is included in all the letters and documents we have of the early church. We can find no place where the fathers of the church ever taught anything less than the miraculous conception of our Lord Jesus inside the womb of a woman with no man involved in any way. It's not up for debate. Jesus, the only Savior of the world, the only sinless human being, born impossibly and miraculously.

Jesus' unique birth is a major clue to His identity and mission. Bam.

3 fully God and fully man
is there anyone who can plead our case before a holy God?

"THE HIGH PRIEST SAID TO HIM, 'I CHARGE YOU UNDER OATH BY THE LIVING GOD: TELL US IF YOU ARE THE CHRIST, THE SON OF GOD.' 'YES, IT IS AS YOU SAY,' JESUS REPLIED."
MATTHEW 26:63-64

Can something be inanimate *and* animate at the same time? A whole number *and* a fraction? Alive *and* dead? Not if words have meaning. Can one individual be both God and man? Not half and half. Completely *both*? Only one in the universe can be: Jesus Christ, conceived by the Holy Spirit, born of a virgin. In Him the fullness of the Godhead dwells bodily. It's not understandable, just the honest, inarguable truth. If He weren't that way, He couldn't be our Savior, so let's just enjoy the mystery!

Jesus is God made flesh. The sentence you just read is familiar to everyone who has ever paid attention during Christmas, but it's actually the stickiest sentence ever written. Five words, and I dare you to explain them to anybody. You can't because they are inexplicable. Just thought I'd save you the trouble and frustration of trying, but knock yourself out if you want to give it a shot.

I'm not a math wizard, but I don't have to be to understand that 100 percent of anything is all there is. I realize that when you spend more than 100 percent of your money that you're spending money that's not there. The government struggles with that idea, but I get it.

Don't give me the line that anyone who believes that Jesus is completely 100 percent God and completely 100 percent human is not smart. There are plenty of smart people who don't understand things—like how electricity travels down a copper wire—and yet they still flip the light switch as expectantly as anyone. Christians don't understand the fully God and fully man thing, but they *believe* it. Hey, it's true! So why <u>not</u> believe it?

There's not another like Jesus. There are other rabbinical teachers, gifted storytellers, great moralists, charismatic leaders, traveling preachers, controversial figures and certainly other carpenters. Sure, Jesus is the best the world has ever seen of all those categories.

But know this: in all of history, in the present time and the future to come, there's no other *Savior of the world*. And when we say Jesus is fully God and fully man, we're saying of all the people who've ever lived, He's the only possible sin payment available. We're saying this God-man is humanity's only hope—someone who can span the divide between a holy God and depraved humankind.

This unique condition of being both fully God and fully man is the key to being able to understand *how* He does *what* He does. Some may complain that it's easy for Jesus to be the Savior because He's God. So what? If I'm drowning in my own sin, I want a lifeguard who has one foot on dry land and can reach out and pull me to safety. I don't mind the fact that Jesus is divine if He's my rescuer from the waters of death. Jesus being God is really okay with me.

In Jesus, we don't have an emissary from God, nor a teacher of the things of God, or a prophet, a wise man, or a guru. We have *God in the flesh*. Jesus and God the Father are indistinguishable due to the simple fact that there is absolutely <u>no difference</u>. See one, see the other.

Jesus Himself said it. The apostle Philip asked Him if He could get them tickets to sneak a backstage meet and greet with the Maker of Heaven and Earth (John 14:8). Jesus was disappointed in Philip's powers of deduction. "Have I been with you this long and you still haven't figured out that when you see Me, you're looking at the one and only God?"

This isn't the first time someone's claimed to be God, but it IS the first time that His closest friends (inseparable for three years) completely agreed. When people try to seem infallible, they keep others away. Those closest to them know too much. Being God is impossible to fake with your closest friends! Jesus' disciples agreed that this man they walked around with every day, Jesus, is God in person. They were willing to die grisly deaths rather than recant.

What does this tell us about whether Jesus is God? Would we be tortured and killed for someone we knew was a fraud? Not a chance. Jesus convinced those who knew Him best that He's God for a simple reason: He actually *is*.

Fully God and fully man is one of those mysteries like the Trinity. Don't try to do the math. It'll only confuse you.

4 the fulfillment of the prophecies
ever googled Babe Ruth's called-shot home run point?

"Do not think that I have come to abolish the Law or the Prophets; I have not come to abolish them but to fulfill them."
Matthew 5:17

There's a true story about the famous baseball slugger, Babe Ruth. Baseball is a game where you try to hit a tiny ball with a slender bat as someone tries their hardest to throw it past you at 90 miles an hour. Ruth came up to the batter's box, tapped the opposite side of the plate, spit in his hands and pointed to a spot in the bleachers as if to say, "I'm not just going to somehow miraculously connect my bat with this ball, but I'm going to clobber it into a home run. Moreover, I'm calling it a home run ahead of time. And even more than that, I'm showing you where the ball is going to end up after I crush it."

It happened exactly the way he called it.

The Bible is a record of promises that God has made, where He pointed to a spot in the bleachers of the future and let us know what He's going to do so we could watch Him do it. Some of His promises have already come true; in the end, they will all have happened just like He said they would. Scripture is like a to-do list with check boxes, many of them already checked off—already accomplished. At some point, every single entry will be marked completed and fulfilled. Count on it. The sun will forget to rise before God lets one of His promises fail.

God's promises are called prophecies. They have one single unrelenting theme: they're all about Jesus. Hold it. Jesus is only in the New Testament, you say. Au contraire, mon friendère. The Bible talks about Jesus from Genesis to Revelation and every book in between. There's not a theme in the Bible that doesn't reveal something we need to know about Jesus. He's the magnetic north to which all biblical compass needles point.

Before I became a Christian I remember thinking that Jesus had quite an ego, because everything seemed to be all about Him. Now I know why I had that idea! Everything _is_ all about Him. Jesus is the unavoidable starting point of all rational thinking, of all uplifting aspiration, of all redeeming love in all its manifestations. We can't avoid Jesus no matter how cleverly we try.

There are fulfilled prophecies: that Jesus would be born in Bethlehem of a virgin, that He'd come from the tribe of Judah, that He'd have to travel to Egypt, that He'd teach in parables, that He'd enter Jerusalem in triumph, be betrayed by a friend, go through unspeakable suffering, have none of His bones broken, be executed among rebels and buried with the rich, rise on the third day and that He would destroy death itself.

There are also prophesies yet to be fulfilled: that He'll rule the nations for a thousand years, that the lion and the lamb will graze together and weapons of war will be used to grow food. There's a prophecy that Jesus will bring peace on earth and good will to men, that He'll restore righteousness and justice to a dog-eat-dog world, bringing God's mercy and grace to a planet without either. There's a prophecy that Jesus will crush Satan's head and give total victory to all those who've been oppressed. There's a prophecy that Jesus will bring healing to those who are broken, hope to minds who are in despair, a vision of God's glory to the humble in heart, freedom to captives in all kinds of prisons, joy to the lonely and bereaved who cry tears of anguish, light to the travelers in darkness, good news to the discouraged who are sincerely hungry for God. Sounds like prophesy about Jesus is everything we could ever dream of.

Any doubts that only Jesus can fulfill these astounding promises? Has there ever been anyone like the carpenter's son from Nazareth? In all the pages of history, does anyone else hold a candle to Him? Can you show me a more compelling figure in the record of great leaders? Can you name another who's had more of an effect on mankind than this Jewish rabbi who was executed by the government of His day at the request of the religious leaders? Two thousand years after His death, there have been more inspired lives who give *Him* the credit than all the other inspirations put together.

Jesus is the embodiment of every hope ever hoped, every wish ever wished. If the Bible had never been written, if we had no concrete record of the promises of the coming Christ, we'd still have an inescapable yearning and anticipation of Him anyway. In our hearts, know it or not, every one of us longs for Him.

Isn't it risky for God to let Satan know precisely how He's going to crush the cosmic rebellion and restore the Kingdom of Light to the world of man? To telegraph what He's about to do? To give the enemy a chance to prepare for what's coming? To give away the plot? Nah. Nobody can stop Him anyway.

The prophecies are so specific, they have no choice but to describe the most remarkable man to ever walk the earth.

5 the Savior of the world
who else in all the world compares closely to Jesus Christ?

"THE NEXT DAY JOHN SAW JESUS COMING TOWARD HIM AND SAID, 'LOOK, THE LAMB OF GOD, WHO TAKES AWAY THE SIN OF THE WORLD!'"
JOHN 1:29

We're hopelessly vain. We have this idea we can't shake that we're rock-star special. Unique. Privileged. Inside. Elite. Remarkable. Exceptional. We think we have God's singular favor: He puts everything else on hold when He sees our text message come up on His smart phone. Well, what would you say if I told you it's all true in God's way of looking at things?

God would pay any price to win your heart back. Of course He'd do that for anybody. Not just would do it, *has* done it. For the world. God so loved *the world* that He gave His only Son. Jesus died for every single solitary one of us. There's no one beyond His saving grace. Somehow, each person on earth is God's favorite. It's one of those things that makes Him God.

Isn't Jesus the Messiah of the *Jews*, the Savior and Ruler they've awaited for thousands of years? Absolutely. That doesn't mean He's limited to one people group, however. Jesus is not the Savior of the Jews only (or of the Gentiles only). God told the Jews that *all nations* would be blessed through Israel. Genesis 18:18, **"Abraham will surely become a great and powerful nation, and all nations on earth will be blessed through him."** Jesus is the Hope of *all* nations and He came through a Jewish ancestry, just as was promised. There's no one He doesn't love, no one He didn't die for, no one He doesn't prize more than anything on earth.

Jesus loves Buddhists, Jesus loves Hindus, Jesus loves Muslims, Jesus loves Atheists, Jesus loves Secular Humanists, Jesus loves Materialists and Pantheists, Gnostics and Agnostics, Cultists and Occultists, and those who don't give a flying leap about anything.

There is no one beyond the reach of Christ's love and His offer of salvation. 1 Timothy 2:4 says God wants all men to be saved and come to a knowledge of the truth. For those who say God is an angry, unforgiving God, chew on *that*.

What would you say if I told you that God turned us over to our own worst instincts so that He could save us from them? It's true. Romans 11:32 says it this way; **"For God has bound all men over to disobedience so that he may have mercy on them all."** There's a principle all lifeguards learn about saving a drowning person: never jump in the water until they give up and stop flailing around or they'll grab you and you'll both go down. Wait until after their last feeble effort.

The Law doesn't save anyone; it's not a lifeguard. It is solid, unforgiving, huge. Far from saving us, it's a weight around our necks, a millstone dragging us down in conviction. It was given to show that we've fallen short of God's holiness, and His righteous expectations, to show that we have no hope of saving ourselves. God has sentenced all to disobedience, showing us the depth of our depravity. At least all we could stomach. And then He Himself jumped in the deadly waters to rescue us from a shipwrecked and capsized world.

Is there any other Savior? God asks and answers this question in Isaiah 43:11, *"I, even I, am the LORD, and apart from me there is no savior."* What about the Muslims who are good people, not trying to murder infidels, but just going about their lives, loving others as best they can? What about the nice Buddhists, the good Hindus, the gracious spiritists and happy New Age holistic Christian Science Unitarian Ecumenical Humanist Environmentally Green Gnostics?

I'll tell you. They're hopelessly lost in their sin, just like you and I were, until we surrendered to the sovereignty of Jesus Christ. The deal isn't who can be nice most of the time; the deal is who can pay sin's bill when it comes due. There's only one who can. If Buddha and Mohammed and Gandhi and Mother Teresa are in heaven, it's not because they were *good*, it's because *God* is good. They all had Adam's fallen nature. They all had their own sins to pay for.

The Savior of the World hears every cry for help and rescues all who cry out for Him in humble desperation. We may be surprised at who ends up in heaven, but we won't have to wonder how they got in. They got in like we did: through the unique Savior of the World, Jesus Christ, because there IS no other way.

Should we tell anyone about this great salvation?

6 the holy Son of God

how do we access our inheritance from the heavenly Father?

"WHEN THE CENTURION AND THOSE WITH HIM WHO WERE GUARDING JESUS SAW THE EARTHQUAKE AND ALL THAT HAD HAPPENED, THEY WERE TERRIFIED, AND EXCLAIMED, SURELY HE WAS THE SON OF GOD!"

MATTHEW 27:54

An odd thing. The demons of Jesus' time knew who He was, while the religious leaders were clueless. Well? Who did the demons say Jesus was? Luke 4:24 tells us: Jesus was in church (I know it was a synagogue but that's the church Jesus attended) and there was a man possessed by a demon who screamed, "You're not fooling anyone! I know who you are! The holy Son of God!" THE Son of God.

And when Jesus was being tempted in the desert, Satan kept starting sentences with, "If you are the Son of God ..." Why did Satan keep saying that? What was so important about being the _Son_ of God? Why not just ask, "If you are God?"

I think I know. God's Son is the _heir_. God wants us to inherit the riches of the Kingdom. So He becomes a son and through that son gives us the estate.

When did Jesus become God's Son? People disagree. Jesus is God and has always existed. Yet Psalms 2 speaks of the Father saying to Jesus, "Today you have become my Son," but when that happened no one can say for sure. Some say the incarnation, but I think it happened before the creation of the world.

Regardless, we know when the inheritance is transferred: upon the death of the owner of the estate. Jesus in His own body provided both the death of the owner and the heir of the estate. Through Him, you and I are given the inheritance of our Heavenly Father. 1 Peter 1:3-4, **_"In his great mercy he has given us new birth into a living hope through the resurrection of Jesus Christ from the dead, and into an inheritance that can never perish, spoil or fade kept in heaven for you ..."_**

Over the entrance of the Dome of the Rock, the Muslim mosque in Jerusalem, is an inscription that reads, "God has no Son." Pay close attention. Go back to Abraham (as the Muslims do). The eldest of his two sons was Ishmael, the father of the Arab/Muslim world, rejected by Abraham (not God) and thrown out of the household. The other son was Isaac, the miraculous child of God's promise, and Abraham's heir even though Ishmael was older. This has never gone over well with Arabs: being cast aside by their ancestor. And so the Muslims claim Abraham rejected Isaac, not Ishmael. Hmmm.

In the way of this world, a king's eldest son is the default heir of the king's position and possessions. This is woven into the fabric of the universe.

God wants us to understand something about Himself—that He's a Father and He has an eldest Son who has inherited everything. Hebrews 1:2 says, **_"In these last days God has spoken to us by his Son, whom he appointed heir of all things."_** Since Jesus owns everything, in Him we also own it all. Romans 8:32 says this: **_"He who did not spare his own Son, but gave him up for us all how will he not also, along with him, graciously give us all things?"_**

The Sonship of Jesus is crucial to get. The Jewish high council convicted Jesus of a capital crime using the Law of Moses because of something He said. Do you remember what that was? It's the night that Jesus was arrested in the Garden of Gethsemane, the night before He was to go to the cross. In the early hours of the predawn, the religious leaders have Jesus on trial and they are hammering away at Him, producing false witnesses, lying, yelling, conniving, trying to convict Jesus of something so they can send Him to Pilate to be crucified. Jesus says NOTHING. Nothing at all. Not a single word.

But then His silence is broken when the priests stumble upon the one question Jesus has been waiting to answer. Luke 22:66-70, *"At daybreak the council of the elders of the people, both the chief priests and teachers of the law, met together, and Jesus was led before them. 'If you are the Christ,' they said, 'tell us.' Jesus answered, 'If I tell you, you will not believe me, and if I asked you, you would not answer. But from now on, the Son of Man will be seated at the right hand of the mighty God.' They all asked, 'Are you then the Son of God?' He replied, 'You are right in saying I am.'"* This is the most fantastic courtroom bombshell ever. The Jews had nearly two millennium of instructions by God that only God is God and here Jesus is, claiming to be God as bold as brass. No one could believe it was happening. The authorities pounced on what they thought was a slip-up on Jesus' part.

John 19:7 recounts the charge by which the Jewish leaders presented Jesus to the Roman authorities to be put to death: *"The Jews insisted, 'We have a law, and according to that law he must die, because he claimed to be the Son of God.'"*

You can be evil and claim you're God's Son. You can be nuts and claim you're God's Son. But you can't be a good man, a beloved teacher, a leader of a group of men who later died rather than deny that you're God's Son if you claim to be God's Son and you're just another man. So where does that leave us?

There can be no doubt about it. The inscription on the Muslim's Dome of the Rock is dead wrong. God does indeed have a Son.

And in that Son, Jesus Christ, God's born-again children have their inheritance.

7 the only way back to God
do drowning men complain that there's just one lifeline?

"No one comes to the Father except through me."
John 14:6b

The two most important words in any list of God's promises have to be "*in Christ*." Unavoidably so. Ever since The Fall and the severing of our Garden relationship with God, man has tried everything he knows to "bring back that loving feeling," from the hit song by—well gee whiz, the *Righteous* Brothers! Sorry, I didn't plan that irony.

Anyway, we've tried to get "righteous" with God every way but *His* way. We've tried being really good, we've tried being really bad. We've tried to substitute things like reason and science. We've tried to get in tune with harmonic convergences and we've replaced biblical repentance with ecological sorrow for our carbon footprint trespasses. We're pathetic. Our right standing with God hinges on being able to grasp two words. Two simple little words. We already said what they are at the first of this paragraph, so I won't repeat them.

Forget *that*, here they are again! *"In Christ!"* In Christ we have forgiveness. In Christ we have hope. In Christ we have purpose. In Christ we have newness of life. In Christ we claim the promises of God. In Christ the wrath of God is deflected. In Christ the wonder of relationship is restored. In Christ we have fulness of joy, and we could go on and on. Everything we have that's any good, we have in Christ.

There are at least 90 Biblical references to this awesome pair of words, this treasure trove of a phrase. Ninety! Each time it's used, the phrase "in Christ" unlocks more of the riches God has freely given us. Do you open all of your Christmas presents or just some of them? Why not try to get into all that rightfully belongs to us *in Christ*?

Remember what God announced proudly to the world at Jesus' baptism? ***"This is my beloved Son in whom I am well pleased!"*** When we're in Christ, God says that wonderful stuff about *us*. He knows we stink, yet chooses to smell the pleasing aroma of Christ who lives inside us. Talk about a sweet deal. Christ in us is way more than just air freshener.

When we say that people have tried every way to get right with God, I don't mean to say we have a ton of desperately determined people. People are lazy. We'll settle for the first thing that halfway works. If you took your car into the shop because the engine block had split, would you settle for a pair of ear muffs and a blindfold, or do you want a new engine? Our spiritual engine is busted and worthless. We need a major overhaul. Every other solution to fixing our problem of being wrong with God? Nothing more than ear muffs and blindfolds. They may make us feel better, but the car still won't go.

The problem is not that we're low on good deeds and our bad ones are piling up. *The problem is that we have even one bad deed*, since it only takes one of them to wreck our chances with Go (James 2:10). Why can't we violate just one little tiny command? Because the One who gave the command is holy. He will not put up with less than totally clean, totally whole, totally redeemed people.

What? Is there something wrong with how God feels about sin? Would <u>you</u> eat a bowl of soup if it only contained *one* used bandaid? God hates sin. All of it. He'll have sinlessness or nothing, just like you'll only eat soup with no used bandaids, not even just one.

Jesus is the only way to have this perfection that God demands. God is high and holy, infinitely above us and our low standards. One day we will see Him face to face. And in that day, all of our good deeds will be like a teaspoon of sugar sprinkled on a giant rotting carcass of our bad deeds unless we turn our lives over to Jesus. His life is perfect. His credentials are the cross and the empty tomb. He says for us to come home; all is forgiven. In Christ. In Christ ...

In Christ. There's no other way.

• CRUCIFIXION
why execute the only perfect man there ever was?

"JUST AS THERE WERE MANY WHO WERE APPALLED AT HIM, HIS APPEARANCE WAS SO DISFIGURED BEYOND THAT OF ANY MAN AND HIS FORM MARRED BEYOND HUMAN LIKENESS, SO WILL HE SPRINKLE MANY NATIONS."
ISAIAH 52:14-15

The cross is the cruelest form of brutality ever devised.

The Romans came up with it. It compels the condemned to pull up on spikes driven through their wrists and feet to be able to expand their lungs enough to draw the next excruciating breath. It's technically a hanging, but on a hellishly different scale: a hanging is over in moments, while a crucifixion can go on until the victim finally bleeds to death.

God knew before He made the world that He Himself would undergo this heinous death out of His love for the very ones who would nail Him to that cross. Before He said, "Let there be light!" He had already decided that He would let men do their worst to Him. And man, *did we ever.*

Sleep deprived night of seeing it coming, manhandled during the arrest and in the courtroom. Mocked by His own people for being who He is, beaten by the Romans for no reason whatsoever. Deserted by His friends and then finally even deserted by his Heavenly Father. The actual nails were just one part of that whole hellish ordeal.

When the Roman soldier pierced Jesus's side with a spear, the blood in Jesus' body had separated into serum and water: a medical sign of extreme heart trauma and oxygen depletion. Some say that Jesus died of a broken heart, but His heart was broken when Adam ate the fruit, and today it breaks every time we turn away from Him.

And yet the Bible declares that there's nothing that *could* kill Jesus. Of this there can be no doubt: Jesus told His disciples that the right to give up His life was given to Him by His heavenly Father according to John 10:18.

And there's this fact: 1 Corinthians 15:56 says, ***The sting of death is sin.*** Well? Jesus was without sin. He did not have to die. He could have gone right on living forever. But John 19:30 and Matthew 27:50 tell us that He *gave up His spirit*. He allowed Himself to die so that He could be the Lamb of God who takes away the sin of the world.

He <u>surrendered</u> His life to be used as a ransom payment for sin. He allowed cruel men to beat Him, to mock Him, to spit upon Him and to nail His wrists and feet to an upright pole. He loves us. Of that there is no doubt.

No other religion has a Savior, nor could they have, since there is only one Jesus Christ. Only one person who ever lived on this earth with a sinless life of perfect obedience to God's law that enabled Him to die a substitutionary death for the sin of the whole world. Your sins and mine.

The cross is not just a fiendish form of execution, it is also a powerful symbol for the Mediator between mankind and God. The cross stood on a hill, raised above the earth, but still very much connected. Jesus was "lifted up" on the cross. A curious phrase, to be sure—read Numbers 21:8-9. The Israelites were having a problem with snakebites, due to their sinful rejection of God. God told Moses to make an image of that snake and lift it up on a pole, so that anyone who was bitten could look up to the pole and live.

John 3:14 says that Jesus took our sin upon Himself and was lifted up so that anyone who has been fatally bitten by the deadly serpent of sin may look to Him and be made whole.

There comes a point in the travels of our lives where we come to a *crossroads*. The cross is such a decision point. We can choose to turn to the left or the right, or we can take the straight road laid out before us. The left and right roads lead to darkness and death, we've already tried the one behind us and it's no good. The one ahead leads to light and life.

Maybe we're afraid of the light of God because there are things about our life that we don't want revealed. This is funny and ignorant. Darkness can't hide our wrongdoings from God! He doesn't even need night vision goggles. We might as well take the narrow path, walk right up to the cross and fall to our knees. He'll reach down, lift us up and give us a new heart, a new mind, and a new mission.

The most beloved figure in all of human history made it the centerpiece of His ministry to die a bloody, excruciating death for the crime of claiming to be who He actually is. From that time onward, what used to be a grisly, brutal apparatus for torturing a human being to an agonizing death became a thing of immortal magnificence. Now people who don't even know what it is wear replicas adorned with diamonds around their necks. I'm speaking of the cross.

If Jesus can transform the cross into an object of beauty, He can transform us too.

1 the suffering Servant
for what possible reason would Jesus go through all that?

"HE WAS DESPISED AND REJECTED BY MEN, A MAN OF SORROWS, AND FAMILIAR WITH SUFFERING. LIKE ONE FROM WHOM MEN HIDE THEIR FACES HE WAS DESPISED, AND WE ESTEEMED HIM NOT. SURELY HE TOOK UP OUR INFIRMITIES AND CARRIED OUR SORROWS ... BUT HE WAS PIERCED FOR OUR TRANSGRESSIONS, HE WAS CRUSHED FOR OUR INIQUITIES ... AND BY HIS WOUNDS WE ARE HEALED."
ISAIAH 53:3-5

If you've ever studied the various paintings of what Jesus may have looked like, you'll notice something curious about the ones from the last hundred years. Jesus is happy and smiling, a very clean and muscular man with a well-groomed beard who is laughing and playing with children, a meek and mild weightlifter. I have no doubt that Jesus at this moment is clean and strong and loves to play with kids. And the people of the Bible certainly had good hygiene. They *did* wash the dust from their feet and they used lye for laundry detergent, while on themselves they mostly used water and olive oil.

On the other hand, look at the pictures of Jesus painted centuries ago. What do you see? You see a much different Jesus. You see a more complex, less handsome face.

This man has seen life at its ugliest and has wrestled with the problems common to all of us. This man has been to the bottom of the scummy pond of humanity and has rolled up His sleeves and started pulling people out. You don't do that and stay clean and fresh.

Jesus wasn't a pretty boy. He had no home, no bed, he had one outer robe with no seams, and while he dined with the well-to-do, he also walked the dusty back roads, muddy lake shores and the smelly streets of towns. He was seldom alone and often surrounded by hot throngs of sweaty people.

He could become angry. He could walk unhurt through murderous mobs. He could drink wine and attend the feasts of the rich and powerful and then sit around a fire on the lake broiling fish on hot coals.

He could find himself talking to a prostitute as if they'd known each other all their lives, and the next minute face a raving, threatening demoniac who'd been a holy terror to everyone until this moment when Jesus steps into his life and leaves him master of his own mind again.

Jesus is a man of action. He's a man in motion. Nobody who meets Him remains unchanged. Ask Zacchaeus. Ask Pilot. Ask Paul.

What Isaiah 53:3-5 wants us to know about Jesus is that He is a man of *sorrows*. Sure, the marriage supper of the Lamb is coming and there'll be music and dancing and amazing food and drink and laughter and joy and a sense of family and wonder beyond anything we can imagine. But when Jesus came to earth the first time, He was a man of *sorrows*.

Even when the crowds cheered Him on, Jesus knew, He simply *knew*, that they'd soon be calling for His blood (John 2:24).

Imagine voluntarily coming to visit a place where people are zombies, mouldering and rotting away before your eyes and the stench of death is everywhere. That's the world Jesus came to save. That's the correct picture of what sin has done to God's good creation.

When Jesus stood before His friend Lazarus' gravesite, He wept, not because death was a fearful mystery to Him, but because He never wanted His world to be a place where people had to grow old and get sick and die. He came to bring life in all its fullness of joy, not death in all its morbid, bewildering finality. He wept over Lazarus because He never wanted His beloved creation to fall from the Garden, to rebel from the Kingdom, to slide into sin.

He wept for us and *our* sorrows. He took upon Himself our heartbreaks. He came to share with us in our misery, so that He could lift us up into His own fierce joy. He already had that joy when He came down to earth. But the mind-numbing sadness? *Jesus took that on* for our sakes. He bore our weakness and sickness and yes, even our sorrows. Our Savior is not a romantic utopian. Jesus is a joy-powered realist who weeps for our condition and suffers for our redemption.

We have a God who knows exactly what we're going through because He Himself has gone through it too.

2 forgiveness

what's the bookkeeping term for retiring a debt?

"Forgive us our sins, for we also forgive everyone who sins against us."
Luke 11:4

Go to a bank and somehow take out an impossibly large loan with no collateral. Congratulations, you're in debt up to your eyeballs. Now, go back to the bank and tell them you're *not going to be able* to pay back the loan and watch their faces. I'll bet they're not thinking of naming their kids after you. You'd have a couple of options.

Do away with yourself. They can't garnish your wages after you're dead.

Go to jail, although you'll never pay off the loan from in there either.

Or! Ask the bank to *forgive* the debt and if they do, spend the rest of your life a grateful debtor to their generosity.

Well guess what? We have a sin debt that's beyond our ability to pay. That debt is owed to God. We've taken advantage of His kindness, played fast and loose with His riches, trampled His house and His rules, and spurned His love.

We have the same three options from above. We can hope death will bring oblivion ... it won't. We can think that hell isn't all that bad ... it is. Or we can come to Jesus and beg for mercy, ask Him to *forgive* the debt ... He will. He promises to. He's wanting to. He'll not only cancel the debt, He'll pay it Himself out of the glorious riches of His own lifeblood given at the cross. Then we can spend the rest of our lives as joyous and grateful debtors to His amazing grace.

Some say that God throws our sins into a sea of forgetfulness, but that term is not in the Bible. Nor should we think of God as having a faulty memory. He does cast them into the *depths* (Micah 7:19). Read Hebrews 10:17, **"Their sins and lawless acts I will remember no more."** God doesn't forget our sins. He chooses not to remember them. The difference has to do with who God is. He makes a conscious choice to forgive. Pretty mind-boggling, if you think about it.

He volitionally purposes to forgive us and irrevocably decides to close His mind to the memory of our transgression. He takes the blood of Jesus and cleanses our account from the red stain of sin, putting our lives back on solid footing, giving us a fresh start, lifting our heads, giving us new hope and another chance. He does this for every one who comes to Jesus in humble contrition.

Is there any feeling of relief to match the realization that we are forgiven? Imagine a calf let out to pasture: running and skipping and leaping high in sheer joyful exuberance of being newly alive (Malachi 4:1).

Okay. Why does God forgive us? Because it's His nature. He enjoys forgiving everyone who asks. He lavishes His love and kindness on all who will receive. God's blessings of providence, including His mercy and grace, fall on everyone. Matt. 5:45, **"He causes his sun to rise on the evil and the good, and sends rain on the righteous and the unrighteous."** God's forgiveness is freely poured out on all.

What about us? Can we take this odd forgiving behavior of God and pass it on? We not only *can*, we'd <u>better</u> if we know what's good for us! Matthew 18:23 tells the parable of the unforgiving servant and what became of him. A servant owed his master a hopelessly large debt. The master graciously forgave the whole thing. Immediately, this servant turned around and started beating a fellow servant who owed him five bucks. When the master heard about it, he was furious and ordered the unforgiving servant to be tortured in prison until his debt should be paid in full. Stern measures from a kind master.

That should make us stop and think before we decide to hang on to grudges and past hurts. We should be quick to forgive as we have been forgiven, quick to seek God's forgiveness and the forgiveness of those we've wronged.

Forgiving each other should be modeled after God's forgiveness of *our* sin. Here's why we forgive: we've been forgiven and we're only passing God's forgiveness on to the next person. If our forgiveness must be like God's, then we too can forgive someone before they ask. We don't have to announce it. We can just quietly DO it and move on.

Our feelings have nothing to do with forgiving others. Forgiveness springs from determination, not emotion. We may not put ourselves in the same situation with that person again, we may retain the wisdom we have gained, we may not be as vulnerable next time, but we can surely forgive the trespass.

When asking for forgiveness, we should avoid ultra lame comments like, "Sorry if I did anything to hurt you." Forgiveness is bookkeeping, not whitewashing. Who cares if you're *sorry*? Saying you're sorry is nothing more than announcing your present emotional status. Big deal. Be specific. You can't call up your mortgage holder and say, "If I owe anything, I'm really sorry." Your lender can supply you with a detailed list of what you owe. God will detail our trespasses if we ask Him. Our words should sound something like this: "I was wrong to speak angrily to you yesterday. I wouldn't want anyone to speak to me that way. Please forgive me." It's up to us to man up ... or woman up.

In the Lord's Prayer, we ask God to forgive us the same way that we forgive others. Go back over it if you don't believe me. We oughta be careful about how we deal with this doctrine of forgiveness! We'd better do it right!

Amazing grace, how sweet the sound. Oh look at the next chapter. What a segue ...

3 grace
are you okay that God loves you in spite of everything?

"FOR YOU KNOW THE GRACE OF OUR LORD JESUS CHRIST, THAT THOUGH HE WAS RICH, YET FOR YOUR SAKES HE BECAME POOR, SO THAT YOU THROUGH HIS POVERTY MIGHT BECOME RICH."
2 CORINTHIANS 8:9

Ever tried to define grace?

Maybe you know what it is, but can you explain it to someone else? Grace is overlooking faults in others. Yes, but that's not all grace is.

Grace is elegance in deportment and movement. Grace is simple courtesy, giving someone extra time to repay a debt. It's a short prayer said before a meal, or grace is also just polite behavior.

Grace is <u>G</u>od's <u>R</u>iches <u>A</u>t <u>C</u>hrist's <u>E</u>xpense. It's merciful provision. Grace is, and this is my personal favorite, *God's unmerited favor.*

Grace is hard to pin down, glorious to receive. The hymns help us get a handle on this elusive idea of grace. Apparently, it's not a new concept! It's one that humankind has marveled at for quite some time.

"Grace, grace, God's grace: grace that will pardon and cleanse within;
Grace, grace, God's grace: grace that is greater than all our sin."

Grace is the gospel in a nutshell. Titus 2:11-12 says grace is found in the person of Jesus, who has appeared in flesh and blood, bringing us a way out of the deadly cesspool of this world and its ungodly and unsatisfying lusts. Grace teaches us and calls us to stand against destructive choices and to behave like the children of God, for that's who His grace says we already are (1 John 3:1).

Though the word grace does not appear, this hymn wonderfully describes our need for grace:

"Could my tears forever flow, could my zeal no languor know;
These for sin could not atone, Thou must save and Thou alone;
In my hand no price I bring, simply to Thy cross I cling"

The Law, even though it is good, could not help but condemn us because we could never measure up to its perfection. But grace gives us a chance, and more than a chance—*it gives us the same test scores that Jesus earned.* What? Yes.

The Law brought a sense of hopelessness. Grace provides a certificate of adoption into God's own family. The Law brought death, but God's grace bestows life, welling up from the Holy Spirit living in us by God's grace.

John 1:17 says, ***"For the law was given through Moses; grace and truth came through Jesus Christ."*** Jesus is where grace originates; He's the wellspring. Jesus does not want fearful cringing slaves, nor robotic religious followers. He sends His grace to capture us with unimaginable love, and frees us to be who we are.

"Oh to grace, how great a debtor daily I'm constrained to be;
Let thy goodness like a fetter bind my wandering heart to Thee"

Grace is freely given, but grace itself was not without cost. It was only free to *us*. Jesus paid a terrible price on the cross to buy this gift of grace.

That's why Christians despise the idea of _cheap_ grace, where salvation is a one-time prayer-in-the-past that punches our heavenly ticket but makes no change in our thinking or our behavior. Instead, Christians sing the praises of God's _amazing_ grace, that teaches us to fear God and to love and obey him with our whole hearts.

*"Twas grace that taught my heart to fear, and grace my fears relieved;
How precious did that grace appear the hour I first believed."*

Romans 6:14 says that we used to be under law, but since we were born again, we're now under grace. Grace supersedes law as rocket fuel supersedes baking soda and vinegar. One will only get you so far; the other will take you to the stars.

The law was a system whereby we tried to obey a set of rules and ended up condemned when we found we couldn't do it. All world religions are systems based on that kind of law. Every single one of the world religions says if you do *this*, then you'll get *that*. Don't do *this*, don't get *that*. Soda and vinegar religions.

Grace, on the other hand, is the freedom whereby we now please God in a new way: by exercising the faith He's given us in His grace. We no longer struggle to produce good works, but find ourselves doing right as naturally as a grape vine produces grapes. It's rocket fuel religion with a never-ending supply.

The old system—the law—was a standard that was impersonal and impartial; the new system—grace—is an apprenticeship that is close and extremely personal.

Grace does not consider the cost. Grace is beyond price. Grace is lavish. Grace is unrestrained. And grace is the opposite of "earned."

We may not be able to define grace, but we know it when we're swimming in it.

4 the holy Lamb of God
can the sacrifice be sort of just um ... good enough?

"FOR YOU KNOW THAT IT WAS NOT WITH PERISHABLE THINGS SUCH AS SILVER OR GOLD THAT YOU WERE REDEEMED FROM THE EMPTY WAY OF LIFE HANDED DOWN TO YOU FROM YOUR FOREFATHERS, BUT WITH THE PRECIOUS BLOOD OF CHRIST, A LAMB WITHOUT BLEMISH OR DEFECT."
I PETER 1:18-19

We may have some wrong ideas about Jesus. He's not a nice teacher. He's not an example for us to pattern our lives after. He's not the picture of how we ought to behave. He is a unique, one-of-a-kind *sacrifice*. He came to die. Matthew 20:28, ***"The Son of Man did not come to be served, but to serve, and to give his life as a ransom."*** His lifeblood was pure and undefiled. His behavior was faultless. His whole being was irrevocably devoted to God the Father in thought, speech and action. He never once said or did anything wrong whatsoever. His cousin John, in recognizing Him before the crowd, called Him the Lamb of God Who Takes Away the Sin of the World. Don't think the Jews didn't know that was a reference to blood atonement— a reference to His mission to come and die for us. That kind of lamb is without a single fault.

This is breathtaking if we'll stop and think about it. Jesus was holy perfection while in the flesh, not as an exalted spirit-being but in a body exactly like ours. While He walked the earth and dealt with the same circumstances you and I face everyday, He didn't just pass the big public tests. He passed the moment-by-moment tests with a perfect score. And why in the world do that?

So he could be crucified. As a sacrifice. Pure and holy. According to plan.

God really drilled this idea into the Jews. The Mosaic Law included lengthy descriptions and instructions on how to take the blood of a spotless lamb and use it to cleanse a sinner. Blood symbolizes life says Leviticus 17:11, ***"For the life of a creature is in the blood, and I have given it to you to make atonement for yourselves on the altar; it is the blood that makes atonement for one's life."***

An innocent life pays for the sin of a guilty life. This is of course not fair. But it's absolutely lawful. Not equitable. But prescribed. Not nice. But effective.

They had endless ceremonies with slaughtered animals as the centerpiece. Gruesome? Maybe, but from God's holy perspective, sin is even *more* gruesome than blood and guts and the terrified cries of animals as they are slashed with knives. Sin is the uglier thing that necessitates the ugliness of animal sacrifice.

Which brings us to today: the Tabernacle is gone. The Temple is torn down. The Jewish religious leaders no longer function as priestly butchers. It is a different Lamb that we must look to. Jesus Christ the righteous.

This Lamb is not only the innocent Sacrifice, but also the righteous Judge and the One who has been wronged. Jesus plays all the parts in this scene except the defendants, the perps. That would be us, caught *redhanded*.

"Redhanded" is a word that pictures the bloodguilt evident on us all. We're guilty of mayhem and bloodshed, and only the prescribed slaying of the holy Lamb of God will wash our bloody hands clean. The people watching the trial of Jesus shouted, "His blood be on us and on our children!" They were accepting the culpability for the murder of an innocent man. And we each would have done the same thing if we'd been there. As He listened to them scream for His blood, Jesus yet loved them; loved them so much that He DID put His blood on any who turned to Him, and He became their holy Lamb of God who took away their sins. You see, either you let Jesus wash you with His cleansing blood, or you will one day float in your own(Revelation 14:20). Have a barf bag ready as you read that verse. It's not for the faint of heart.

The ancient Israelites would ceremonially place their hands on a goat, transferring their sins and then chase the goat away. It was called the "scapegoat." Even today, we use this word for an innocent person who assumes the crime of another. Jesus is *our* scapegoat. We place our sins upon Him, and He carries them away to where God chooses to not remember them any more.

The KJV uses the word *propitiation* in 1 John 2:2. Propitiation is more than just forgiveness. It's *the deflection of God's wrath*, regaining for us favor and right standing. It's the hope of everyone who's ever cried out to God, that He'll not only forgive us, but restore us to Himself. Propitiation says Jesus has become our atoning sacrifice, completely shielding us from God's righteous anger.

Jesus lived 33 years without ever once committing a single sin. Passing up chance after chance to show off, He only did what the Father was doing, only said what the Father told Him to say (John 5:19, and John 8:28).

In Gethsemane, He drank the vile cup of the world's sin, and took into Himself the vomitous ugliness of human sin and absorbed the righteous anger of God against it (Matthew 26:42).

The leaders of the Sanhedrin told disgusting lies about Him at His mock trial. Pilate, Herod, and the civil authorities treated Him as a circus show freak. The crowd in the marketplace spat at Him and shouted "Crucify." The Roman guards administered a beating that left Him without a recognizable face. The cross tore Him apart as it crushed His lungs. And the cup of God's undiluted wrath was poured like unquenchable fire down His willing throat. The holy Lamb of God died for the sins of the world. Not figuratively. Not symbolically. Bodily.

What happened after Jesus had taken upon Himself the full fury of a holy God against the transgressions of the world? Brace yourself. He laid down His life and He died. You'll never read a more bewildering sentence than that last one. Life Himself, who gives viability and breath to everything else, *died*.

How can God die? No one has an adequate explanation for it. It's a paradox wrapped inside a mystery. The thing about God is that He's eternal, right? So how can the eternal just jerk to a halt? How can everlasting ever come to an end? How can Life Himself, the Holy Lamb of God, lay down His essential nature and die? Nobody knows.

But we do know one thing: the only one who *could* do it *did* do it. The holy Lamb of God.

5 substitutionary death

ever heard of someone "taking a bullet" for a friend?

"GOD MADE HIM WHO HAD NO SIN TO BE SIN FOR US, SO THAT IN HIM WE MIGHT BECOME THE RIGHTEOUSNESS OF GOD."
2 CORINTHIANS 5:21

In baseball, it's called a pinch hitter. In teaching it's called a substitute. In movies, it's called a stunt double.

In broken dishes, it's called a replacement. In airplanes, it's called redundancy. In households and governments, it's called an emergency fund.

In wild west gun fights, it's called a derringer in your boot. In planning, it's called a contingency. In computer files, it's called a backup. In dating, it's called a wing man. In your home, it's called a gas-powered generator.

In each of these cases, what's being described is whatever steps in when the first thing goes down.

We went down. Jesus stepped in.

We walked with God until the day we blew the Garden of Eden up and launched ourselves out of God's grace. Now we're nothing more than a rag-tag rebel army trying to make a last ditch stand against the overwhelming forces of devouring spirits arrayed against us. It looks as if we'll be wiped out.

But Someone stepped in when everything was lost, stepped into our place and took the deadly blow delivered by the hand of justice and the spitefulness of the kingdom of darkness. That pounding was meant for us, but it never reached us because someone got in the way of it, intercepting the blow.

Now, you might say, that's not fair. No argument here. It's *abominably* unfair—to Jesus. No, no, you protest, it's unfair to let people get away with sin. Again we agree. It's not fair to Jesus that He had to die for other people's sin, prompting an increasingly frustrated you to say you don't mean it's unfair to Jesus, it's unfair to *everyone who's doing the right thing*. It's unfair that some get away with it while some have to just do the right thing with no special attention from Jesus. To which we reply, oh, who *are* these hypothetical people who are doing the right thing? Righteous people are one of the greatest fictions invented by Satan.

But you resolutely respond that there must be *someone* who's righteous. And we shake our heads and quote Romans 3:16, ALL have sinned and fallen short of God's impossible standard of perfection. "All" = everyone in the whole world. That is *except* Jesus. He took the punishment we deserved. The light comes on. Praise God that Jesus doesn't care about fairness. He cares about *us*.

If Jesus weren't the perfect, holy, sinless Son of God, there'd be no one available who could substitute for us on execution day. No one. This is why Jesus says in John 14:6, ***"No one comes to the Father except by me."*** He's not trying to bully the other religions, or exclude the other religions, or put down the sincerity of other religions. In a sense there *are* no other religions, because there are no other *saviors*.

No one else *could* take our place because everyone else has to appear at their own hanging and can't double up at ours. Mohammed is bankrupt and can't pay my sin debt. So's Buddha, so's Karl Marx, so is every would-be prophet of whatever belief system you want to name.

Only Jesus can save. Only Jesus can step in and fend off the crushing weight of God's wrath. Only Jesus can take the bullet that was fired at our hearts. Only Jesus can go to the cross to die *in our place*, taking our sins upon Himself. Only Jesus can free us from the penalty of sin and death and release us into new life.

The substitutionary death of Jesus is the very definition of the love of God for us. It was love that brought Jesus to this planet, and love that laid Him in the manger in Bethlehem, love that lived a sinless life, love that took Him to Golgotha, love that lay down His life upon the cross, love that was lifted up on spikes through His hands and feet, love that was dying for my sin and your sin. I know God loves me because Jesus put Himself in my place when it was time to pay the punishment of death for my sins.

Oh the deep, deep love of Jesus. I was awaiting my chance to die for my sins. Jesus was safely and comfortably in heaven.

Substitution means that Jesus and I got to switch places.

6 justification
what do you call it when you straighten something up?

"CONSEQUENTLY, JUST AS THE RESULT OF ONE TRESPASS WAS CONDEMNATION FOR ALL MEN, SO ALSO THE RESULT OF ONE ACT OF RIGHTEOUSNESS WAS JUSTIFICATION THAT BRINGS LIFE FOR ALL MEN."
ROMANS 5:18

Bookkeeping has a term for making sure that income and outgo of funds are evened up. When that happens, the books are said to be *justified*.

When typing lines up left, right or center, the page is considered to be justified. If you rightly display anger that was provoked, you are said to be justified in that anger. Justified means your ducks are all in a row, your numbers add up, there's nothing that jumps out as undone or unresolved. Nice and neat.

When used in theology, the word "justified" has been defined as "just-as-if-I'd," as in, just as if I'd never sinned. Our sins have not been whitewashed or covered over, they have been *expunged* from the record with no trace left. It's not that snow has fallen on the trash heap, hiding the ugliness; rather, a dump truck has hauled the trash off and a landscaper has finished transforming the site into a theme park. Our sins ... never ... *happened.*

God is not going to come back to us someday and say, "We still need to talk about such-and-such that you did. I let you skate on that for a while, but now we need to deal with it." *The child of God has no sin record.*

Justification doesn't mean we *are* righteous; it means we're *called* righteous, but when God calls us righteous, we *are!* Put that in your pipe and smoke it. When God looks at the books where our sin would be recorded, He chooses to see Jesus' lifeblood on the ledger in our account instead of our sin. God has decided to say to the redeemed what He said to Jesus at His baptism: ***"You are my beloved child; in you I am well pleased."*** We're totally justified by the grace of God.

Our righteousness is said to be *imputed* to us by God. Connected. Assigned. By fiat. By royal decree. Because, with His own children, that's how God keeps books. You want to be righteous on your own? Okay, let's see how you stack up to the standard of perfection called "the glory of *God*" (Romans 3:23). Oh? You're not as holy as God? Me neither. Well, we may both want to try the only <u>other</u> way to be right with God: the one that comes by faith *in Christ* (Romans 3:21-22). Surrender our will to God and find we've been assigned the holiness of Jesus Himself. Honestly, it's such a great deal that very few will even believe it.

Satan, AKA the Accuser, is not happy with this arrangement and he'll hammer away at us every chance he gets. He'll bring up unconfessed sin. We should turn this tactic around on him. Confess the sin immediately, taking away his weapon and cleaning our own consciences as a twofer (Matthew 5:25). He'll then say that God's tired of forgiving our recurring sin and we should give up repenting of it. Don't give him that satisfaction. Instead, tell God that you'll repent until your dying day if that's what it takes to conquer the sin habit.

The thing is, Satan just wants to kill and steal and destroy, according to John 10:10. We shouldn't be surprised when he pulls his stuff on us, rather we should be aware and ready. Quote him Acts 13:39. Quote him Romans 3:24. Quote him 1 Corinthians

6:11. Quote him Titus 3:7. That'll boil his oatmeal.

Justification is something we've been given, but also something we must stand in. Don't let the enemy mess with us about it and somehow rob us of the knowledge of this amazing gift. Think of justification as the armor of God in Ephesians 6 and see what that passage has to say about being immovable.

If you have come under the Lordship of Jesus Christ, you're *justified by faith* as part of the deal. There's no paperwork that has to be filled out, no coupons to redeem, no receipts that have to be kept, nothing more to do at all. Justification is included in the part where we get to have the Holy Spirit living in us. Clean and purified and ready for God's use.

Justified: straightened up and ready to fly right.

7 reconciliation
what do you call it when opposing sides come to an agreement?

"God was reconciling the world to himself in Christ, not counting men's sins against them. And he has committed to us the message of reconciliation. We are therefore Christ's ambassadors, as though God were making his appeal through us. We implore you on Christ's behalf: Be reconciled to God."
2 Corinthians 5:19-20

Reconciliation is just basically this: making things *right*.

Reconciliation is the breaking down of barriers between estranged parties, the resumption of diplomatic relations.

Reconciliation is the healing of the wounded and separated members of a family. We were the ones who walked away from God. He was the one who ran after us, caught up with us, and made a way for us to come home.

Once an account has first been justified, it can then be *reconciled* with other accounts. Once a person has first been justified, they can then be reconciled to others. If we've not been reconciled to Jesus, we can't really experience healed relationships with others, but if we've asked Jesus for *His* forgiveness, it should be easy as pie to give forgiveness and ask others for *their* forgiveness.

Jesus taught the importance of reconciliation. He said in Matthew 5:23-26 that if you're praying, or worshipping, or feeding an orphan or preaching a fabulous sermon to a stadium crowd and you remember that something's not right between you and someone else, stop. Go to that person. As far as it depends on you, make things right. Immediately.

Why? I'll tell you why. Because Jesus said to. No other reason's needed. But there *are* plenty of great reasons to do what Jesus says about being reconciled. If we don't make things right, we'll wind up in prison, emotionally and spiritually, held captive by the solid walls of our own unforgiveness (Matthew 18:35).

Maybe we think that we're okay regarding the category of getting along with others. Let's run a check. Ever secretly hated someone? Not hated what they've done, that's okay, but hated *them*, perhaps even without cause? Matthew 5:21-22 says we're a murderer! Have we ever wanted what belonged to someone else? That's the tenth Commandment broken right there. Have you ever said something that wasn't strictly true? Ever snuck a pencil out of the pew? Oh! Ever disobeyed your parents? Under Levitical Law, that's a capital offense.

Do I really need to go on? We're doomed. There's no such thing as a truly good person. If you think you know someone, ask *them* if they're perfect! Because of our sinfulness, our relationship to a holy God is irreparably severed. That's the bad news: we're fallen creatures, dropped from the guest list of the Garden, cut off from the joys of fellowship with God and each other, unable to change anything by our own effort. The situation is desperate.

Enter God. Fully aware that we would fall away from a right relationship with Him and with each other and become estranged, He decided before the foundation of the world (1 Peter 1:20) that He would die a sacrificial death on the cross to bring us back together. Bring us together emotionally, bring us together legally, and even shrink the distance gap: promising to live inside of us, to "tabernacle" with us, to make His home in us as it says in John 14:23.

Matthew 18:23 says our Master has forgiven our unforgivably enormous sin debt, so it makes no sense for us not to forgive others who owe us peanuts. Being reconciled is not only crucial, it just makes good sense.

After getting reconciled with God in Christ, getting right with each other will be a natural outflow, not a Herculean effort on our part. Just as we're commanded to forgive as we have been forgiven, we are commanded to reconcile with others as God has made possible our reconciliation.

Just think. Relationships that have seemingly been damaged beyond repair, festering and decaying, can now be healed and restored because God was in Christ reconciling the world to Himself. People we haven't given the time of day can become our dear friends.

Restored, renewed, returned to relationship. I want some of *that*.

• RESURRECTION

what's the most used plot device of all time?

"JESUS SAID TO HER, 'I AM THE RESURRECTION AND THE LIFE. HE WHO BELIEVES IN ME WILL LIVE, EVEN THOUGH HE DIES; AND WHOEVER LIVES AND BELIEVES IN ME WILL NEVER DIE. DO YOU BELIEVE THIS?'"

JOHN 11:25-26

No one doesn't get resurrection.

It's a repetitive theme in creation, appearing in every season, every seed, every sunrise. All our most beloved stories are saturated with this idea of the comeback. All the world's civilizations have legends that picture it. Although there are a few among us who claim they don't believe in life after death, not one of us would risk two dollars betting against it.

1 Corinthians 15:17-19 makes the case logically. If there's no such thing as resurrection, our faith is futile, our sins are unforgiven, our loved ones who have died are gone forever and we're pitiable idiots if we try to live to please God. If there is no resurrection, we'd be smarter to just do as we please, feasting, drinking, reveling and living life for what we can get out of it before we're toast, or worm food, or whatever you want to call being dead. Argue with that if you can, but you'll lose. If there's no resurrection, do whatever you feel like doing. Nothing has any meaning, *especially* meaning.

If there's no resurrection, life has no purpose, no joy, no payoff, no hope. Love is a cheat, death is a mercy. It's no good to live a good moral life, giving of yourself to others, since life is a passing hiccup in a dying universe.

We might as well believe in Darwin's magical sun rays, Freud's scientific licentiousness, Marx's murderous collectivism, and Nietzsche's hopeless materialism. Can there be any higher purpose for Darwinist brutes who've fought and clawed their way to be simply alive for the moment? Where would the Freudian acolytes come up with selfless love in a world where the passions are simply psychiatric chemical responses? Where is true charity in a Marxist world where one group unites to dominate another? And in a Nietzschean context, where is meaning in a meaningless world? If there's no resurrection, we're left with total despair. When Darwin, Freud, Nietzsche and Marx rejected the resurrection, they were left with absolute nothingness to promote.

The world follows these ideologies like lemmings over the cliff. But the truth of the gospel will free us from these deadly philosophies. The truth is that God made us, so God knows us—knows us better that we know ourselves and still loves us. He loves us for no reason other than He's got way too much love to hang on to, and it's spilled over into whoever will receive it.

You and I are the chief objects of His lavish love. Because He loves us, God left His Godness behind … left His throne … left His crown … left His omnipotence … left His omniscience … left His omnipresence, divested Himself of unlimited power and authority and became one of us. He lived a perfect, sinless life. He went to the cross as a sacrificial lamb strictly by the Mosaic Law, using actual priests and raw secular governmental jurisdiction. He gave up His life so we could have it.

He died. Dead. Not pretend dead. Real dead. Actual dead. Certifiable dead.

God was dead. Can you hear me say that? God was DEAD. For three days. And then …

Glory! Trumpets! Thunder and lightning, fire and hail, earthquakes and mountains tumbling into the sea! Up from the grave comes Jesus! Not recovered. Not restored. Not restocked. Not reenergized, rebooted, rediscovered, redesigned, retooled, rebuilt or rereleased. RESURRECTED. Lifted from the dead in *new life*. Jesus wasn't healed, wasn't saved. He was RAISED in a brand new way never before imagined.

This is stunningly great news. This is exactly why people can laugh and dance and cry tears of *joy*! This is festival, this is parade, this is celebration and wonder. Christ is no longer dead. Christ is risen. He shall come again in glory with a multitude of the heavenly host. He is risen *indeed*. Amen!

Hey. Where do you think we got the expression, "You can't keep a good man down?"

1 the ascension of Christ
ever tried to hold an inflated float at the bottom of the pool?

"AFTER THE LORD JESUS HAD SPOKEN TO THEM, HE WAS TAKEN UP INTO HEAVEN AND HE SAT AT THE RIGHT HAND OF GOD. THEN THE DISCIPLES WENT OUT AND PREACHED EVERYWHERE, AND THE LORD WORKED WITH THEM AND CONFIRMED HIS WORD BY THE SIGNS THAT ACCOMPANIED IT."
MARK 16:19-20

What did Jesus do after he rose from the dead? He appeared to the disciples and taught them over a period of 40 days.

And then? He *ascended*. Stay with me here.

The disciples met Jesus at the Mount of Olives and while Jesus was speaking to them, He rose up in the air until He was out of sight. Anybody else in history you can name who's done *that*?

I mean, we get all worked up over guys who can jump and stay in the air a few seconds to dunk a basketball! Jesus has stayed up for 2,000 *years*, and He'll stay up as long as He needs to. That's real hang time, so to speak.

Jesus, using a mode of propulsion that we still can't even imagine let alone replicate, simply lifted up beyond the visual range of the disciples. Oh, and their visual range was fairly good considering they were already standing on a mountain.

The ascension was such a mind boggling event that angels had to come and explain it to those who had just seen it happen! In Acts 1:11, they say (I'm paraphrasing), "Okay, you can pick up your jaws and go on with your lives. Jesus will return the same way you just now saw Him go." The people needed help understanding what they witnessed with their own eyes. Jesus said He was going to do it, they just never envisioned what that would be until they saw it happen and the angels gave them some context.

Let me ask you a question. Why didn't Jesus vanish into thin air? Why didn't He fly around the room and out the window? Why didn't He step into a titanium rocket ship and zoom away? Why didn't a giant blinding white hand or a fiery chariot come to take Him away? Why did He do it the way He did? I don't know, ask Him! I think the way He did it was the best, but that's me: I dream of flying.

The point is that Jesus ascended. The Apostles, the Nicene and the Athanasian Creeds all clearly proclaim this as basic Christianity 101. Jesus has gone back to heaven and we know exactly where He is: seated at God's right hand.

The ascension of Jesus is easily misunderstood, especially in this age of Mormonism, so let's be clear. For one thing, Jesus is already God. There never was a time when He wasn't God. He did not ascend to *become* God, okay?

And for another thing, Jesus is at God's right hand, even though God does not have hands or a right side: God is spirit according to Jesus in John 4:24. "At God's right hand" is a positional equivalence, not a GPS coordinate. As our Advocate, Jesus is closer to the Father than anyone, in a place of honor and trust and counsel (to the Father) and advocacy (for us)!

And still another thing, it's wrong to think of God as three different persons because God is one person. So God the Son is sitting at His own right hand, which is the Father's and the Son's and the Holy Spirit's hand. Since Jesus ascended, He has returned to us as the Holy Spirit who is also the Father and the Son. But Jesus is still ascended at this moment even while He has returned as the Holy Spirit. We mentioned Athanasian Creed—it drills this truth into us.

Only the highest can descend to the lowest. Why else would pearl divers start from high up on the cliffs? From the highest heavens down to a Bethlehem stable is quite a drop. And yet, Jesus would descend further still. He took upon Himself the sins of the whole world. Every evil thing that's ever been done or imagined in the dark heart of man was what Jesus carried in His own flesh to the land of the dead, the bottomless abyss, the lowest point in the Universe.

Then the Father reached down and raised the Son to new life and from new life, raised Him again to highest honor praise. Jesus ascended from the depths of death to the heights of highest heaven.

There's a song that says it beautifully: ***"You came from heaven to earth, to show the way; from the earth to the cross, my debt to pay; from the cross to the grave, from the grave to the sky, Lord I lift your name on high!"*** He has ascended! Jesus is *exalted*!

Exalted means to be placed in a lofty and powerful position. Our Savior is the ultimate well-placed friend. Majestic, preeminent and all powerful; He conquered Satan and his demon hosts, singlehandedly defeating death and ascended to the right hand of God the Father (Colossians 3:1). Seated in glory, He spins the planets, steers the stars, and directs the cosmos.

If He can do all that sitting down, what will happen when it's time for Him to return and He *stands up*?

2 the authority of Christ
does Jesus need to ask anyone's permission?

"THEN JESUS SAID, 'ALL AUTHORITY IN HEAVEN AND ON EARTH HAS BEEN GIVEN TO ME.'"
MATTHEW 28:18

What is authority? It's the *right* to do something. It differs from power: the *ability* to do it. Does Jesus have authority or power? In other words, does He have the right to act or does He have the ability to act? The answer is … *yes*.

Have you ever heard someone say, "Well, who DIED and put YOU in charge?!" In our case, Jesus died and the Father put Him in charge. Of everything. Bam.

As we'll see later in the part entitled "The Great Commission," the One in charge of everything has been very specific in laying out what He wants done. No need to ask WWJD. The memo from Him is on the bulletin board.

The Bible says Jesus has all authority. *All* is a word that's hard to misunderstand. If a robber says, give me *all* your money, you're not confused. If a person says they love you with *all* their heart, you don't ask them how much that is. If Jesus says that *all* authority in heaven and earth is His, there's not a lot more to say. He's got it all. Period. So what authority does the Devil have? or the nations? or the rich and powerful? Nothing except what Jesus allows.

Consider what Jesus having all authority implies. Who will ultimately triumph between the forces of good and evil for the planet earth? The One with all authority. Does Jesus have authority over diseases and economies and nuclear armaments and disasters? Can He have authority over the future and the past, the things you'll end up doing and what you've already done? Could He maybe have authority over the weather, whether the planet gets colder or warmer? Could He possibly have authority over politicians, who gets elected and who gets shellacked? Does He even have authority over the wicked and powerful people in the world who abuse and steal and kill and seem to get away with it?

Yes. Absolutely. With ultimate authority comes ultimate responsibility. The world is not out of control. It is in a pre-planned, controlled free fall. Jesus is still at the wheel, and everything, *everything*, happens for a purpose with Him. Have hope, Jesus is the one with all authority. It's all taken care of.

Quick disclaimer. Having authority over everything is NOT the same thing as *causing* everything. Jesus is NOT the author of evil. Jesus is responsible only for allowing the continued presence of evil, but has nothing whatever to do with planning and execution. I hope that's clear. It's a little sticky, but it's tied up in the doctrine of free will, which is in this book if you want to check it out.

So who *used to have* the authority? What did Jesus do to *get* it? And what will He do now that He's *got* it?

The Father had all authority. He gave a little bit of His authority to Adam to be fruitful and multiply and to fill the earth and subdue it, ruling over the other creatures. Some say (and I agree) Adam then surrendered his authority to Satan when he listened to the serpent and ate from the forbidden tree of the knowledge of good and evil. Then Satan had the authority God originally gave Adam. That is, he had it until Jesus died on the cross, went to wherever Satan was and rightfully won that part of God's authority back.

Check out Colossians 2:14-15, **"[Christ] canceled the written code, with its regulations, that was against us and that stood opposed to us; he took it away, nailing it to the cross. And having disarmed the powers and authorities, he made a public spectacle of them,** *triumphing over them by the cross."* Jesus now has the keys of death and Hades (the place of the unrighteous dead), according to Revelation 1:18. When Jesus ascended, the Father gave Him all authority, not just the authority Adam lost but also authority never before delegated—over the heavens, over the seen and unseen, over the past, present and future. Nothing is left outside of Jesus' authority.

With this authority, Jesus will one day renew all things (Matthew 19:28).

It's a little startling that Jesus downloads some of His all-authority to His people. We're His ambassadors, His liaisons, His representatives, His front men. We're the face of His organization, the Kingdom. In His name and for His sake, we do things, say things, pray things, accomplish things, call things to be. Jesus says we'll do greater things than He did, because He is lobbying the Father for the power (John 14:12). Don't ask me for an explanation of that. I don't have one.

Matthew 28 tells us not only that Christ has all authority, but in that authority He sends us out to make disciples. Not to make Christians, to make *disciples!* There shouldn't be a difference, but there is. Maybe. I think you know what I mean. It's the difference between getting saved and getting sanctified. But forget I said any of that. Back to the authority of Jesus Christ.

Just as we despair when bad men are in charge of our sports teams, businesses, schools, governments, and even churches, so we rejoice when good men are put in charge of them. How much more should we rejoice that Christ has been elevated to CEO of the space time continuum!

Evil will someday be a forgotten memory now that Christ has *all authority*.

3 redeemer
ever had to pay to get your own impounded car back?

"I KNOW THAT MY REDEEMER LIVES, AND THAT IN THE END HE WILL STAND UPON THE EARTH. I MYSELF WILL SEE HIM WITH MY OWN EYES I, AND NOT ANOTHER. HOW MY HEART YEARNS WITHIN ME!"
JOB 19:25 AND 27

We once belonged to God. We sold ourselves to evil. Then Jesus *redeemed* us.

To redeem something is to buy it back again. To reacquire. To fulfill a previous promise with a coupon or voucher. To get something out of hock.

More than buying a thing for the first time, this is more akin to a _repurchase_, buying your own stuff from the second hand store where it was sold. You, the former owner, have come to buy back what once was your own stuff. It's complicated and it's straightforward as well.

Look at one of the greatest love stories of all time: Ruth. Not only does the story have its own book in the Bible, but God had it named after the character who represents *us*, not the hero representing Him (whose name is Boaz, I know, *Boaz!* Sheesh). Ruth and her mother-in-law Naomi are widows with no inheritance and no prospects ... just like we used to be before we were redeemed. Ruth faithfully serves her mother-in-law and, in the course of doing so, meets Boaz. In Ruth 2:20, Naomi praises God, adding, ***"That man is our close relative; he is one of our kinsman-redeemers."*** Have you ever considered your relatives as potential kinsman redeemers? No? Me neither. What is that, anyway?

Leviticus 25:47-55 supplies the legal precedent. A *kinsman redeemer* is a relative who looks after those in his family who cannot fend for themselves. In the kinsman redeemer model, the closest relative gets the honor of providing for those who need help, perhaps taking them into his household, even offering marriage vows in the case of young widows to ensure their security and their honor since simply living together would be a scandal. Just so you know, Ruth was the widow of one of Naomi's wicked sons, so Boaz did not marry his cousin. Details. But you might have wondered and I wanted to spare you that.

Boaz didn't just feed Ruth, he quietly watched out for her best interests, guarding her from a dangerous world. One day he went to their closest relative to see if he had plans to redeem his kinfolk. The man said he wouldn't do it, so Boaz did something with a shoe (you'll *have* to read it now) and married Ruth, bringing along his new wife's old husband's mother. Whatever it was he ceremoniously did that day reacquired for him the primary right to take care of his long lost relatives. We don't usually go to great expense and trouble to find people whose burden we can assume. But God does this constantly.

As we have already noted, this story is not only about Boaz and Ruth, it's about Jesus and us. Jesus is *our* kinsman redeemer: watching over us, protecting, initiating, drawing. He buys us back from the clutches of sin, taking full responsibility for our welfare and our future. We used to be orphans and widows, abandoned and bankrupted by our sin and the fallen world around us. We had no hope, no plan, no prospects.

Little did we suspect that our Maker had a great desire to become our main provider just as Boaz (and ultimately God Himself) did for Naomi and Ruth. Our kinsman redeemer bought us back, exchanged His own blood for us in a legal ceremony and paid with His own life to repurchase our lives.

Redemption also provides for us a second chance; hence, the idiom, "They finally have a shot at redemption." We needed another shot at life, having badly botched our first try. Jesus gives us that second chance ... and a third, fourth and fifth if we need it. Like pitching to a batter who is just learning to hit the ball, God let's us take as many swings as we need to connect.

Psalms 49:7 says, **"No man can redeem the life of another or give to God a ransom for him."** We're no help to anyone else. We don't have the wherewithal to redeem a flea. The cost is too high; it's beyond the combined riches of all the realms in all the world. No one can make even a simple downpayment against the sin debt we've incurred by our transgressions.

But there's a Savior who's ransomed the whole world from the power of death and from the inevitable judgment—One who can make Psalms 49:7 eat its own words and have to admit, "There is no man _[except one]_ who can redeem the life of another."

We can say with Job, "I _know_ that my Redeemer lives!"

4 the supremacy of Christ
who in the world could stand up against Jesus?

"FOR BY HIM ALL THINGS WERE CREATED: THINGS IN HEAVEN AND ON EARTH, VISIBLE AND INVISIBLE, WHETHER THRONES OR POWERS OR RULERS OR AUTHORITIES; ALL THINGS WERE CREATED BY HIM AND FOR HIM ... AND HE IS THE HEAD OF THE BODY, THE CHURCH; HE IS THE BEGINNING AND THE FIRSTBORN FROM AMONG THE DEAD, SO THAT IN EVERYTHING HE MIGHT HAVE THE SUPREMACY."
COLOSSIANS 1:16 AND 18

"So that in everything, he might have the supremacy!" I _LOVE_ that.

In all things, Christ is supreme. This is solid fact. Jesus is not merely a great teacher. He's not just another one of the wise men of the world. He's not simply a great philosopher or a leading advocate of a healthy lifestyle and He's not the champion of any economic class or political party. He's the King of all the other kings. He's the Most High God. There is no up-line from Jesus. Even death itself, the last enemy which He soundly defeated at the empty tomb, is underneath His feet.

After acing His mission to rescue the rebellious ingrates also known as us, He left in an odd manner—He just went straight up. No cables, no propellors, no rocket pack, no nothing. He just lifted off and kept going. The angels who were there told the astounded crowd who saw Him go: Don't worry, He'll be coming back the same way you just saw Him go. Christ has supremacy over space and time. He accomplishes intergalactic travel without help from a spaceship. He can appear in any age without assistance from a time machine. Size, speed, breathable air, gravity, importance, degree of difficulty, danger, intricacy, technology, possibility: *these are not considerations that limit His actions.*

He has no rival, no equal, no nemesis, no archenemy. He is unmatched, unparalleled, unrestricted, unbounded. Nothing's too hard for Him, too far for Him, too big or too small for Him. He can't be overthrown, upstaged, outdone, capped, topped, beaten, transcended, outmaneuvered, or surpassed. You can take it from there.

So if He's so supreme, why is His name used as a curse word? Why do people belittle the word "crucified" and use it trivially? Why are His people, Christians and Jews, hounded and beaten and treated horribly all over the world? Why do the godless seem to have all the power and the money and the machines of culture at their command? Why does it <u>seem</u> like Jesus is anything *but* supreme?

I'll tell you why. Jesus is not insecure about His position. If an army comes against you with pea shooters and you have an atom bomb, you can afford to wait while they bluster and blather about all they're going to do to you. Jesus can rest in assurance of ultimate victory, allowing His enemies to exist a little while longer. He's giving His enemies time to surrender their hearts and repent.

Still you question? If Christ is so supreme, why does it look like this world is firmly in the clutches of the devil and his henchmen? If evil is triumphant, then Jesus may be good but not powerful enough, or powerful but not good enough.

In C.S. Lewis' book <u>That Hideous Strength</u>, the leading character, Mark, is told to trample and insult a crucifix as part of his initiation into a demonic circle. Failure to comply will result in his death. Mark doesn't believe in God and believes Christianity is a hoax, but he begins to think about the person represented on the crucifix. He wonders why the wicked always seem to hate the good, why the crooked always do horrible things to the straight. He reflects upon the irony of what Jesus is hanging from—a *cross*—and realizes that it is a junction of good and evil and this man is caught in the middle. Mark even thinks at this point that it looks like the evil has already won and this crucified man had known it as he cried out that even God had forsaken him. But Mark realizes that even if the evil looks as if it were triumphant, he still didn't want to join sides with it. He'd rather go down with the light than shake hands with the darkness. This stark contrast between the crooked and the strait preached the gospel to his unbelieving heart better than any sermon.

The joke will not be on God. Darkness never even had half a chance. The seeming success of evil is transitory. Satan is presently prince of this world, just like Edward John Smith was Captain of the Titanic. The devil is in charge over this world like a fly is in charge of a blob of dropped ice cream on a hot sidewalk. The same way the White Witch was queen of Narnia. Wickedness may triumph for a time, but one day, all will be made right and every title returned to its proper owner. It's gonna happen and nothing or nobody can stop it.

There is only one true and everlasting King, after all. Christ is *supreme*.

5 transformation
what do a butterfly and a caterpillar have in common?

"AND WE, WHO WITH UNVEILED FACES ALL REFLECT THE LORD'S GLORY, ARE BEING TRANSFORMED INTO HIS LIKENESS WITH EVER-INCREASING GLORY ..."
2 CORINTHIANS 3:18

Mark Twain's character Tom Sawyer once whitewashed a fence. The inherent nature of the fence did not change, only its outward appearance. If you were to chip off the whitewash, you could see the old fence. God doesn't want to whitewash us like the Pharisees of Matthew 23:27. He wants us to be totally new from the inside out.

Transformation is a radically different process than any kind of a repair job. It seems almost magical. Forget that, it *is* magical. When a tadpole becomes a toad, he changes nearly everything about himself—from breathing underwater to breathing in air, from feeding off the bottom of the pond to catching food with a sticky tongue, from smooth skin to rough, from swimming with a tail to hopping with no tail, like Harry Potter at the Tri-Wizard Tournament who grew gills and webbed feet, only in reverse. Bizarre in the extreme. Just ... *creepy*.

Transformation is a self-defining word: *"trans"* means across. *"Form"* means, um ... form. Transform: to form across, to become another thing entirely. When a caterpillar transforms, it's other-worldly. Metamorphosis is the big descriptor for a worm-thing with lots of little knobby feet *digesting* itself from the inside out. Undergoing a near liquefaction that's called *histolysis* (*"histo"* means tissue, *"lysis"* means decomposition), followed by a period where the soupy mess of a creature builds entirely new cells. From fat to skinny. Leaf nibbler to nectar drinker. Crawler to flier. We're told that the butterfly actually remembers things the caterpillar learned. I told you it was whacked out.

But not half as weird as when a Christian is *born again*! You've seen people at a crusade or an altar call, repenting of their sins and asking Jesus to be their Lord? Freaky stuff is happening. Nothing you can see by just looking. There's some histolysis and histogenesis going on. Those at the *altar* are being *altered*.

Maybe that's why they call it an altar: everything changes. We get rid of our old way of life, and as it melts and dissolves, we receive new construction and new instruction. We get a new want-to, a new set of godly desires. We're not just revitalized or rejuvenated, we're re*made*.

God is totally *other* than us. He's outside our daily experience, beyond what we ordinarily run across. Transformation is us joining God in His *other*-ness. It isn't something we can control or cause, but it's inevitable for the child of God to be transformed into the image of Christ (Romans 8:29). Jesus doesn't expect us to change our habits or our appearance by force of willpower. He must do the transforming work in our hearts, which then works outward into our habits and our outlook. It shows in our eyes. It manifests in our faces. It comes up in our conversation, and is seen in our checkbooks and calendars.

Transformation, newness of life, is something that happens inside everyone who responds to the call of Jesus to follow.

2 Corinthians 5:17, ***"Therefore, if anyone is in Christ, he is a new creation!"*** Jesus takes charge of our old selves in order to transform us into a new something new: something that looks more and more like He looks. That's why we can wear His armor, like it says in Ephesians 6 that we look like Him. That's why we can be His ambassadors, 2 Corinthians 5:20—we're like Him. That's why we'll see Him "as He is" one day, according to 1 John 3:2. We'll be like him. Romans 6:8-11 says we died to our old sorry life when Christ died for us, so now we can fly above and beyond the reach of death. Transformed to walk in newness of life.

Is it any wonder that the most powerful word in advertising psychology is the word *"new"*?

6 Christ the only Savior
Is it okay to tell the truth about the number of Saviors there are?

"SALVATION IS FOUND IN NO ONE ELSE, FOR THERE IS NO OTHER NAME UNDER HEAVEN GIVEN TO MEN BY WHICH WE MUST BE SAVED."
ACTS 4:12

The Church that belongs to Jesus includes the Protestants, the Eastern Orthodox, the Catholics, and one glorious day the Jews, according to Paul in Romans 9 (remember, Jesus himself is *still* Jewish). If you think part of Christ's body is off-base, that's okay. They probably think the same thing about you. Parts of our bodies face forward, parts face to the side, and even some parts face backwards, though we won't dwell on that!

But something's happening these days that we should watch with a sharp eye. It is called the interfaith movement or universalism. Jesus is good for the Christians, they say, but we shouldn't discount all the *other paths* to God. Some wish to find common ground between all world faiths, legitimizing and combining Christianity with belief systems such as Buddhism, New Age, Islam, Spiritists, Animists, the occult, and any number of man-invented belief systems in the name of *tolerance*.

But there's a problem. God says in Isaiah 43:10-11, ***"Before me no god was formed, nor will there be one after me. I, even I, am the LORD, and apart from me there is no savior."*** So if someone says the God of Abraham, Isaac and Jacob and His only begotten Son Yeshua Ha Mashiach, are just *one* of the paths to heaven, they're horribly, outrageously, dangerously wrong. *I* don't say it. God said it in that scripture passage from Isaiah 43.

Say you wake up one morning and someone has taken a chain saw to the side of your house? You demand to know what they think they're doing and they calmly tell you they can jolly well bust into your house any way they want to. What do you say? What do you do? Do you have the right to make the rules about your own house? How do you feel about what they're doing?

Well? Maybe heaven IS God's house. Maybe He does get to make the rules about it. Maybe what He thinks about it trumps anything we might feel. How do you suppose God feels when someone says they're coming into heaven any way they sincerely feel like coming?

Did Jesus haplessly undergo incarnation and endure an unimaginably horrific crucifixion when all along there were actually tons of *other ways* to restore us to fellowship with Himself?

There's a big fat reason why the man-invented, demon-inspired religions of the world don't impress God: <u>sin</u>. The problem is not *sincerity*: just *sin*. And none of the man-invented, demon-inspired religions of the world have any mechanism whatsoever to deal with sin. They have no savior. It's a fatal oversight.

Before going further, we need to be clear. There may be well-meaning and morally upright people in the world's religions, some of whom are much <u>better</u> people than you and me. But *better* is not even close to *perfect*, and perfection is God's standard. Sincere is nice, but it's possible to be sincerely wrong. And ignoring the problem of sin, which all other religions do, is a deadly mistake. As Dr. Ravi Zacharias said, "Jesus did not come to make bad people good, He came to make dead people live."

If we sin, and all have sinned and fallen short of the glory of God (Romans 3:23), then we come under condemnation according to the Law of Sin and Death. This is a universal law. No religion can simply annul it. No penance can shield from it. We reap what we sow. If you jump off a high bridge, you will fall. You can be as sincere as you want all the way down. If we plant an apple tree, an apple tree grows, not a pear tree, no matter what religion the tree planter is. No matter how good the tree planter tries to be. No matter how sorry the tree planter may say they are. Again, universal law. Everyone is under the Law of Sin and Death with zero exceptions.

World religions are invented by men in an attempt to solve this problem. And all the world religions have something in common: they *just* *don't* work. They can't deal with our problem of sin. It has nothing to do with how clever or fun or hard or sincere the religion might be.

Nothing against entering a Hot Wheels trike in a NASCAR race, but it's not going to do what you hoped it would, no matter how hard or sincerely you pedal.

The difficulty with trying to escape the Law of Sin and Death is that we have fallen short of the glory of _God_ (Romans 3:23). I don't know if you've noticed, but the glory of God is fairly easy to fall short of. Every one of us is in the same boat. Except one guy. The only one who hasn't fallen short is Jesus Christ the Righteous, the Savior of the world. His perfect life which He sacrificed for you and me on the cross is our only hope.

Ever heard the question, "If you knock on heaven's gate and they ask you why you should be allowed in, what will you say?" If for any reason you don't already know the answer, it goes like this: "The blood Jesus has given for my sins. Jesus is my Master and my Friend. He said I could come in. He's been preparing a place for me in His Father's house. I'm *expected*. I have a reservation." I have one of those.

If you don't have a reservation, *get* one.

7 the Great Commission
what should we be doing until He comes again?

"GO AND MAKE DISCIPLES OF ALL NATIONS, BAPTIZING THEM IN THE NAME OF THE FATHER AND OF THE SON AND OF THE HOLY SPIRIT, AND TEACHING THEM TO OBEY EVERYTHING I HAVE COMMANDED YOU."
MATTHEW 28:19-20A

The Starship Enterprise (it never seemed like just a TV show to me) had a prime directive and a five-year mission. Well, follow this: Christians worship the Prime Director and have a Great CO-mission. The Great Commission is the heart of Christianity, the heart of the gospel. Forget the approved haircut and black leather Bible with gold engraving. Forget the dental hygiene and swearing off swearing. Forget the once-a-week church meetings where everyone acts differently than we do the rest of the time. Forget boycotting DisneyWorld and voting Republican. Forget all the guilt about watching Seinfeld and laughing. Forget switching from pot to coffee pot.

The Great Commission is very nearly the only part of the Bible that we need. Of course, that's hyperbole for the sake of making a point. None of the Bible is superfluous. We need every word that proceeds from the mouth of God, says Jesus in Matthew 4:4. But if the only part of the Bible we really *get* is the Great Commission, we'd have a healthy idea about what God is up to and what our part in it is.

By the way, what *is* a disciple of Jesus? If we're supposed to make and baptize and teach disciples, it would be helpful to know what one is, right? Easy. A disciple of Jesus is someone who looks at the world and operates in the world the same way Jesus does. By faith. Using spiritual discernment and spiritual discipline exercised in the power of the Holy Spirit. As the disciple John said in 1 John 2:6, ***"Whoever claims to live in him must walk as Jesus did."***

This is huge. Disciples of Jesus are not simply to obey Him when we can, tend to His affairs at our leisure, consider His Kingdom at our liberty. We are to become the same as He was when He walked the earth. Too bold? Too extreme? Didn't Jesus say we would do greater things than He did? Didn't Jesus say that we have overcome the world just as He has? Didn't Jesus say that we are the light of the world just as He is? Yes, yes and yes.

So a disciple is someone who is learning to be and to do as Jesus is and does. Simple.

Jesus begins His Great Commission saying, ***"All authority has been given to me ..."*** He establishes the chain of command and flashes His credentials. The authority that He wields is absolute, giving Him the right to send His followers out to do whatever He commands. And He's very clear, so we don't have to go back and try to figure it out ourselves: *go, make, baptize, teach.* Let's look at these details.

"Go and make disciples ..." This is why we're not dead yet. We're not on earth to become more prosperous or more wonderful but rather to engage the world around us with the single-minded purpose of making disciples for Jesus. This is our theme song, our mission statement, our insignia, our charter and our ambition. To "win souls" is the primary job in the Great Commission. Once they are brought into the family by rebirth (John 3:7), there are two steps in the ongoing process of ongoing discipleship.

Step one: ***"Baptizing them in the name of the Father and the Son and the Holy Spirit ..."*** To be baptized is to be committed. In some parts of the world, Christian baptism is a way of getting yourself thrown out of society, if it's not an actual death sentence. Jesus himself was baptized because it is what God said to do (Matthew 3:15).

We shouldn't make more of baptism than the Bible does, nor make *less* of it either.

It's a sacrament whereby we publicly identify with the death, burial and resurrection of Jesus (Romans 6:3-4). In the New Testament, baptism immediately followed conversion. We can think of it as the official beginning of our new life in Christ.

Step two. ***"Teach them to obey all I have commanded you."*** Discipleship is the best way to pass along new life from God. Jesus modeled this process with twelve men. What happened was that they did life together, and Jesus showed them how to be in the world and not of it, both teaching and demonstrating all that meant. In the context of relationship, they were taught a new way to walk and a new way to talk, a new way to think and a new way to both act and react. 2 Corinthians 3:18 says it like this: you and I are being ***"transformed into his likeness in ever-increasing glory."***

Discipleship is the best way to imprint a way of life: "Do as I do." It's not unique to Christianity. Virtually every group of like-minded people has some form of it, but what IS unique to Christianity is *who it is that we're following!* We're not trying to become a great spot welder, or a master salesman, or a dedicated Buddhist. We're invited to begin the process in which we end up becoming like Jesus. Not like Billy Graham, Mother Teresa, Peter, Paul, Moses or Abraham ... but like *Jesus*. If this is hard to believe, read 1 John3:1-3. It's true.

Plus, there's a big picture purpose of this discipleship thing. The Great Commission is God's master strategy in a war that's being fought to free the captives of sin from the dark forces of evil that infest the planet earth and restore them to their rightful King. Pretty cool, huh?

Make and baptize and teach disciples. Go!

Is it a second chance? A change in the wind? More of the same only a little better? No, it's way beyond any of those things. It's something that's never been before, something beyond the other side of the far edges of our wildest imaginations. Something we've never dreamed, but it was what we really wanted all along. This is the wonder of what God has planned for us after He brings the universe to a burnt stop. The old world is dead. Long live the new ... um, whatEVER it is!!!

....

¬chapter five
NEWNESS: OUR DEEPEST YEARNING

don't you love that new universe smell?

"HE WHO WAS SEATED ON THE THRONE SAID, 'I AM MAKING EVERYTHING NEW!'"
REVELATION 21:5

Have you ever been absolutely clobbered for the bazillionth time in some game and said, "Give me just one more try"?

Sin had us whipped, time and time again, but Jesus came and swapped His life for ours and said, "Let's _you_ _and_ _me_ give it one more try!" And this time around, we finally came out on top. Now instead of being losers, we're "more than conquerers" according to Romans 8:37. We have a new outlook on this present life—not wishful daydreaming, but a full-bore _evidence-of-what-we-cannot-see_ kind of hope! We know beyond a doubt that this life is only a place holder. It will soon be gone. And whatever's on it's way will be indescribably beyond all we can ask or imagine (Ephesians 3:20).

It'll be the kind of life we don't now have words to begin to talk about, not that *that* should stop us. We can't describe the colors, the smells, the sounds, the light, the view, the air, the buoyancy of heart, the total absence of evil, the fierce joy that will for endless ages roll over us in waves of blissful glory.

We can't imagine it, but we can prepare to be part of it. This present life will determine our final destiny. We'd better not ignore God's call. He speaks to each of us, commanding us to leave behind our own selfish will just like the fishermen left their nets. New life awaits. New worlds beckon. New modes of being are just around the corner.

Fasten your seatbelt.

• NEW COVENANT
what if God kept OUR end of the deal too?

"THE TIME IS COMING WHEN I WILL MAKE A NEW COVENANT WITH THE HOUSE OF ISRAEL AND THE HOUSE OF JUDAH ... THIS IS THE COVENANT I WILL MAKE WITH THE HOUSE OF ISRAEL AFTER THAT TIME, DECLARES THE LORD. I WILL PUT MY LAW IN THEIR MINDS AND WRITE IT ON THEIR HEARTS. I WILL BE THEIR GOD, AND THEY WILL BE MY PEOPLE."
JEREMIAH 31:31 AND 33

On the mount of transfiguration (Luke 9:28) Jesus is shown transformed in shining glory. Moses and Elijah (*wait, aren't they supposed to be dead?*) appear with Jesus. Powerful visualization of the truth that the Law (Moses) and the Prophets (Elijah) find their fulfillment in Christ. These two men, Moses and Elijah represent the *old deal*, the *previous* arrangement, where God requires the lifeblood sacrifice of a perfect animal for every single transgression of His law.

The two men did not stay with Jesus. They only verified Jesus whom they'd prophesied would come, *and then they were taken away.* Only Jesus was left. Nobody else. No other system. No other path. No other Messiah. The old is *gone.* Then the disciples who were with Jesus were engulfed by a frightening cloud of glory from which a voice spoke saying, "This is my beloved Son. Listen to *Him.*"

There's a new sheriff in town—a new reality. There's a new way of doing things.

We no longer have to keep the impossible law of Moses. We no longer have to slaughter animals to cover our sins when we break God's law. We are no longer required to make ceremonial offerings and blood atonement. There's a new agreement God is offering every one of us.

He says instead of defaulting on our own sin debt and falling into the foreclosure of eternal separation from His holy presence, we can opt for the transfer payment of Jesus' death on the cross. If we take Him up on this new covenant, we're more than just forgiven and back to square one. We become part of God's very family. You heard me right, His *own family*. It's hard to see why anyone would refuse to opt into this provision of the contract.

Time travel with me to spring of AD 33. Jesus is about to have His last meal with eleven men He's chosen to carry out His plan to save the nations. He has foreshadowed this meal in the institution of the Passover. But Jesus adds a new twist: He departs from the well-known script. It's recorded in the three synoptic gospels and revealed directly from Jesus to Paul who recorded it in 1 Corinthians 11:23-26. Jesus takes the unleavened bread and tells the disciples that this is *my body*, broken for you. Then He takes the cup and says this is *the new covenant in my blood*.

Stop. Listen. Think. What is Jesus possibly saying? What could these words mean: *my body broken for you, the new covenant in my blood*? Is this some new teaching? Yes, no! It's the covenant God was always preparing, says Jeremiah 31:31. God didn't try something in the Garden of Eden and when that failed, attempted to fix His mistakes by instituting the Law and the judges and the prophets and the kings and then when those plans bombed, He had to go to plan C, then D and down the alphabet. This new covenant thing was the target all along. He's always been planning the manger, the cross and the empty tomb. God stays on plan A. Believe it. He's God!

God has *not* been frustrated in His attempt to win back our hearts. He doesn't misfire or suffer setbacks.   He made covenants with people like Adam, Enoch, Noah, Abraham, Jacob, Moses, and David. He kept all of His covenant promises, and yet none of them were intended to be the last word.

We're not under the Noaic covenant, or the Abrahamic or the Mosaic or the Davidic. We are under the NEW covenant, the covenant made by the blood of Christ. Paul calls it the Law of the Spirit of Life in Christ (Romans 8:2). It's a covenant that enables those who enter in to fully please God, a covenant kept by God on His side <u>and</u> on ours. God is eternally faithful to *His* promises, and, living in us, He fulfills *our part* of the new covenant as well.

The new deal needs a new deal-maker, and that go-between is of course Jesus Christ the Righteous (Hebrews 9:15). Jesus, the only Savior of the world, the unique mediator between wicked, rebellious, estranged human beings and their holy Creator who loves them as only He can. This new covenant is the best deal we've ever been offered. It's *way* too good to pass up. The old deal was rightly imposed on us. The new deal is freely offered to us—to whoever will.

The old agreement was never meant to save us. The new agreement already has, if we'll let it.

1 repentance
does anybody really go for a bogus apology?

"THE TIME HAS COME. THE KINGDOM OF GOD IS NEAR. REPENT AND BELIEVE THE GOOD NEWS!"
MARK 1:15

Repentance isn't popular. Few Christian studies dwell on it. I was so concerned with the more glitzy doctrines I almost left it out of this book. I mean, we repented once already, can we just move on? But there's a reason the Bible refers to repentance over 120 times. Some of the most powerfully convicting, healing and liberating Scriptures have to do with repentance.

Let me ask a question: What's the problem with the world around us? If you're stumped, here's the correct answer: THE FALL. We abandoned God and because of that, *we've lost our minds*, severed our connection with the only source of wonder, wisdom, joy, satisfaction and life. We're left with endless hour—dry, empty, purposeless, frustrating, hurtful and hellish.

What's the solution? Get right with God. How do we begin that process?

Repentance. That's it. That's the answer. Repentance. Repentance means to stop going the wrong way. Turn around. It's not complicated, just sticky.

The process goes like this. First, The Holy Spirit calls to our hearts. "Come back," He says. "Turn from your sin. Humble yourself under God's mighty hand." He draws our hearts to respond. Then we respond in repentance. God cannot "repent" us. He cannot make us sorry for our wicked attitudes and warped behaviors and undone assignments. He can only make us aware and give us grace to repent. Then it's up to us what we do from there. Ever seen this extraordinary scripture from Romans 2:4, ***"Do you show contempt for the riches of his kindness, tolerance and patience, not realizing that God's kindness leads you toward repentance?"***

It's in our repentance that the grace of God can reach us and give us the ability to want whatever God wants, to be able to hear the words of life from the heart of Jesus who loves us. Stop. Turn. Repent.

C.S. Lewis said that if you make a mistake in arithmetic, the quickest way forward is *back*—correct the error and go on from there. That's the picture of repentance. We have made a gross miscalculation, if you will, in keeping God's law. We are trespassers, convicts, rebels, scofflaws. And the way forward is the way back, back to where we scoffed at God's law. We must correct our error by repenting and getting a fresh start from the Holy Spirit.

Who needs to repent? Whoever's going the wrong way. God calls sinners to repent from being the small "k" king of our own kingdom, thinking we can live for ourselves and make up our own code of conduct. Until then we can never come into God's eternal Kingdom. So we must surrender our will to His. Have you done that? If not, do it now. It's the only sensible thing *to* do.

Who else needs to repent? God's own born-again children. We know what God expects and we know He has given us His Holy Spirit to empower us to meet His expectations. Still we persist in our boneheaded wrong choices. Belonging to Christ changes our desires, but not our willfulness. We still sin, but it's not as fun as it used to be! It's more natural for a child of God to repent, because sin has become a vile thing to us like it is to our Father.

We may need to repent from false doctrine. We should never give up the essentials: Christ's death, burial and resurrection. But we ought to allow for mystery (Calvinism versus Arminianism for example). We respect some truths as too big to reduce to formulas to beat each other up with. A little doctrinal humility on *inessential* matters is a good thing. We *must* repent of being theological know-it-alls.

The way back to God begins with repentance. Some say we can't do this ourselves, others that it's the only thing God really asks of us. Maybe both of those ideas are absolutely right. Maybe we must do it ourselves with the help of the Holy Spirit. I know, that sentence was a contradiction. Well, maybe it is and maybe it's not.

Repentance: key doctrine, crucial move. Let's be ready. Let's be quick to repent.

2 born again

how does one enter into a whole new existence?

"I TELL YOU THE TRUTH, NO ONE CAN ENTER THE KINGDOM OF GOD UNLESS HE IS BORN OF WATER AND THE SPIRIT. FLESH GIVES BIRTH TO FLESH, BUT THE SPIRIT GIVES BIRTH TO SPIRIT. YOU SHOULD NOT BE SURPRISED AT MY SAYING, 'YOU MUST BE BORN AGAIN.'"
JOHN 3:5-7

How do we get into this world? We're born. How do we enter the world-without-end? We're born *again*.

Nicodemus thought Jesus was saying he would have to be born *one more time*, but he misunderstood. Jesus was saying that he must be born *again*. If that confuses you, think how Nicodemus felt. Jesus wasn't talking about a do-over, a mulligan, another shot. He was saying we must be born *from above*. The gospel of John returns often to this idea in 3:3, 3:7; 3:31; 19:11 and 19:23.

Jesus says we MUST be born again: an imperative, a command, not a suggestion. Maybe this is why the man in Matthew 22 who shows up at a wedding without the required garment gets tossed. It's not just another block party, it's strictly a family affair. Don't think you'll live in God's house without being part of the family.

You get to be family by birth. Or adoption.

What would you think of a man who put 200 dependents on his tax return and when the IRS questioned him said that it's not his fault, his dependents just hadn't yet been born? Birth is a kind of necessity if you want to be counted in an existing world.

The world gets this born-again thing ... not that the world *is* born-again, but they get the *idea*. If a politician has a dramatic change of heart about an issue, they're said to have a *born-again* moment. If a hardened criminal becomes remorseful, they've had a *"come to Jesus"* experience. *Mountain top, revival, crusader, resurrected, redeeming, saving grace, newly converted.* The world *understands* these words. They are used and maybe even overused in songs that have nothing to do with Jesus or His command to Nicodemus.

To be born again is to receive and wake up to a totally new life. We're not talking renovation, we're talking bulldozing the existing structure to the ground and starting fresh with a whole a new indestructible foundation, using brand new and absolutely permanent materials. This is expressed many ways: *born again, born from above, new life, second birth,* and one of the best, the principal of *regeneration*.

We're not talking about simply restoring what was there with some patchwork fixes, a repair or repaint, or covering the bad parts with a fancy facade. We're talking new, down past the molecular level.

It's not just reformed. It's more than reconfigured or built back to look like the original. It's something totally other than what we had before. Totally ... well, *brand spanking new*.

Being born again is the only way we'll ever make it out of this world of darkness and despair. Consider: we inhabit bodies that get sick and die. We were made in God's image, but that's been ripped to pieces by our own selfishness. Our minds are full of deathly junk. Our future is thrown away in brainless pursuit of instant gratification. Our whole world revolves around what *we* want and what everyone else can do for *us*. We're sliding down a greased tube that empties out in the graveyard. Did I say that strongly enough? *How in the world* can we ever be fit for heaven with such baggage clutching at us and pulling us down?

How in the world indeed! There's no way *in the world*. So it must be *in Christ* that we overcome, in Christ that we're reborn, *remade*. There's no part of our lives that God will not transform if we let Him work, and it will be on His timetable and at His speed. We must surrender to His plans for us, trusting that He knows exactly what He's doing. Caterpillars can't fly south in winter; they have to be transformed into flying machines of tremendous form and function and grace.

Let God transform you. Give in to Him and pray He'll start the work that will equip you for the coming ages. Be thankful that you don't have to ride this world all the way into the fire, but that we can lift off the surface of this wicked planet as we are born from above. Whoever's been born once can be reborn in Jesus. Let God's Spirit give new life to your spirit.

Be born again.

3 adoption

how great is it to be wanted?

"THIS MYSTERY IS THAT THROUGH THE GOSPEL THE GENTILES ARE HEIRS TOGETHER WITH ISRAEL, MEMBERS TOGETHER OF ONE BODY, AND SHARERS TOGETHER IN THE PROMISE IN CHRIST JESUS."
EPHESIANS 3:6

Adoption can mean simply to claim something as your own. An assembly may adopt a motion, a country may adopt a policy, a teen may adopt an attitude.

But in the case of parents, adoption is much more specific. It's making an outsider to the natural born family a legal member thereof, with all the perquisites. It's circumventing the blood relationship with a lawful ceremony or certificate. It's not just getting any child that happens to come along, it's requesting a very specific child. A focused love on that particular child.

If the highest form of love is to die for someone else, this has to be close—to make a decision to take the responsibility for a person's nurture and well-being. Nobody can force someone else to adopt them. Adoption is proof positive of the love of the *adopter*. Never doubt that God loves you. He adopted you!

The root words for *adopt* mean, "to choose." Adult couples *choose* a child to adopt.

The parents take on all the legal, emotional, and societal rights and responsibilities of being the child's parents and the child is subsequently awarded the legal, emotional, and societal rights and responsibilities of a son or daughter. It's entirely volitional and speaks volumes about the heart of the parents. What's happening is not in any way an accident; it's a conscious decision. A child may be conceived in any number of "unintentional" ways, but no child was ever unintentionally adopted.

So when we understand that God intended all along to adopt the Gentiles into His family—the Jews—we have to be impressed. How do you know God always intended to do this? The same way I can know it—I read my Bible!

God told Abraham, the original Hebrew, that through him all nations would be blessed. According to 1 Peter 1:20 and Revelation 13:8, God decided before He made the world that He'd love the world with such intensity that He would give His only begotten Son. His love was always extended to every people group, not just the Jews. He loves the heathen nations every bit as much as He loves the children of Israel! Read the end of Jonah sometime and get the picture of God's compassion for the Assyrian city of Nineveh, steeped in idol worship and godlessness. God loves to take in wandering kids.

God adopts His Gentile children and transfers to them all the rights and privileges of full family status of the Israelites. 2 Corinthians 1:20 says that *all* the promises of God are "yes" in Christ. In Galatians 3:28, Paul, a Jew himself, says that in Christ there is neither Jew nor Gentile. Ephesians 2:12-13 infers that the Gentiles are now included in the commonwealth of Israel! Love the word "commonwealth."

This is astounding, considering the scriptures that announce that the Gentiles are part of the shared riches of Israel were generously written by Jews! Since God pounded the idea of national separation into the Israelites as a matter of holiness (and the word "holy" *means* "set apart from"), you'd think that no Jew would ever proclaim the doctrine of Gentile inclusion. Here's another proof that the Scriptures were inspired and written, not by the hand of man, but by God Himself.

Remember Peter's dream in Acts 10? A sheet of "unclean" animals is lowered to him from heaven and Peter is told to eat them. Peter says he's never eaten those animals because Jews are commanded not to. God tells Peter it's now okay. The rules excluding the "unclean" Gentiles have been updated to begin the next stage of God's plan: get the worship of the one true God from the people of Israel to the rest of the world. Christ's death on the cross has broken down the wall between the Jews and the heathen nations. The Jewish covenant of circumcision is over, and believer's baptism is instituted, some go so far as to say *substituted*. God is doing something brand new and Peter needs to get his head around the Kingdom of Christ. The family of God is getting bigger with tons more kids ... not less holy, more accessible. Not watered down, washed in blood—the blood of The Lamb.

When the Holy Spirit selects the word *"adopt"* in Ephesians 1:5, it's not because another word wasn't available, it's because it's the best word to describe what's going on when, as Gentiles, we're made part of God's family. God makes a conscious decision. He *chooses* us to become part of His family and He takes on the legal, emotional and societal rights and responsibilities for our well being.

We were unwanted, orphaned, seemingly left behind by a God who had selected Abraham and his descendants to tell His story and be His family. But now we know God intended all along to bring us into His family too, for in His promise to bless Abraham, He said, ***"All peoples on earth will be blessed through you"*** (Genesis 12:3).

In John 15, Jesus describes Himself as a robust and healthy vine, with us as His branches. Some of His branches are natural, such as the Jews. Others are grafted on says Romans 11:17. This grafting process is a picture of adoption—taking a branch with no root and bonding it with a strong and growing tree, partaking of all the sappy support! Selected and added on purposefully.

Welcome to God's family, adopted waifs. There's plenty of inheritance to spread around.

4 the church
do knucklehead sheep comprise an exclusive elite club?

"Do not leave Jerusalem, but wait for the gift my Father promised, which you have heard me speak about. For John baptized with water, but in a few days you will be baptized with the Holy Spirit ... you will receive power when the Holy Spirit comes on you; and you will be my witnesses in Jerusalem, and in all Judea and Samaria, and to the ends of the earth."
Acts 1:4,5 and 8

Forty-nine days after Jesus was crucified, there was no church. The very next day, there was. What happened that fiftieth day? It was the arrival of the promised Holy Spirit sent by the risen Christ to His beloved flock of ragtag followers. In an instant, those misfits became the most lethal army of all time, upsetting religious apple carts, replacing man-made dogmas, toppling powerful world rulers, infiltrating every nation on earth, altering the course of countless millions of lives and rewriting the totality of history forwards and backwards.

Look out world, here comes the church. We don't look like much, but it's the all-powerful God who's at work among us.

Forget traditional, contemporary and mixed services. Forget denominations and non-denominations. Forget theological distinctives. Forget the apostolic age, the rise of the papacy, Constantine, Augustine, Martin Luther, the reformation, Cromwell, Wesley and Whitefield, the Puritans, the first Great Awakening and the ascendance of Christian Radio (just kidding about the radio). Forget Jew and Gentile. Forget the distinctives. There's just *one* Church. That's all there's ever been and that's all there'll ever be. This is the truth. There is one. Count it—one church.

Think. Is the church the bride of Christ? Revelation 19:7 says yes. So, will Jesus be coming back for a profusion of brides or just one? Hint: Jesus is *not* a polygamist. As much as we may want to kick some Christians out of the fold that don't see everything as we do, a bride cannot pull her own nose off! A disgusting visual and rightly so. Jesus is the ultimate judge of who's in and who's out of His church. He has, however, given us a hint about this matter.

The requirements to belong in the church are laid out in Matthew 16:13-18, where Jesus asks the disciples who they say He is. Simon makes his great confession, ***"You are the Christ, the Son of the Living God."*** Jesus then tells Simon his name is Rock because he correctly identified the Messiah. Jesus told Peter his confession was revelation knowledge, and specifically, revelation about who Jesus <u>is</u>: the question that was being discussed. For Catholics, this section identifies their first Pope, and that's okay, since Jesus said other things that singled Peter out. Don't sweat it.

Because the church isn't ultimately about popes, or pedigrees, or politics. Not about immersion, or smoking or drinking. Not about transubstantiation, immaculation or instrumentation. Not about dunked or sprinkled or dancing, or speaking in tongues or personal holiness or lattes in the sanctuary or any of that stuff. That stuff is important, but it's not deep down what defines the church. It's all about correctly seeing Jesus as the Christ, the Son of the Living God. Who do we say that Jesus is? What place do we give Jesus Christ in our lives? Million dollar question. Is He the Christ, the Son of the Living God or is He just a nice idea, a model citizen, a slogan, a magic prayer, a rhyme in a song? *Is He central to our lives and do our thoughts and actions revolve around Him and what He likes and thinks and wants and expects and commands?* If so, I'm sorry to tell you, but you're part of <u>the</u> church.

The church is made up of people who follow Jesus. End of story. Period. It's all about Jesus. Jesus plus nothing. Jesus alone. Jesus and only Jesus. Of course we add other stuff, but it doesn't make us more Christian, and in some cases what we add is wrong! Not saying I know where everyone is wrong, just saying that the only definitely right part is the Lordship, the dominion of Jesus in our lives. Bang.

The church is the visible extension of the love of Christ in the world today. That's why the church must engage the world round about. Christians believe the present world is where Luke 10:25-37 can be lived out in the lives of real people—the lost and the hopeless, the cynical and the sinful. The Holy Spirit has given His church spiritual, material and motivational gifts not merely for edifices but for edification.

Brick and steel are not the church, they are only the place where the church can *gather*, where the flock can ... well, *flock*. From here, the church seeps into the community, the workplace, the schools, the culture, the art, the thinking, the entertainment, the scholarly endeavors, the imagination, the discovery, the politics, the philosophy, the fabric of the world that surrounds us with the saving message of the Kingdom of God. Jesus said to start in Jerusalem, then go to Judea and Samaria and then take the message to the ends of the earth (Acts 1:8). Start right where you are and go on from there as far as God leads. The church is involved with people, wherever those people are. This is a distinctive of genuine Christianity.

There is only one church, but it's helpful to think of it in three distinct ways (we are Trinitarian people, we Christians!). Firstly, the *local church* is vital to God's plans for the Kingdom. Paul, Peter and John use the phrase "one another" 35 times in their letters to describe how the church should behave. These scriptures are impossible to live without *local* fellowship. Alarmingly, many of the people who love Jesus in our day have become disillusioned with "church" and have pulled away, as if a church could be more perfect than the people of which it is made! Satan likes nothing better than a family of God that is wounded and estranged. We should pray and reach out with wisdom and grace to our fellow Christians who have left the local church. Christians should always be involved locally. This is where the tithe is paid in money, in worship, in prayer, in service. No local church? You're a wandering sheep and an easy target.

Secondly, there's also a *worldwide church*, which is the church throughout the earth. Existing under different political, geographical, cultural and economic conditions, the worldwide church is incredibly eclectic. God loves variety, just look at snowflakes. Though there may be times of peace, persecution is the norm, for the world system is diametrically and violently opposed to Jesus Christ. When one part of the church rejoices, all parts rejoice; when one part suffers, all parts suffer. Each part has a function. Just as we should be *involved* in the local church, we should be *connected* with the church around the world, and in this age of communication and technology, it's not that hard. This is where our alms and offerings rightly belong. Those alms and offerings can be time and talent as well as money; think mission trips. Travel. Going to a new culture. Across the world, across town. Leaving something and finding something else because God said to go. Mission *trips*.

And thirdly, there's the *catholic church*, the saints who've gone before us, who wait for us beyond the sleep of death, who cheer us on as we live each day for Christ and His Kingdom. We spell catholic with a small c because it is historic and universal and it's different from the capital C Catholic church which is a subset of the small c catholic church! We should remember the Hebrews 12:1 witnesses who are pulling for us to run our race well, having lived through the same trials we face and much worse. God has made His people to be victorious over this world says Romans 8:37. Be encouraged. We're part of the historic church that stretches from this moment back to the morning of the fiftieth day after Jesus ascended, and continues without pause into the future when the Father says it's time for this world to end. The one church of time and space, faithful through the years because of the faithfulness of God in Christ.

We're the church. We sing off key, we're a little out of step, we're slightly annoying. Nothing special to look at, just those whom God has selected to be His own.

5 baptism
is it all over for a seed when it gets buried in the ground?

"WE WERE THEREFORE BURIED WITH HIM THROUGH BAPTISM INTO DEATH IN ORDER THAT, JUST AS CHRIST WAS RAISED FROM THE DEAD THROUGH THE GLORY OF THE FATHER, WE TOO MAY LIVE A NEW LIFE."
ROMANS 6:4

Dietrich Bonhoeffer wrote, "When Christ calls a man, he bids him come and die." The way *into* this world of sin is birth; the way out is death. When we are baptized, we are baptized into Jesus and His death. It's a sacramental burial that frees us from this world. And also, it's a sacramental resurrection into new life.

The word baptism can mean either *immersion* or *washing*. It's also slang for an *initiation*. When you join a society, there are ceremonies that are observed. Ask the Boy Scouts, ask the Kiwanis Club, ask the Daughters of the American Revolution. Ask the Marines and the Seals, for crying out loud! These ceremonies have deep significance to the members of the society as well as the inductee. Baptism is *that* ceremony for the follower of Christ.

Strangely enough, baptism is a divisive doctrine in the church today. How important is it in your salvation, how deep in the water must you be submerged, what phrase should we speak as we dunk the disciple, whether it is effective for infants and children. It really shouldn't be this hard, dear family. We know what baptism is, but there's no manual about the correct way to do it. Apparently, the execution must not be as important as the participation!

The Bible *does* say that [1] Jesus was baptized Himself to fulfill all righteousness, [2] the apostles invariably and immediately baptized new believers, [3] there were times entire households were baptized when only one of the parents had professed belief, [4] we are to baptize people into the name of Jesus *or* into the name of the Father and the Son and the Holy Spirit (and the name of those three, I think, is *Jesus*), and [5] baptism represents cleansing, burial and resurrection. Cleansing is the washing away of guilt upon the declaration of a repentant heart. Burial is an identification with the substitutionary death of Christ. Resurrection is the start of a transformed life in Christ. Other stuff can be mined from the Scriptures, but it's harder work than the ones I've given you.

When a baptism happens, the whole church family gathers around. It's a solemn occasion, so solemn that believers shout for joy and clap and sing praises to God. It's a wildly formal party. Serious fun.

Water baptism is a big part of the gospel message, but there are other baptisms too, since baptism simply means *washing*. There's the baptism of *repentance* (Mark 1:4), which is a public declaration of sorrow for sin. There's the baptism of *fire* that John the Baptizer and Jesus both spoke about. I'm not sure what this is, but I think it means the fiery trials God allows to mature our faith, the kind of baptism Jesus asked James and John if they were ready for in Mark 10:39. And Paul, in Hebrews 6:1-2, speaks of other baptisms that he calls elementary teachings. In Titus 3:5, the new birth is called a "washing", a baptism, if you will.

There's also the baptism of *the Holy Spirit*. Again, what do I know? But, I think this is the already indwelling Holy Spirit being released in new ways in our lives. At times, this comes with an outward indication such as speaking in unlearned languages, but always in commissioning for a new *work*, not merely a new *experience*. Don't go off the rails in any direction. Leave room for mystery with God.

Baptism is a step of obedient faith. It's never forced. It's strictly voluntary. In the New Testament, it immediately follows conversion. In our time it seems to follow the believer becoming serious about their relationship with Jesus: "owning their faith" so to speak. Baptism is more than simply a symbolic gesture. In many cultures, baptism is the sign of a new allegiance to the sovereignty of Christ and rejection of the kingdom of darkness. Quite often, being baptized into Christ leads to being kicked out of family and society. Many around the world know their baptism is a literal death sentence and yet still obey the command of Jesus to do it.

Baptism isn't necessary before being admitted into God's family, the dying thief wasn't baptized but still Jesus said he'd join Him in paradise (the waiting room of the righteous dead) that very day (Luke 23:43). Still, the record of the early church strongly emphasizes the baptism of the *repentant disciple*: see Acts 2:38, 8:12, 8:36, 9:18, 10:48, 16:15, 16:33, 18:8, and 19:5. The message of the early Christians was simple: Repent. Be baptized. Follow Jesus Christ.

The attitude God loves toward baptism is found in Acts 8:36, spoken by the Ethiopian who, upon discovering Jesus in the book of Isaiah, asked Philip, "Is there any reason I *shouldn't* be baptized?"

Baptism is a command of our Lord Jesus. Have you obeyed this one?

6 the Lord's supper
what will we become as we partake of His life?

"THE LORD JESUS, ON THE NIGHT HE WAS BETRAYED, TOOK BREAD, AND WHEN HE HAD GIVEN THANKS, HE BROKE IT AND SAID, 'THIS IS MY BODY, WHICH IS FOR YOU; DO THIS IN REMEMBRANCE OF ME.' IN THE SAME WAY, AFTER SUPPER HE TOOK THE CUP, SAYING, 'THIS CUP IS THE NEW COVENANT IN MY BLOOD; DO THIS, WHENEVER YOU DRINK IT, IN REMEMBRANCE OF ME.'"
1 CORINTHIANS 11:23-25

We'll appreciate the Lord's Supper better if we can get a handle on the first Passover, 1,500 years before the upper room. The story is in Exodus, or if you'd rather, you can just watch the animated feature *Prince of Egypt*. Just kidding. Read the Bible. But the movie's still great.

Passover is all about the Messiah, the promised Deliverer. It's a picture of the Grand Story, the gospel. The Israelites walked freely into the land of Egypt but later became oppressed and enslaved, in the same progression that we become slaves to sin. In time, 400 years to be exact, God answered the Israelite's cries for help and sent a deliverer, Moses, just as He sent the Savior of the World, Jesus. Moses displayed miracles, yet Pharaoh couldn't see the hand of God, just as Jesus' miracles made no impression on the "blind" legalists. Moses told the Jews to sprinkle their doorposts with lamb's blood, just as the blood of Christ covers the believer in Christ. The angel of death then would *pass over* the faithful, just as Jesus has triumphed over death for us. More could be said, but you get the picture.

This exodus from slavery meant glorious freedom for the Israelites, but absolute catastrophe for Egypt. It was the end of their future namesakes, the end of their family fortunes, and the end of their prominence as a nation, just as Christ's death and resurrection has ended the dominance of the power of the devil over this world. Egypt not only released Israel, but showered their former slaves with the better part of their wealth to get them to leave! The world system rewards those who defy God, but one day we will leave this world, rich beyond our dreams.

As usual, God brings His children out better than they were when they went in. It's just the way He does things. Check out the lives of Job and Joseph and Daniel. But back to our story. As the Israelites left Egypt, God instituted the feast of Passover and the Jews have kept it ever since.

For the Passover feast, you start with a perfect lamb (Malachi 1:8). The lamb is then slaughtered and its blood drained by hanging. Recognize the cross? Then it's roasted and eaten with unleavened bread which symbolizes a humble heart, not puffed up with pride. There are four cups in the ceremony: *sanctification, deliverance, redemption* and *restoration*. You can make those comparisons to the work of Christ yourself by now. Scholars believe it was the third cup, the cup of redemption, that

Jesus offered to the disciples saying, *"This is the new covenant in my blood."*

Today, Christians celebrate the Passover as the Lord's Supper. We don't recline around a table in an upper room after washing each other's feet. We might not even have unleavened bread or wine, but perhaps specially prepared crackers or wafers or a loaf of leavened bread with grape juice. The important thing is not the groceries, but the reverent remembering of Jesus Christ and the new covenant He purchased for our sake with His physical body and blood.

In the new covenant, the sacrament of the Lord's Supper takes two of the elements of Passover: the bread, and the cup. The bread is called Jesus' body, according to the 1 Corinthians passage. Moses and the Israelites also knew it as heavenly manna, a miracle of God's provision (John 6:48-51). Bread is considered a staple food, one that can supply what is needed to sustain life. No wonder, Jesus calls Himself the "Bread of Life." He is all we need to sustain us in this world and the next.

Likewise, the cup is called the blood of Christ, which He shed for us at the cross. Both the Old Testament and modern medicine recognize that the **"life is in the blood"** (Leviticus 17:11). The blood brings oxygen and nutrients and carries away deadly toxins while fighting disease and bringing healing. Blood is *vital*. Christ's blood has been poured out for many for the forgiveness of sins (Matthew 26:28).

Catholics strongly believe that a miracle called transubstantiation occurs and the substance of the bread and the cup become the body and blood of Christ, even though the outward appearance and taste do not change. Protestants strongly believe the bread and the cup are a physical representation of a spiritual reality. Both acknowledge the mystery of the Lord's Supper. There is ample scripture and church tradition to uphold either view, or even both. Who knows? Just understand that the Lord's Supper is something Jesus instituted that our rational minds cannot contain. The only way to come to the table of the Lord is by faith, giving thanks for His provision for us in His sacrifice at the cross. Jesus is the crucial idea, not what happens or doesn't happen to the food and drink in front of us.

The Lord's Supper is many things to a Christian. It's a rich and powerful way to experience the presence of God ... an unforgettable reminder of Jesus' broken body and poured-out lifeblood ... a strong declaration that we all partake of the same Jesus Christ as we eat from the same loaf and cup ... and a powerful way to pass along the faith to our kids, acting out the narrative of our deliverance from sin and death. We participate in the mystery of salvation, the great story told through the ages. We embrace the parts we can't understand in wonder and thankfulness.

Communion is a physical celebration of a spiritual reality: we belong to Christ and in the bread and in the cup, we take in His life and death and resurrection. Jesus calls us to share His life together around His table, where we declare our total dependance on Jesus Christ and His complete sufficiency for us.

In the Lord's Supper, Jesus bids the hungry and thirsty come, where we gather around Him in a reality that has confounded the wise men of the ages. Eat. Drink. And remember Him.

7 perseverance
when is it time to give up on God and His promises?

"BUT THE SEED ON GOOD SOIL STANDS FOR THOSE WITH A NOBLE AND GOOD HEART, WHO HEAR THE WORD, RETAIN IT, AND BY PERSEVERING PRODUCE A CROP."
LUKE 8:15

Perseverance is persistently, unrelentingly pushing forward, never calling it quits.

Calvinists have a central belief they call "the doctrine of perseverance," which is a once-saved-always-saved kind of teaching. But we're not talking about that use of the word perseverance. We're talking about the scriptural command that says don't give up—stay the course, run the race all the way to the finish line, keep on keeping on. A Christian is not only what we are, it's what we continue to become.

The false doctrine of "cheap grace" has made it hard to find the concept of "sticking with it" in our churches. Cheap grace is the lie that if we say a magic prayer one day, then the rest of our lives we can do whatever we want, since we've already punched our ticket. There is no magic prayer. There never was.

The excuses are easy. It's too hard. We were tricked. Nobody told us it was going to take this long. I have to stop a minute. Are we there yet? The sun was in my eyes. The ball took a bad bounce. How can God expect us to be faithful longer than our 20-minute attention span, or acknowledge Him more than on Sundays?

But while anyone can make excuses for mailing it in, we all idolize people who have dedicated their lives to achieving greatness. Such as the elite athletes described in 1 Corinthians 9:24, *"Do you not know that in a race all the runners run, but only one gets the prize? Run in such a way as to get the prize."* Simply doing whatever's necessary to rise up and become champions. Running with purpose and *perseverance*.

The Bible says nothing about a shortcut, a ticket or some kind of trick. It only talks about an ongoing relationship with Jesus, such as the one in Colossians 2:6, *"So then, just as you received Christ Jesus as Lord, continue to live in him."* See the word "continue" in that last sentence? Oh, and this one from Matthew, Mark, AND Luke (it must be something we should consider), *"If anyone would come after me, he must deny himself and take up his cross daily and follow me."* Keyword: "daily." There's no hint of a one-time event, but rather an ongoing, persistent operation.

Jesus uses tons of agricultural references describing the kingdom, not because the people He was talking to were ignorant peasants. He used agricultural references because life in Him is a growth process, not a one-time event. Christians through the ages have used the analogy of _walking_ in Christ, as in, "Hey, how's your walk?" Walking is step by step, one foot in front of the other. Keep on truckin'.

The Christian life is also referred to as a _pilgrimage_, which is a long and difficult journey, not a sprint. Until we cross the river of death, nobody but _nobody_ has arrived. To finally reach our destination we must doggedly pursue it. This is the principal of perseverance and a key to living a victorious life in Christ. But it isn't taught as often as it ought to be. It's not stressed as it should be stressed. Why would we lose sight of such an important teaching as perseverance?

Maybe we don't teach perseverance because of the seeming squabble it has with the doctrine of grace. Grace works in us to sovereignly accomplish God's purpose. Check. So why are we expected to persevere and put forth some effort? Are you kidding me? Grace is cool because it requires no effort from us. Perseverance expects us to contribute to the process. Grace wins! But it shouldn't be like that.

Perseverance and grace are not incompatible. They mark the opposite points in the most distant zip codes of a giant truth. As one coin has two sides, so do grace (unmerited favor) and perseverance (gut-check determination) describe a conundrum in Christian theology. Consider the following two scriptures. Jesus said in Mark 13: 13, **"All men will hate you because of me, but he who stands firm to the end will be saved."** Make of that what you will, but it sounds like perseverance is somehow important. At the same time, Romans 14:4 says, **"[The servant of Christ] will stand, for the Lord is able to make him stand."** I think I said it's a mystery, didn't I?

Perseverance just makes sense. If you offer to buy someone dinner and then can only come up with part of the money to pay the check, you look like an idiot. If you start to build a house and halfway through the process you decide to give up, you look like a loser. If you get ready to fight and then before the end of the battle you run away, you look like a coward. The Bible calls us to persevere, to run until we cross the finish line, whatever it costs. We must finish what we start, by God's grace. See how I threw that in? The mystery remains intact!

Sure, being a Christian is hard, but not nearly as hard as being an unbeliever. Being dedicated to anything is hard, so if we're going to be committed to _something_, why not the most worthwhile something there could be? As Paul says in 1 Timothy 4:8, **"Godliness has value for all things, holding promise for both the present life and the life to come."** Nobody lay on their deathbed and wished they'd spent less time doing what they knew God wanted them to.

Perseverance produces character, according to 2 Peter 1:5-9—a list of the steps of Christian growth. Character is doing the right thing when nobody's watching.

Character is all tied up with the fruit of the Spirit and reaching spiritual maturity and becoming more like Jesus. Perseverance is the necessary ingredient to this acquisition of character. Do we want to produce fruit in our Christian faith?

Then, we must persevere. 2 Timothy 2:1, 3, 6 and 7, *"Be strong in the grace that is in Christ Jesus ... Endure hardship with us like a good soldier of Christ Jesus ... The hardworking farmer should be the first to receive a share of the crops. Reflect on what I am saying, for the Lord will give you insight into all this."*

What options do we have outside of perseverance? Jesus once asked His disciples, "Will you leave me too?" Peter's reply was vintage Peter, "Leave to go where? You're the only real thing going."

As the Spirit gives us strength, we will persevere.

• SECOND COMING

were we starting to think He'd never come back?

"AT THAT TIME MEN WILL SEE THE SON OF MAN COMING IN CLOUDS WITH GREAT POWER AND GLORY. AND HE WILL SEND HIS ANGELS AND GATHER HIS ELECT FROM THE FOUR WINDS, FROM THE ENDS OF THE EARTH TO THE ENDS OF THE HEAVENS."

MARK 13:26-27

Look at Luke 4:18-19. Jesus read this Scripture in the synagogue, but He stopped before He got to the "day of vengeance" part. This was a clue that the Messiah had a two-part mission. Only one part was to be accomplished on His first visit. The disciples were convinced (as we would have been) that Jesus would accomplish all the prophesies about Him in one go. We have the benefit of quasi-omniscient hindsight, so we shouldn't get too smug. Put yourself in their shoes.

They expected Jesus to mop up the Roman Empire, establish the eternal Kingdom, and start everything new. That's why they were so surprised when Jesus kept trying to tell them that He was going to Jerusalem to be *killed*. They had no theology that included a dead Messiah. They had no theology that provided for the Messiah to leave or to later return. Sure they had a Passover, and a lamb and the concept of blood atonement, but nothing to prepare them for the Messiah to actually *be* that lamb. But the Messiah was going to straighten things out *politically*, right? The Romans were the end-time enemy of God, right? The world couldn't go on much longer the way things were, right?

But Jesus understood the different purposes of His first coming and His second, at which time He'll set up His 1,000-year reign on earth and stage the final showdown between good and evil that will end the present space-time universe.

Sandwiched between the first and second coming of Jesus is what the Bible calls in Luke 21:24 the Age of the Gentiles, a time where everyone who's not Jewish gets a chance to be adopted into God's family. For that alone we should be grateful that Jesus always planned to make two trips. Many believe that we're in the season of the Lord's return, and if that's so, the age of the Gentiles is nearly over.

You may have heard the put-down, "He thinks he's the second coming!" What does that mean? It means the person has a God-complex. They think they've got all the answers and the world revolves around them. This insult is one of the best-known modern references to Jesus and His return, with a major caveat: Jesus doesn't have a God-complex, He *is* God, with all the answers plus a few more. Oh, and the world actually does revolve around Him according to Hebrews 1:3!

You may also have heard the expression, "Keep looking up!" Why do we even have an encouragement like that? What's up there worth looking for? Are the clouds good omens? Are we afraid of bird droppings? What warrants an upward gaze? We look up because our redemption will one day come ... in the sky. When Jesus ascended 40 days after the resurrection, the angels told the flabbergasted crowd that He would return in the same way (Acts 1:11). No jet pack. No space suit. No titanium galactic cruiser. Just too bright to look at, riding a shining horse with a robe dipped in blood, coming with thousands of glorious angels. That's all.

Job 19:25 states a powerful truth, ***"I know that my Redeemer lives, and that in the end he will stand upon the earth."*** At the end of all things, our Redeemer will return. The first time He came as the Lamb of God to die for the sins of the world. The second time He will come with power, which is curtains for the bad guys.

Tons of people have written tons of books that try to tell us what's going to happen when Christ returns. Pre-rapture, post-rapture, no-trib, whole-trib ... there are even Christians who believe we're in the millennium reign of Christ *at this moment.* Don't ask me to explain anything. Read all the books you want, but it won't help you much. There's a deliberate mystery about it all that God will reveal in His time. Our part is to know the Scriptures *and to look up.* We don't have to figure it out ahead of time if we just do what He told us to.

In Mark 13:35-37, Jesus says this to you and me: ***"Therefore keep watch because you do not know when the owner of the house will come back, whether in the evening, or at midnight, or when the rooster crows, or at dawn. If he comes suddenly, do not let him find you sleeping. What I say to you, I say to everyone: Watch!"***

Word to the wise: stay awake and keep a sharp eye out.

1 the times of the Gentiles
does God have an amazingly inclusive plan or what?

"WHEN YOU SEE JERUSALEM BEING SURROUNDED BY ARMIES, YOU WILL
KNOW THAT ITS DESOLATION IS NEAR ... FOR THIS IS THE TIME OF
PUNISHMENT IN FULFILLMENT OF ALL THAT HAS BEEN
WRITTEN...JERUSALEM WILL BE TRAMPLED ON BY THE GENTILES
UNTIL THE TIMES OF THE GENTILES ARE FULFILLED."
LUKE 21:20, 22 AND 24

One of the things Christians ought to know about Jesus is that He's not a Christian.
He's not a Gentile. He is, at this exact moment, the most orthodox *Jew* who ever
lived. He came for the children of Israel, according to Matthew 15:24. So why in our
time, do we see the nation of Israel rejecting Jesus as their Messiah, while the other
nations are coming to Him as the Savior of the World? I'll tell you why. It's because
we're living in a unique pocket of history known as *the times of the Gentiles.*

During this time, God's promise to Abraham that *all nations* would be blessed
through Him is being fulfilled and God's strategy from Romans 11 is being
implemented. God raised up Paul as "the apostle to the Gentiles" (Acts 22:21). Paul
was not one of the twelve, and had never met Jesus during His earthly ministry.
Yet, Paul still knew Jesus face-to-face, according to Galatians 1:12 and 1 Corinthians
15:8. Jesus personally trained and instructed this guy for the Gentile mission.

In Daniel chapter two, we learn that the most powerful king of all time,
Nebuchadnezzar, had a dream about a statue. He told no one of this dream, but
instead asked for an interpretation. All the wise men of his realm said what you
might expect: tell us the dream and we'll tell you what it meant. But the king
responded, if you don't know what I dreamed, how can you expect me to trust your
interpretation? Daniel sought God about it. The dream was revealed to him and is
described in Daniel 2:32-35: *"The head of the statue was made of pure gold, its chest and
arms of silver, its belly and thighs of bronze, its legs of iron, its feet partly of iron and
partly of baked clay. While you were watching, a rock was cut out, but not by human
hands. It struck the statue on its feet of iron and clay and smashed them. Then the iron,
the clay, the bronze, the silver and the gold were broken to pieces at the same time and
became like chaff on a threshing floor in the summer. The wind swept them away without
leaving a trace. But the rock that struck the statue became a huge mountain and filled the
whole earth."*

The statue represented the empires that crushed the nation of Israel: Babylonian,
Medo-Persian, Greek, Roman, and Western Civilization. The Rock not hewn by
man that crushed the statue and filled the whole earth is the Kingdom of Christ.
Nebuchadnezzar's statue is a prophetic vision of the times of the Gentiles, as they
dominate Israel for an age, but that age will draw to a close, and the great empires
will blow away in the wind one by one. When the time of the Gentiles is over, *great*

things are set to happen on earth.

Here's Paul's explanation in Romans 11:25-26: ***"Israel has experienced a hardening in part until the full number of the Gentiles has come in. And so all Israel will be saved."*** The Gentiles who will receive Christ are numbered, according to this Scripture, and that number will be gathered in. Israel has rejected Christ and received a hardened heart from God, just as God hardened Pharaoh's heart. But one day, God will soften those hearts again and Israel will turn to Jesus!

That time will be action-packed. Romans 11:15 ***"For if [Israel's] rejection is the reconciliation of the world, what will their acceptance be but life from the dead?"*** Just wait until God's chosen people turn to Jesus Christ. There are going to be fireworks! The time of the Gentiles is ending, and the time of Israel's return is at hand. Satan has been given a free hand to persecute the Jews, and before the end, he'll get together the most terrifying army ever seen to try to wipe Israel off the face of the earth. Fat chance. Strap in, cause the ride's about to get bumpy.

Big stuff is about to bust loose.

2 the antichrist

what do you call a person diametrically opposed to Christ?

"BUT EVERY SPIRIT THAT DOES NOT ACKNOWLEDGE JESUS IS NOT FROM GOD. THIS IS THE SPIRIT OF THE ANTICHRIST, WHICH YOU HAVE HEARD IS COMING AND EVEN NOW IS ALREADY IN THE WORLD."
1 JOHN 4:3

The Antichrist is marked by his making the claim that Jesus did NOT come in the flesh. There have been many people who have taught this, and they are all of the *spirit* of the Antichrist. The Antichrist from this perspective doesn't seem to be a single man, so much as a demonic influence that resurfaces here and there. This lying demon spirit may one day possess a single human being who will represent the culmination of every wicked scheme Satan's been working on throughout human history.

I'm not an authority on Revelation or Daniel, and frankly, it's hard to tell who IS. Those are tough books! Even thoughtful commentaries can sound wild and unbelievable. Revelation and Daniel are full of allegory, with dreamlike symbolism that can frustrate any attempt to plot a timeline of the narrative. Humility is a necessary character trait of all who study these two books. It's confusing for us who live in sequential time, because biblical prophecy skips around. Mixed up with events that have already occurred for us today are events that haven't yet happened. We must stay flexible and study diligently. Hebrews 12 is great advice—

keep your eyes on Jesus. So with fear and trembling, let's take a stab at tracking the Antichrist through the foggy marshes of prophecy. Your results may vary!

The Beast, the second Beast, the False Prophet, the Dragon, and Satan get a lot of ink in Revelation 13 and Daniel 9. It appears (and I emphasize *appears* through this section) that the Antichrist arises after a period of worldwide turmoil, hardships and horrors greater than have ever been before. That's why every generation thinks it's living in the end times. It's hard to imagine greater turmoil than the present.

The Antichrist will seem to have all the answers. He's also called the Beast. The False Prophet that arises with him to do counterfeit miracles is also called the second Beast. The Antichrist will sign a treaty of peace with Israel, but, true to his deceitful nature, he'll violate his own agreement, turn around and make war on Israel, and set himself up to be worshiped. Then Christ will return, defeat the armies of the Antichrist and the False Prophet in the famous battle of Armageddon, and toss both of them into the Lake of Fire.

Angels will then bind Satan and throw him into the Abyss for a thousand years while Jesus reigns and makes everything right on earth. At the end of that time, also known as the Millennial Reign, Satan will be released for a short time to take his last shot. Failing a second (or third) time to subdue God, (and what does it say about Satan's powers of reasoning that he actually believes he _can_), he gets mopped up and thrown into the Lake of Fire along with the Antichrist and the False Prophet, the wanna-be trinity of darkness.

And that will be that.

For now, just know that if you're not a child of God, you're cannon fodder for the devil, the Antichrist, the False Prophet and their lies. You'll be deceived, used, abused, and finally get eternal damnation as you spend the rest of your existence, whatever that will be, in burning sulfur.

This news isn't usually included in the gospel when we tell it, but maybe it should be. The good news would have a lot more punch if we told people the horrific truth of the bad news before we announced the Savior. Telling someone they have to give up their beloved house sounds a whole lot better if you include the news that the structure from top to bottom is irrevocably on fire and is burning to the ground.

The Antichrist is a twisted, evil, irredeemably wicked man. He'll do and say things that don't even belong in nightmares. Many have come as his forerunners. But when he appears, he'll top them all. Scared? Maybe you should be if you haven't surrendered your life to Jesus. Yet in the end, the Antichrist will be sent packing to the land of dry, empty, burning nothingness and Jesus will reign in ever-increasing wonder, joy and life. Bye-bye, Antichrist. You are TOAST, son.

In the words of James Weldon Johnson, "Your arms are too short to box with God."

3 the Day of the Lord
does God ever get really, really mad?

"WAIL, FOR THE DAY OF THE LORD IS NEAR; IT WILL COME LIKE DESTRUCTION FROM THE ALMIGHTY ... SEE, THE DAY OF THE LORD IS COMING: A CRUEL DAY, WITH WRATH AND FIERCE ANGER TO MAKE THE LAND DESOLATE AND DESTROY THE SINNERS WITHIN IT."
ISAIAH 13:6 AND 9

I'm sure you've heard the good guy say to the bad guy, "You'll never get away with this!" They're probably not theologians, but the Bible says they're exactly right.

Inside, every person on earth knows about it. It's a day of *reckoning*, where accounts are tallied and debts called in, bills come due, and all credit ends. Time to put up or shut up. No more wait and see, just read and weep. No more Mister Nice Guy. No more you *will* be sorry, the godless *are* sorry on that day—the day of the Lord.

Imagine the excitement of the last 15 minutes of every movie ever made rolled into a nanosecond of retribution. The bad guys don't just get shot, they get blown up, blasted, boiled, bombed, vaporized, drowned, dropped, spewed, strewed, hewed, liquidated, lit up, incinerated, melted, nuked, exploded, extruded, steamed, fried, fricasseed, flattened, fumigated, flogged, fragmented, fractured, and fire-bombed. The bad guys don't survive to resurface in the next movie. It's curtains, baby.

Is God trying to scare us? No question about it. Absolutely. Affirmative. Yes. Scare the <u>pants</u> off of us. He doesn't want *anyone* to meet the day of the Lord unprepared (1 Timothy 2:4), so He tells us in the Bible what's coming and also that we can't possibly know when it will arrive. So we'd better get ready *now*.

Both 1 Thessalonians 5:2 and 2 Peter 3:10 say it will come like a thief in the night—a total surprise, bringing destruction and loss in hyper-biblical proportions. Obadiah 1:15 tells us God is getting ready to enact the golden rule. It will be done to us as we have done to others. Joel 2:31-32 tells us that even though the day is coming of God's fierce wrath, if we will call upon His name, He will save us from that day.

Ever wondered how God can forgive a murderer, even when the family of the murdered cannot? It's because, from God's perspective (and His perspective is all that really counts), the sin was against Himself. God will ultimately take perfect care of the innocent victims of evil actions. Beyond mere compensation or petty revenge, God offers complete *healing* of the physical and emotional trauma and total wipe of the hurtful memories. He makes *all things* new, according to Revelation 21:5, and memories and trauma are part of *all things*. I'm not saying it's easy for the injured party or even that God promises to fix anything this side of the grave, I'm only looking at the big eternal picture.

Hard as it is for us to identify with, God ALSO has concern for the *evildoer*, in peril of eternal hellfire. In Jonah 4:11 He says, **"Nineveh has more than a hundred and twenty thousand people who cannot tell their right hand from their left, and many [animals] as well. Should I not be concerned about that great city?"** You can't name a more wicked idolatrous city than Nineveh, yet God bent over backward to warn them. God is never happy to see the wicked die. God's wrath is *righteous*. There is no hint of sadistic enjoyment of His retribution.

If you see a stranger about to walk off a cliff, don't you cry out a warning? Do you think you're better than God, that He wouldn't? No one's a stranger to *Him*. He made each one and loves each one. This is why He says in Matthew 5:44 and Luke 6:28 to pray for those who persecute and mistreat you. They're dangerously balanced on the very brink of cataclysmic destruction. Pray they'll find God's forgiveness. Give them yours. Have God's heart by calling on His Holy Spirit for discernment and wisdom. The Day of the Lord is coming.

Isaiah 13:7-13: **"Because of this, all hands will go limp, every man's heart will melt. Terror will seize them ... See, the day of the Lord is coming: a cruel day, with wrath and fierce anger to make the land desolate and destroy the sinners within it. The stars of heaven and their constellations will not show their light. The rising sun will be darkened and the moon will not give its light. I will punish the world for its evil, the wicked for their sins. I will put an end to the arrogance of the haughty and will humble the pride of the ruthless ... I will make the heavens tremble; and the earth will shake from its place at the wrath of the Lord Almighty, in the day of his burning anger."**

We get a small taste of this event in the worldwide catastrophes that seem to happen more frequently day by day—earthquakes, volcanic catastrophes, tsunamis, and hurricanes—bringing devastation and tremendous loss of life. When God is through waiting for those who will not repent, we'll have an event that makes all these other events look like picnics in the park. Zephaniah 1:18b warns, **"In the fire of his jealousy the whole world will be consumed, for he will make a sudden end of all who live in the earth."**

This is the prophetic equivalent of taking out the trash. It's no different from erasing a bad hard drive on a computer. It's the same thing as burning leaves in the fall. It's what happens to photos of old romances when we get married. It's like shredding old tax returns. It's identical to dealing with whatever arrives at the waste treatment plant.

Be wise. Be warned. Don't be caught off guard. God has given us a chance now to make peace with Him and to call our loved ones and those we meet to do the same. God is good, but His righteous anger is nothing to toy with.

The day of the Lord is coming. Are we ready?

4 Jerusalem raised up

remember angels, shepherds, and "peace on earth?"

"IN THE LAST DAYS THE MOUNTAIN OF THE LORD'S TEMPLE WILL BE ESTABLISHED AS CHIEF AMONG THE MOUNTAINS; IT WILL BE RAISED ABOVE THE HILLS, AND ALL NATIONS WILL STREAM TO IT. MANY PEOPLES WILL COME AND SAY, 'COME, LET US GO UP TO THE MOUNTAIN OF THE LORD, TO THE HOUSE OF THE GOD OF JACOB. HE WILL TEACH US HIS WAYS, SO THAT WE MAY WALK IN HIS PATHS.'"
ISAIAH 2:2-3

Is America the apple of God's eye?

Are you kidding me? Not even close. I mean, God dearly loves America as He does all nations, but ever since Abraham, the Jews have been His posse, their welfare the foremost thing on His mind. Since Melchizedek, the king of Salem (Jerusalem in Genesis 14:18), He's always had the world revolve around Jerusalem!

Think of it. The footprint of the nation of Israel is the size of New Jersey for crying out loud. And yet, America owes its entire legal and moral system to the Israelites. The banking system of the globe is shaped by the Israelites. To this day, world news events can't ignore Israel, as crazy as that sounds. Whole groups of people and even nations exist seemingly just to hate Israel. Some in Congress have made their careers on their support or their rejection of Israel.

Surrounded by countries with many times their population full of crazy people shooting machine guns in the air as they scream for Israel's destruction, Israel has fought and whipped every one of them! There's no logical explanation for the existence of the nation of Israel or for its reappearance in our time, and no conceivable reason why it's still there this morning, other than the tiny fact that God loves those guys. Inalterably and finally they belong to Him. Exodus 19:5, **"Out of all nations you will be my treasured possession."** That about says it.

Jerusalem has a unique history. As we said, Abraham meets Melchizedek the King of *Salem*, probably the early site of Jerusalem. The Canaanites called it *Urusalimum* after one of their gods. King David made Jerusalem his capital. A transliteration by the Hebrews turned it into Jerusalem which means *"the rain of peace"*! That's just like God, to make a Messianic promise to a tiny town and then make that town the talk of the world.

The mountain of the Lord's temple mentioned in the Isaiah 2 passage above is Mt. Zion—you guessed it, the mountain Jerusalem sits on. Right now, Satan has a mosque on it. That will be gone, count on it, probably by the hand of God Himself. Mt. Zion, now a couple hundred feet high, will be chief among all other mountains. Maybe "chief" simply means that it will be the most important, but I mean, what makes a mountain a mountain? Height. Mountains are high; highness is what mountains do and who they are. It's not unthinkable that Everest and Denali and all the rest of the great mountains will either be brought low, or Mt. Zion will be higher than 29,000 feet.

This orogenic apocalypse (d'ya like that? I made it up) isn't clearly laid out in scripture, nor is it of paramount (I did it again) importance. What we *do* need to know is that Zion will become the ***focus*** of everything that happens in the world. Sort of like now, only magnified exponentially.

The nations will "stream" to it, a wonderful word picture of the river of humanity flowing to the heart of God in Israel. And the nations will give more than just lip service to Jesus, since He just whupped all the armies of the world combined, all by himself. For a thousand years, the nations will be awed by the presence of the Lord and will want to know Him (Hosea 6:3). The earth will be full of the knowledge of the Lord as the waters cover the seas, says Isaiah 11:9 and Habakkuk 2:14.

The second of those passages adds the fact that everyone will know God, or at least know *about* Him. I think for a season, the world will just want to be on God's good side. Jerusalem will be raised up and the headlines in all the news, the main course of study in academic institutions, the prime topic of discussion will be Jerusalem, the city of God set high on a hill, a hill raised up to display the sovereignty of God's Kingdom. Then, after the thousand years are over, Jerusalem will again, for the whatevereth time, be surrounded by God's enemies, but fire from heaven will fall and burn them up (Revelation 20:9) and the end of the world will have arrived. Talk about "global warming!" Not sure what that fire will be, but ouch.

Pray for the peace of Jerusalem, says Psalms 122:6. When Jerusalem is at peace, the rest of the world be at peace as well.

5 Christ's millennium reign
can you picture this world in perfect harmony?

"BLESSED AND HOLY ARE THOSE WHO HAVE PART IN THE FIRST RESURRECTION. THE SECOND DEATH HAS NO POWER OVER THEM, BUT THEY WILL BE PRIESTS OF GOD AND OF CHRIST AND WILL REIGN WITH HIM FOR A THOUSAND YEARS."
REVELATION 20:6

People in the millennium will live happily ever after to a ripe old age in wonderful health with sparkling white teeth. Early death will be odd. Anyone who lives less than a couple hundred years will be considered to have died young! Kids will play unafraid in the streets. Crops will flourish, rain will be sweet and in season, we'll have lifelong friends for much longer lifetimes, literature and music will soar to previously unknown heights and who knows what people will accomplish under the righteous government of God on earth. Andy of Mayberry reruns will look like wicked, scary times. Read Isaiah 65 for some of this (not the Mayberry part).

If there's any kind of dispute, King Jesus will settle it with perfect wisdom and justice. No frivolous lawsuits with the King of Kings on the bench! If nations have disagreements, they won't send in their armies, they'll send to Jerusalem to request a ruling. Since the Judge is omnipotent, there'll be no miscarriages of justice.

What the dreamers have always dreamed will be a waking reality in that day. What the poets have always poeticized will be standard operating procedure. All the eco-friendly, idyllic-idealistic, hunter-gatherer, hippie-commune, robes-and-sandals, perfect-planet society will seem pathetic in comparison to the coming reality of the millennium reign of Jesus Christ. All our imaginings of what that time could possibly look like will fall woefully short of the reality.

When Christ reigns, this world will be the kind of world the secular humanists always wanted, or at least *said* they did. Each person will be fed and clothed and given work that brings them satisfaction and joy. No one will be afraid in their homes or in the streets, day or night (Ezekiel 34:28).

In the animal world, the meat eating predators will be best friends with the pacifist vegetarians and every creature will contentedly chow down on your front lawn, says Isaiah 11:6-9. Alligators will let you tickle them on the chin. T-rex will let you climb his back between mouthfuls of oats and hay. Tigers will sleep in your bedroom ... if you want them to.

Micah 4:2-5 says that all people will want to learn about God's ways and that their weapons will be so useless that they'll be turned into farming tools. If socialist-utopian occupy-wall-street protestors had an honest bone in their body, they'd be fervently, loudly praying for Christ's return.

And then, at the end of the thousand years, God will allow evil one last pathetic revolt. There will be a temporary time of upheaval and rebellion. Think of it as the last gasp of the self-worshippers. Psalms 2 will be the screenplay for that time (as it has been for the last 2,000 years). The humanistic armies of the world will get together under Satan and attempt to do what the Dragon could not do in Revelation 12: defeat the Kingdom of God. Good luck with that, guys! Like you've got a chance in you-know-where.

The very name of Jesus Christ describes His dual mission. His name declares two distinct *advents* or appearances. Christians teach that we live in the time between advents. When Jesus came the first time, He came as *Savior*, which is the meaning of "Jesus." But the Greek word "Christ," or in Hebrew, "Messiah," means *The Anointed One*, and implies the titles: *Master, Owner, Ruler*. So the second part of His name announces that He's coming back for a second advent—this time not to suffer and die as a sacrifice to take away sins, but to reign in glory and majesty. When He returns, it will be as the Maker and Master, the Ultimate Absolute Ruler of Creation. Study the principal of Jubilee in Leviticus 25 and you'll see that it is the return of everything to its rightful owner. That's exactly what we're talking about.

Just as surely as His name is Jesus Christ: Savior and King, He will come in glory to rule on earth for a thousand years.

6 angels
are you sure you want to meet one of these guys?

"HE MAKES HIS ANGELS WINDS, HIS SERVANTS FLAMES OF FIRE ... ARE NOT ALL ANGELS MINISTERING SPIRITS SENT TO SERVE THOSE WHO WILL INHERIT SALVATION?"
HEBREWS 1:7AND 14

God doesn't tell us a lot about His angels, just as the Bible doesn't tell us much about a lot of things. The Bible doesn't have recipes, or multiplication tables, or the dimensions of the solar system, to name a few of the things missing from Scripture. There's a reason we don't know about the rules of soccer from the Bible. The Bible is all about Jesus, which is also why it doesn't tell us much about *angels*. But it DOES tell us all we really need to know about them (Colossians 2:18).

Here are some of the things the Bible explains about angels:

- The word *"angel"* is a transliteration of the Greek word for *"messenger"*.
- Humans can't boss angels around. Angels obey God (Joel 2:11, Matthew 16:27).
- Glory has to do with the quick-as-lightning, illuminating power of light:
  at present, we don't have the glory they have, but that's going to change.
  One day, we too will be glorious like the angels (Hebrews 2:9-10).
- They're extremely hard to see most of the time, at times, disguised (Hebrews 13:2).
- A single angel can destroy an army of men, overnight (Isaiah 37:36). However, this
  particular angel is the "Angel of the LORD" with 55 references in the OT,
  and might be a Christophany (a pre-incarnate appearance of Jesus).
- God gave the Ten Commandments through angels (Hebrews 2:2).
- They don't know everything, but there are some things that they would like
  to know more about (1 Peter 1:12).
- Angels are created, like we are. Yet, they're invisible, powerful, fiery, sentient,
  spirit beings, swift and deadly and completely alien to our minds.

Almost invariably, with Mary perhaps as the only exception, when human beings meet angels they develop difficulty in thinking, seeing, breathing, and standing. It's a terrifying and gut-wrenching experience, usually. Whoever came up with the idea that angels were small, cute, effeminate, cheerful or chubby has never read their Bible!

Some confused people worship angels—understandably since angels are glorious and terrifying to look at—but the angels themselves forbid it. An angel will inspire worship, but never accept it. When John, in Revelation 19:10, started to worship the being who revealed the apocalypse, he was told explicitly NOT to do any such thing. Unlike the demons who crave our worship, angels unfailingly deflect praise to God alone. It's a defining characteristic.

Speaking of demons, Satan used to be an angel, but his pride disqualified him and now he's the chief of the *fallen* angels (Isaiah 14:12).

We know the names of only two angels from canonic Scripture. *Gabriel* (which means "God is mighty") is a herald who stands in God's presence (Luke 1:19). I don't know what "standing in God's presence" means and neither do you, but Gabriel does! It may mean that Gabriel is God's favorite angelic communicator. It may mean that Gabriel knows God's heart well. It may mean that even while Gabriel is on earth talking with Daniel or Mary, he's still in direct communication with the throne room in the third heaven. Gabriel's definitely the go-to-guy when God employs angels to deliver tidings.

Michael (which means "who is like God") is an *archangel*. We don't really know what an archangel is, but it's a top rank in the angelic command structure. Michael is the commander of the forces of heavenly beings who watch over Israel (Daniel 10:21). He's portrayed in the Bible as the leader of the angelic armies who defeat Satan and throw him out of the heavenly realms (Revelation 12:7). Some say God and Satan fight for supremacy of our world, but that's silly. When God fights, it's over before it starts. If there's an opposite force to Satan, it would have to be the archangel Michael.

All it takes is a single angel to seize Satan and bind him and throw him in the Abyss according to Revelation 20:2-3. Angels are nothing to mess with.

A great book on angels is <u>The Panoramic Bile Study Course #2 Angelology</u> published by Oak Knoll, only available from the family of the deceased author. The best books in the Bible to learn about angels are Genesis, Daniel, Acts, and Revelation. But don't go overboard on the study of angels. Remember, even the angels will tell you that they're not that big a deal.

As we said, deflecting praise is one of the angels' trademark giveaways.

7 separating righteous and unrighteous
ever come across a bad peanut in the middle of a mouthful?

"ALL THE NATIONS WILL BE GATHERED BEFORE HIM, AND HE WILL SEPARATE THE PEOPLE ONE FROM ANOTHER AS A SHEPHERD SEPARATES THE SHEEP FROM THE GOATS."
MATTHEW 25:32

Let me ask you something.

Would you like a bowl full of cereal that included sticks and hay and tiny rocks and scoops of dirt along with grasshoppers, ants and beetles with a large helping of cow pies? Aren't you glad the cereal company separates the grain from everything else in the field? Is it *unfair* to the rest of the grain field that all you want in your bowl is the grain? Is it prejudice or bigotry? Should the Association for the Hurt Feelings of Cow Pies be allowed to lobby for inclusion? What about the *good* beetles and the *sincere* rocks?

Well? Think. Should God have to let *everyone* in to His home in glory simply to be somehow "fair," or to indulge our idea of how He should act? Will we magnanimously allow God to make His own rules regarding who gets let in and who gets left out? If we think it's okay for us to have ideas about things, maybe it's okay if God has a few as well.

It's God's job and only God's job to sort people out ... easily forgotten, but worth a reminder. We see someone and say to ourselves, *they'll* never get in: Hitler, Stalin, Bin Laden, Saddam Hussein, the other political party we don't belong to, so-and-so at work, and what's-their-name from school. We have it all figured out, and we don't really need to wait for Jesus to show us whether certain people will make it.

If we were doing the separating, we'd have excluded C.S. Lewis long before his motorcycle ride with his brother. We would have condemned St. Francis of Assisi long before his rejection of worldly position and privilege. We would have approved of the damnation of the Apostle Paul (who was zealously dragging Christians out of their homes and doing unspeakable things to them) long before he was struck down on the Damascus road and called to preach to the Gentiles and write most of the New Testament.

1 Corinthians 4:5 warns, *"Judge nothing before the appointed time; wait till the Lord comes. He will bring to light what is hidden in darkness and will expose the motives of men's hearts."* We can't afford to prejudge those around us. Just as God does, we can earnestly desire the salvation of everyone (1 Timothy 2:4). Let's pray *each person* comes to repentance.

At the return of Christ, the Antichrist and the False Prophet will be separated from the world and tossed into the Lake of Fire. Nobody will be sorry to see them go. There'll be an interlude of a thousand years in which Satan will be bound and Christ will rule the world from Jerusalem. Then the devil will be loosed for a time to gather the armies of the earth in a last ditch effort to establish hell on earth. Fire from heaven will devour the armies of the enemies of God and Satan will be cast into the Lake of Fire where the other two members of the unholy trinity already are.

Then comes the judgment, the sorting. All the living and the dead will be brought before the judgment seat of Christ, and the books will be opened (Daniel 7:10, Revelation 20:12). We don't know what's in those books, but we can guess they're an account of what each of us has done. *Those whose names are not in the Book of Life are sent to the Lake of Fire* along with the devil, the Antichrist and the False Prophet. Those whose names <u>are</u> in the Book of Life get to witness the coming of the New Heaven and Earth (it'll be a better show than the creation of the first heaven and earth) and watch as the New Jerusalem comes down to the planet from somewhere up above, a literal "heaven on earth."

When we read about the outcome of the separation of the righteous and the unrighteous in our Bibles, anyone with half a brain will be doing whatever it takes to be sure to have their name written in the Book of Life. Pssst. Here's the secret of how: stop, drop, repent and ask Jesus to take your surrendered life to use however He wants. The prayer goes like this: "Yes, Jesus."

If you've never done that, do it now.

• NEW CREATION

what lies beyond the reach of our imaginations?

"So will it be with the resurrection of the dead. The body that is sown is perishable, it is raised imperishable; it is sown in dishonor, it is raised in glory; it is sown in weakness, it is raised in power; it is sown a natural body, it is raised a spiritual body."
1 Corinthians 15:42-44

Walt Disney had it both right and wrong. Someday our Prince *will* come. But because God loves us, our dreams will NOT come true. We'll get much <u>better</u> than our pitiable, miserable dreams. Ephesians 3:20: **"Now to him who is able to do immeasurably more than all we ask or imagine ..."** If He's planned a world *immeasurably more* than all we can ask or imagine, our dreams will be nightmares compared with what God is *able* to do, what God *plans* to do. Who in the world would want to merely settle for their wildest dreams?

Similarly, those of us who "just want what we deserve" are not very bright. First, what we "deserve" is to be cast out of God's holy presence forever . The standards for admittance into heaven's perfection are a little higher than admission to the movies. Second, why on earth ... scratch that ... why in *heaven's name* would we want to get what we deserve *when we could have what God has prepared?*1 Corinthians 2:9 **"No eye has seen, no ear has heard, no mind has conceived what God has prepared for those who love him."** If someone is trying hard to give you a gigazillion dollars, why would you demand they give you a sharp stick in the foot instead?

Get what we deserve? No, no, no. Lord, we want what You've mercifully offered to us in Christ. Remember Ephesians 3:20? We're in line for God's freely given grace along with His boundless love—far beyond all we can ask, think or imagine.

Will God melt the old world down like silver and use the elements to form new atoms? Nope. As the sign on the store that was going out of business said, "Everything's got to GO!" Read Revelation 21:5. He's salvaging nothing but the essence of us and the things we have rightly loved in this world. The physical stuff of this world will exist no longer. Clean sweep, clean house, clean plate, clean slate, whatever idiom you like. What's on the way is brand new. It sparkles and shines. It's never been seen or even dreamed of. It's not of this world.

What joy we'll experience when we find ourselves beyond the reach of this world's evil. Satan will be history. No, I'm wrong. *He won't even be a memory.* The enemy of our souls will be vanquished beyond a remote possibility of rising again. The odds that this present evil will make a comeback in the new heaven and earth are not statistically approaching zero, they *are* zero.

There'll be no tears or pain, no separation anxiety, no friend will ever be lost, no worry, no fear. There will likely be new challenges, but all the old challenges will have been overcome by the blood of the Lamb and we'll have total victory over them. If you've ever seen a cat curled up asleep in a comfortable chair by a warm and cheery fireplace on a winter's day, that's a picture of the raging joy that's unquestionably on its way for every one of God's children.

Is there something we should be doing to get ourselves ready for the new creation?

Yes. Matthew 28:18-20 is the manual of our present training mission. It precisely details how we are to prepare for this unimaginably delightful world that is on its way. Here it is. Go into all nations. Make disciples. Baptize them into the Name. Teach them to obey all that Christ has commanded.

That's how we align our hearts to the heartbeat of God. That's how we get prepared for what is on its way. That's how we ready our souls and renew our minds. That's how we say goodbye to this world and hello to the world to come. We invite everyone we meet to come with us through Jesus Christ our Lord. Leave behind this sinking, stinking, rusting iron ship and step aboard a star cruiser. Jump off this collapsing ruin and walk the streets of pure gold in the shining city that will never be dark again.

World without end! Amen, amen.

1 the Book of Life

have you ever been glad just to be included?

"IF ANYONE'S NAME WAS NOT FOUND WRITTEN IN THE BOOK OF LIFE, HE WAS THROWN INTO THE LAKE OF FIRE."
REVELATION 20:15

God is very concerned about legality and propriety, and in keeping with that, an account has been kept of every deed ever done, from the stealing of office paperclips to the murder camps of Stalin. God has a *written* record of the actions of every person who's ever lived. Does a good deed cancel out a bad deed? No. Far from it. God appears to *expect* good deeds from us: Job 35:6 and Luke 17:10. No points for doing what God already expects of us.

So surely if we stay away from the bigger sins we'll be okay, right? Nope. Just one slip and it's curtains for our chances of heaven. James 2:10-11, **"Whoever keeps the whole law and yet stumbles at just one point is guilty of breaking all of it. For he who said, 'Do not commit adultery,' also said, 'Do not murder.' If you do not commit adultery but do commit murder, you have become a lawbreaker."** Whoever stumbles *at just one point* is guilty of breaking every law on the books because God made those laws. The Law is not merely a set of arbitrary rules. Our offense is not against some sort of list; we have transgressed the rightful commands which are the outworking of the personality of a very real Creator God. *God* is the one offended when we sin, not some detached standard (Psalms 51:4). Any violation of the law violates *Him*. We can't elevate one offense over another, they're all face slaps to His holiness, to His will, to His Kingdom. They're all mud thrown on *Him*, insults to *Him*, spit in *His* eye.

So it is to Him we must come with a humble heart. God gives grace to the humble (James 4:6). God receives the repentant, the sorrowful, those who mourn for their sin. Because He recognizes the return of His gift of love, producing Godly guilt that we may see our desperate situation and turn again to Him. We learn to rightly fear Him and honor Him. When that happens, not only do the angels rejoice, but ...

God writes our names in a Book. The Book of Life could be a metaphor for the number of the saints, or Jesus' family, or the Father's heart of course; or it just might be a physical object, a guest list, an actual book if you will. Why not?

There is a book mentioned in Malachi 3:16-18. Malachi wrote the last things the Holy Spirit speaks for 400 years before the birth of Jesus. If you had a friend who had said nothing for four centuries, you'd want to think back to their final words before the silence, right?

Here are some of those final words of the Spirit: *"Then those who feared the Lord talked with each other, and the Lord listened and heard. A scroll of remembrance was written in his presence concerning those who feared the Lord and honored his name. 'They will be mine,' says the Lord Almighty, 'in the day when I make up my treasured possession. I will spare them, just as in compassion a man spares his son who serves him. And you will again see the distinction between the righteous and the wicked, between those who serve God and those who do not.'"*

Is this the Book of Life? I think it is, but that's not the important thing. This book clearly reveals the heart of God Almighty. He doesn't write us in His book because we're good or because we attend church or because we have good hygiene or because we're nice or because we don't curse or because we read our Bibles every day or because we've done more good things than bad things. We're in the Book because we love to talk with each other about the love and the wonder of God Himself.

It's our hearts He prizes, that He cherishes. Abraham lied about his own wife when his life was threatened, but God loved Abraham and made a covenant with him because Abraham obeyed God by faith. Abraham returned God's love.

Moses was a murderer and yet God loved him and chose to use him to free one nation and destroy another. Because Moses was the friend of God, Moses included God in everything in his life. Why wouldn't God include Moses the same way?

David was a premeditating murderer and an adulterer and God loved him because David was a man who cared what God wanted and what God thought. He pursued God's heart (1 Samuel 13:14).

Paul was a terrorist and by his own admission, the chief of sinners, yet God loved Paul enough to smack him down on the Damascus road. To take away his sight and give him spiritual _in_sight. Take away his life's mission, replacing it with the Great _C_ommission. Because Paul was all out for God, whether persecuting Christians as he did at first, or being persecuted by the Jews as happened later. God loves those who are all out, because they have the muchness to be all out for Him.

Like these, we want to please God by faith and enter into covenant with Him. We want to include God in every part of our lives in order that we may become part of His. We want to care what God thinks and what God wants as we pursue God's heart. We want to be all out for God so that He can direct and redirect us for His will and purpose. These are the people whose names are found in the Book of Life.

May our lives orbit around Jesus, that whatever our problems and shortcomings, our names may be found in His book.

2 Christ's victory

what's so significant about Christ's empty tomb?

"FOR THE TRUMPET WILL SOUND, THE DEAD WILL BE RAISED IMPERISHABLE, AND WE WILL BE CHANGED. FOR THE PERISHABLE MUST CLOTHE ITSELF WITH THE IMPERISHABLE, AND THE MORTAL WITH IMMORTALITY. WHEN THE PERISHABLE HAS BEEN CLOTHED WITH THE IMPERISHABLE, AND THE MORTAL WITH IMMORTALITY, THEN THE SAYING THAT IS WRITTEN WILL COME TRUE: DEATH HAS BEEN SWALLOWED UP IN VICTORY ... THE STING OF DEATH IS SIN, AND THE POWER OF SIN IS THE LAW. BUT THANKS BE TO GOD! HE GIVES US THE VICTORY THROUGH OUR LORD JESUS CHRIST."
1 CORINTHIANS 15:52-57

In sports, a blow-out is a win so complete that the winning team can play their scrubs for the last part of the game. In our case, God's victory over the Kingdom of Darkness is such a sure thing that we, the scrubs, are in the middle innings! As tough as the battle is, Jesus is still wiping the floor with the enemies of the cross. Christ, the Victor, will bring this world to a dead stop and then He and His friends will start a whole new one.

The thing that throws us is that His victory happened mid-game. The winning goal was scored 2,000 years ago at a place called Skull Hill, in an obscure city in Judea, a far-off province of the superpower of Rome where a wandering rabbi earned the deadly disapproval of the leaders of a curious little religion. The day of the execution was actually marked by the sun going dark, as well as earthquakes and reports of dead people walking, but no big deal. It soon brightened up, the earth settled down, and the graveyard people that came to life that day eventually died again and stayed that way.

Who would have guessed that this was the turning point of the war described in Psalms 2 and Revelation 12? Who could have predicted that the fatal blow would have been struck by a man forsaken by His friends and His God, beat up so badly that Isaiah 52:14 says you couldn't tell He was a human being anymore, spiked onto to an upright wooden beam from which the only escape was death? Who could have understood that this seemingly inconsequential execution so long ago and far away was truly the death knell of the mighty world system of darkness, and the executed man was in reality the only hope of hopeless humankind?

The story of Christ's victory was not one we would've made up if we were telling it. We'd have invented something more like a heroic swordsman (and by "heroic," we mean oversized muscles, improbable good looks and very cool long hair) slashing his way through the ranks of our hapless enemies.

But not the cross. Not this display of *weakness*. Never. Who would have thought of rescuing the world THIS way? On the surface, it's pathetic. Ill-advised. Uninspiring. So all I can say is that it's a good thing that God is God and not you and me! Because this "uninspiring" plan has launched more songs and acts of courage and selfless sacrifice than all other inspirations put together. This "ill-advised" scheme confounded the wisest and succeeded brilliantly. This "pathetic" attempt has ground the machinations of all the glorious kingdoms of earth to a whimpering halt.

Hebrews 2:8b says, ***"At present we do not see everything subject to him."*** Right now, it looks bad. Wherever we turn, it seems as if evil is winning. Hollywood is overrun with those who openly flout God's precepts, portraying Christians as lunatics, vile behavior as normal. The arts these days are largely peopled by those who think a crucifix in urine is worthy of public funding. Our schools have removed the Ten Commandments and banned prayer. Same sex marriage is the law in many states. Babies are killed in the womb by the millions every year. The aged are candidates for euthanasia. Christians worldwide are persecuted in horrific atrocities. God's name is taken in vain and his Son is mocked. Victory? It sure doesn't look like it.

God sees. God knows. He's not ready to panic. Christ's victory is a done deal, and one day, we'll all see it clearly. One day there will be no doubt that God has always had everything under control. I love the old hymn that goes:

"Victory in Jesus, my savior forever: he sought me and bought me with his redeeming blood; he loved me e're I knew him, and all my love is due him; he plunged me to victory beneath the cleansing flood!"

The victory has already been won. Help is on the way and nothing in heaven or earth could possibly stop or even delay it for a moment. Take courage.

3 the coming ages
is God's love really forever and ever and ever?

"GOD RAISED US UP WITH CHRIST AND SEATED US WITH HIM IN THE HEAVENLY REALMS IN CHRIST JESUS, IN ORDER THAT IN THE COMING AGES HE MIGHT SHOW THE INCOMPARABLE RICHES OF HIS GRACE, EXPRESSED IN HIS KINDNESS TO US IN CHRIST JESUS."
EPHESIANS 2:6-7

Beyond half a century we can't imagine time very well. When people talk about millions of years, it's like throwing dust in our eyes. We don't have the circuitry to process the idea of billions of years.

Some people grandly claim this universe is the result of an explosion of gasses 20 billion years ago. Wow, they just used a *really* large number! *"Twenty billion years ago,"* we repeat with a monotone voice and glazed eyes. Who can possibly argue with twenty <u>billion</u>? Twenty *billion*! Good golly, that's a lot of years! Never mind that the very same people who say life began 8 billion years ago tell us the planet is only 4 billion years old, 'cause we're talking b-b-b-billions of years. Don't argue. Just watch the pretty lights and come along quietly. Billions. Billions! *Billions.*

So when we read in the Bible that God inhabits eternity and that we'll live with Him as the ages roll, we have no earthly idea what's being said. We get glazed over talking thousands of years, lose our minds at billions, and shut down at the mention of *unending years*. That's beyond us. I mean, we can't even remember what we had for breakfast. How can God expect us to understand this idea of eternity?

Well, let's think outside the box for a minute. What if eternity is not a measurement per se but a new *state of being* we can't grasp with our present brains?

Ephesians 3:17b and 18 says. ***"I pray that you, being rooted and established in love, may have power, together with all the saints, to grasp how wide and long and high and deep is the love of Christ."*** Didn't that verse use <u>four</u> dimensions? Presently, space only has three. What if time is not a useful measurement in the ages to come and what if there are more than three *spacial* dimensions? What if linear time doesn't make it into the new heavens and earth? I'm just wondering here, don't mind me.

1 Corinthians 13:8-13 tells us what parts of this world will make it through to the other side: ***"Love never fails. But where there are prophecies, they will cease; where there are tongues, they will be stilled; where there is knowledge, it will pass away ... Now we see but a poor reflection as in a mirror; then we shall see face to face. Now I know in part; then I shall know fully, even as I am fully known. And now these three remain: faith, hope and love. But the greatest of these is love."***

There's nothing on its way in eternity that will replace *love* because it's not an emotion but a descriptor of God Himself.

Hope seems like it ought to pass away when the new world comes. I mean, why would we still hope when our hopes are all realized? But maybe hope remains because as perfect as the next world will be, God can always outdo Himself. Hey, He's *God*! He can make a rock too big for Him to pick up and then pick it up! In this life, we hope in our redemption, but I'll bet there'll be something bigger than redemption to hope in.

And *faith*? Isn't faith the evidence of things not seen according to Hebrews 11? So perhaps, even when the new world comes, there'll still be the unseen, the part that we must trust God for, where we continue to live by faith. Why else would we be trained in the use of faith? Just to navigate the next couple of years? Then we throw faith away and replace it with a walk of sight? I don't think so, but you decide for yourself.

Consider that this world may be where we *practice* using faith, hope and love—the economic system of the world to come.

One day soon, we'll see Jesus face to face and we'll have a body like His new one! The very last time we saw Him, He could go through solid rock and closed doors, He liked to eat, and could easily lift off the earth on His own power, traveling wherever He wished to go at the speed of thought. We will know Christ and be fully known by Him—best friends with our Creator God. Everlasting life, love that never ends, never runs out, never stops. No tears, no sadness of any kind, only wonder and delight. The real thing at last. Life and joy and daily adventures that would peel paint off the walls down here. Our lives will revolve around Christ like the planet earth revolves around the sun, except that with Jesus, we'll be closer than any friendship or love we've ever experienced.

Oh *man*. I really just can't *wait*.

4 the healing of the nations
will there ever be a time when we all enjoy each other?

"AND THE LEAVES OF THE TREE ARE FOR THE HEALING OF THE NATIONS."
REVELATION 22:2B

In the Bible, the word "nations" does not refer as much to countries on maps as it does to people groups: descendants. Check out what's called "The Table of Nations" in Genesis 10:32, ***These are the clans of Noah's sons, according to their lines of descent, within their nations. From these the nations spread out over the earth after the flood.*** The nations are all descended from Noah. So it seems that we should all get along, after all, we're all the same family.

But as my friend Steve Geyer says, the problem with public restrooms is the public. As soon as you have distinctives, you have reasons to feel superior, giving rise to wranglings all the way from simple hurt feelings to wars and bombs. The nations in Genesis 10 numbered seventy. Today we have by some estimates ten to thirty *thousand* nations. And nobody likes anybody else. Groups harbor generational hatred for other groups. Some groups have committed unthinkable atrocities upon other groups because those groups committed unthinkable atrocities upon them and some groups have stood by while it all happened. There's not a people group without a sad and sordid history *because every group is made up of _people_*. And people are rats. Ask anyone you want. Ask Romans 3:23. Everything is solidarity this and protect our turf that and *they* are taking over our such and such.

And so we have our world today—a cesspool of conflicting people groups. Groups struggling for available resources, the approval of the public, the moral high ground, the strategic position. Fighting, grabbing, shoving, hurting, maiming, murdering. The battle between groups is sometimes below the surface, but it's never far removed from boiling up. Almost anything can inflame the tensions, and then the conflict begins again in endless repeating cycles.

God, deliver us! What's that you say? He *has?* Why am I not surprised?

There's a tree in the Garden of Eden that appears again in the New Jerusalem. It's the Tree of Life. Is this a metaphor? I'm sure it is. Is it a real tree? I'm pretty sure it's that too! And it could be Jesus Himself. Isaiah 11:10 says, **"In that day the Root of Jesse will stand as a banner for the peoples; the nations will rally to him, and his place of rest will be glorious."** I think the Tree of Life might very well be Christ Himself, for if it *can* heal the nations, it might just be the Great Physician. I could be wrong.

How are *leaves* from the Tree of Life used to heal the nations? I have no idea, and the Bible doesn't say. But we use leaves all the time: applied as a poultice, drunk in steaming cups of hot water, ground up into health foods, made into infusions and tinctures and pills. Leaves keep us healthy. The most widely used medicines are herbs, which are simply leaves. If the leaf of the cone flower is nearly miraculous in its healing ability, I'll bet the leaves of the Tree of *Life* aren't half bad.

But never mind the process, what about the result? People once hopelessly divided become miraculously reunited. The ones once estranged are again friends. God never wanted us to use our differences as bludgeons and knives. If you really want to know, God created our differences to keep us from ... well, getting *bored*. If everyone in the world looked exactly the same, this world would be dull and tiresome. For example, if there were no differences, your spouse would look just like you. Need we go further? Differences are a *good* thing.

In the New Jerusalem, differences among the people groups will surely *exist*, but they will no longer *divide*. The differences are no longer a place of pride, but of fascination, wonder and praise, just like flowers in a garden. The Tree of Life will somehow help us to see each other the way God sees us: enjoying each variation on the theme. The more different kinds of notes we have, the more the chance for delightfully complex *harmony* ("joining in concord"). You don't get *symphonies* ("sounding together") from any single instrument but from an orchestra. Solos are fine, but they get old if that's all you've got!

I mean, look at the city described in Revelation 21:18-20: **"The wall was made of jasper, and the city of pure gold ... The foundations of the city walls were decorated with every kind of precious stone ... jasper ... sapphire ... chalcedony ... emerald ... sardonyx ... carnelian ... chrysolite ... beryl ... topaz ... chrysoprase ... jacinth ... amethyst."** Why so many different stones? They are each delightful and together precious to God, that's why. Ephesians 2:22 says we're being built together like this city, a place where God can dwell among us as we glorify Him, even in or especially in our differences.

The nations will no longer scratch and claw each other; instead, they'll enjoy and appreciate each other, laugh with each other (and I think in a healthy unhurtful way, because we won't take ourselves so seriously), and worship God together in unity and uniqueness, in peace and one-of-a-kind pieces.

God is going to give us an exponentially better world than the godless utopians dream about.

5 eternal life

can we conceivably conceive no limits to existence?

"AND THIS IS THE TESTIMONY: GOD HAS GIVEN US ETERNAL LIFE, AND THIS LIFE IS IN HIS SON. HE WHO HAS THE SON HAS LIFE; HE WHO DOES NOT HAVE THE SON OF GOD DOES NOT HAVE LIFE."
I JOHN 5:11-12

All-you-can-eat buffets. Free oil changes for the life of your car. You're always welcome here. We'll leave the light on for you. These are our ideas of "endless." But sooner or later, the check has to be paid. The free ride dumps you out on the street. The door closes. We can't imagine it otherwise.

But "otherwise" is exactly what God is offering us in 1 John 5:11. He promises there'll be no running out, no final bell, no closing door. Life begins when we bow our knee to Jesus and ends ... *never*. There is everlasting life for those who receive Jesus Christ, who passionately follow Him, who gratefully belong to Him. It's for keeps. Not even death can cancel this kind of existence, for after death comes more and more ever-increasing life ... life that is outside our ability to *dream about*.

In <u>The Great Divorce</u>, C.S. Lewis talks about the afterlife and he proposes through his allegorical brilliance that both heaven and hell begin long before we die. For the person who rejects God, even the greatest joys in life become no more than dispassionate precursors to eternal despair. For those who trust Jesus, the most wrenching sorrows of life will later be recognized as the first transformative steps on the upward path of eternal joy and delight. The future Heaven and hell work their way backwards through our lives and transfigure even our history.

The hymn *"Farther Along"* declares, *"Farther along we'll know all about it, farther along we'll understand why."* Eternal life ensures we'll one day be able to look at this life from God's vantage point and see each setback as a chance for faith, each sorrow as a new place of God's grace and strength. We'll see that Satan got *used*. The devil thought he was knocking us off our game, but he was nothing but a tool on God's workbench, used to beautifully shape the children of God. All the powers of darkness which press in all around us? We will one day understand that He orchestrated them for His plainly revealed purpose—to make us look just like Jesus.

Eternal life will never be boring, never be static, always new and endlessly engaging. We'll need to tell each other to close our mouths because of the drool running out of our dropped jaws, gaping at the wonders that will be revealed to our reborn senses. We'll go from strength to strength, like it says in Psalms 84:7. We won't wear out, we'll keep growing and gaining more and more health. The most vicious diseases of this life couldn't hurt a newborn baby in eternity. Isaiah 40:31 says it this way: ***"Those who hope in the Lord will renew their strength. They will soar on wings like eagles; they will run and not grow weary."*** Isaiah is talking about God's life, new life, that never fails, never flags, ever soaring, mounting ever higher.

As the ages roll, ever more glorious vistas will unfold before us. Fanny Crosby, in *"Blessed Assurance"*, proclaims, *"Perfect submission, perfect delight, visions of rapture now burst on my sight; angels descending bring from above, echoes of mercy, whispers of love."* Keep in mind that Fanny Crosby was blind! Without physical sight, she saw more than most of the rest of us whose eyes are in perfect working order.

Eternal life is the promise of more on top of more on top of more. More what? That's easy. More of Jesus.

John 17:3 says that eternal life is knowing God. Are you studying your Bible to find out more about Christ and His Kingdom? That's eternal life. Are you walking through your day talking things over with Jesus, asking Him questions, praising Him for His blessings, interceding for your friends and your enemies? That's eternal life. Are you praying for more revelation, more opportunity to show God's love, more wisdom and discernment? That's eternal life. Hanging out with God, walking with the Holy Spirit, seeking to glorify the name of Christ? All of this is nothing less than life in Jesus. That's eternal life.

Eternal life starts happening for us right here and now.

6 the new heaven and earth
did God run out of ideas when He made this world?

"BEHOLD, I WILL CREATE NEW HEAVENS AND A NEW EARTH. THE FORMER THINGS WILL NOT BE REMEMBERED, NOR WILL THEY COME TO MIND."
ISAIAH 65:17

Everything made brand new. Just a reboot from a mistake God made? No way. The new heaven and new earth were planned long before the first ones were ever made.

What? You don't believe that? Isaiah 66:22 sounds like the new world foretold in Revelation 22, but it was written nearly 800 years before. Jesus told His disciples in John 14 that He was going to prepare a place for them and then come back to take them there. Paul said the mortal would be swallowed up by the immortal in 1 Corinthians 15:54. It's not a do-over. God takes no mulligans. He has just one plan and He's working it. Sure and steady. Dependable. Like a rock.

Will we travel to other planets in the new universe? I don't see why not. Will there be other creatures there? I don't see why there wouldn't be. Will we help them? Why else would we go? Will we walk on the surface of the stars? Yes, of course, just to show off. The rest of the time we'll be playing in the gaseous clouds of deep space like they were part of our own personal swimming pool. I mean, if 1 Corinthians 2:9 says this is all beyond imagining, I thought I'd give it my best shot.

We are told that the new heaven and earth will be the home of righteousness (2 Peter 3:13). That means evil will not escape the destruction of this old world. It will be sucked in like a collapsing red giant star devolving into a black hole. Does that register? Evil will be destroyed so completely even the *memory* of it will be erased!

The earth will be full of the knowledge of the Lord (Isaiah 11:9). No one will walk in a bad part of town. Every part of town will be the best part of town. No one will go to sleep hungry or lonely, every emptiness will be filled. No one will be anxious about the future, just as no middle-class suburban child ever wondered if supper was going to be cancelled.

This present world is under God's curse. *We have no idea what a world would be like without that curse, for even our imaginations are trapped in the darkness.* If we lived in a wooden box underwater—cold, dank, hearing impaired, without a sense of smell, our sight blurred, air barely breathable, visibility restricted—it would be hard to imagine ourselves soaring above fields and mountains and rivers with the fresh warm air in our face and the sunrise lighting everything below while the delicious sounds and the aromas of the earth waft upwards towards our delighted senses. We have no clue what a world without sin will be like, but it's coming. People get ready. The train is leaving the station.

Will we remember *anything* about the old world? God only knows, but many think, as do I, that we will remember the blessings. Will we remember our friends? We won't have to. The ones who belong to Jesus will be with us, and the ones who have rejected Him won't even be a distant memory.

Will our beloved pets be in the new heaven and earth? I really don't see why not. In Revelation 19:11 and 14, Jesus and the mighty host who follow Him ride horses out of heaven. If there are horses, why not our own beloved furballs? I don't want to argue about it, but be assured of this: whatever *ought* to be in heaven *will* be.

Will we finally get justice? No, praise God. We'll get grace and mercy instead. Trust me when I say that it's better this way.

Will we be beautiful? Will we eat three times a day? Will we need clothes? What will they look like? What will our houses be like, or are we gonna all pile into God's mansion? Will we all be able to sing better than anyone on earth? Will we need to sleep? Will we be indestructible? Will we all be gardeners? Will everyone be great at sports and writing songs, and will there be microwave popcorn?

Nobody knows the answers to these questions, but they're really fun to think about. The new life will be the total enjoyment of the riches of the blessings of the grace and mercy and love of Jesus Christ.

We'll be blessed every which way and sideways!

7 the new Jerusalem
ever heard the phrase "heaven on earth?"

"I SAW THE HOLY CITY, THE NEW JERUSALEM, COMING DOWN OUT OF HEAVEN FROM GOD."
REVELATION 21:2

I may not be a Greek scholar or an expert on biblical prophesy, but it seems very plain that in the millennial reign Jerusalem is raised up. But *the New Jerusalem is lowered down* from heaven. Revelation 21:16-17 says (and it makes a point to say that these measurements are human measurements) that it's 1400 miles long, 1400 miles high and 1400 miles deep with 216 foot thick walls. The new city is way too big to fit on this planet; I mean, if you tried to land it on the present-size world, you'd alter the path of the earth around the sun and drag the moon into a decaying orbit. Not something God would do—put His new city on a planet too small to support it.

So what gives? Well, *the New Jerusalem won't be on the old earth. It'll be on the new one.* I'm guessing since the New Jerusalem is a whole lot bigger than the old Jerusalem, that the new Earth will be the same thing. Bigger, better, higher, wider, and a whole lot more fun. God never downsizes.

The New Jerusalem won't need electricity or sanitation or firemen or policemen. It won't have a crooked city council. Everyone who wants to visit will be able to afford it. Jesus has paid all expenses at the cross. It will be lit by the face of God the Father, powered by the presence of the Holy Spirit, and made the most interesting spot in the universe by the glory and the joy of the Lord Jesus Christ.

Wait. When we say, "New Jerusalem," aren't we just talking about a metaphor for the Bride, the Church? Well, perhaps. But the old Jerusalem was a city, why not the new one? Revelation 22:12-27 describes its foundation, its streets, its guests, its gates and i's wall. If this is just an analogy, that's carrying it a little too far, don't you think? We should always watch for metaphor in the book of Revelation, but I believe this is a real city. On the other hand, it could be both! Don't you just love God's mysteries?

A careful study of the measurements given in Revelation 21 reveals that this city is constructed on a whole other scale than any city we know. The gates are magnificent, and they're never used. They're always open. Why does everything have to have a use? Why can't some things just be beautiful? Art! These gates *could* be closed but they never will be. There's no need to shut them because there's no enemy left to challenge the walls. Only the children of God are still around. Remember, this is after the destruction of wickedness and the making of the new heavens and new earth.

The New Jerusalem looks like home base for everything that happens in the world which is to come. Perhaps we'll travel across the universe on God's business, serving the crazy creatures that God might sprinkle across the new cosmos. Or there'll be other errands that wouldn't make sense to our earthly brains if God told us all about them. But wherever we are, I'll bet base will be the New Jerusalem. Home is where the heart is, and our hearts will definitely yearn for that city. It's big enough to hold the entire holy-catholic, universal, time-space church put together.

The bright white city of transparent gold, adorned with monstrous jewels of unthinkable brilliance, lit by the healing light of God Himself and inhabited by the glorified children of God. Everybody who loves Jesus will be there. Oh, and Jesus Himself will be there every day, hanging with us while He rules the universe, laughing and dancing and singing and swimming and running and flying and just *being* with us. The sun will never set and yet the colors of the sky will still take your breath away. There'll never be another heartbreak, no more pain, no more loneliness. The eats will be astonishingly delicious as well as bottomless, the jokes will all be riotously hilarious, and we'll never ever have a bad hair day. If you can't get a lump in your throat over the New Jerusalem, your imaginator is broken!

One thing is sure about the people of that glorious city. We'll live happily *ever after*.

¬extra stuff
APPENDIX
HOW DO WE *APPLY* DOCTRINE?

1. Imprint it on your family as "just who we are"

"THESE COMMANDMENTS THAT I GIVE YOU TODAY ARE TO BE UPON YOUR HEARTS. IMPRESS THEM ON YOUR CHILDREN. TALK ABOUT THEM WHEN YOU SIT AT HOME AND WHEN YOU WALK ALONG THE ROAD, WHEN YOU LIE DOWN AND WHEN YOU GET UP."
DEUTERONOMY 6:6-7

This scripture says to talk about the things of God *all the time*. The great evangelist Charles Spurgeon wrote a catechism (a set of doctrinal teachings using question and answer format) for family use. Why? To combat widespread error in the church. Families are God's original church and still the winner as far as all important *quantity time*. I mean, how can one measly hour on Sunday morning compete with the whole rest of the week? The family setting is great for teaching sound doctrine. Start by memorizing the Apostle's creed and go from there.

2. Discuss it with your friends instead of other stuff

"THEN THOSE WHO FEARED THE LORD TALKED WITH EACH OTHER, AND THE LORD LISTENED AND HEARD. A SCROLL OF REMEMBRANCE WAS WRITTEN IN HIS PRESENCE CONCERNING THOSE WHO FEARED THE LORD AND HONORED HIS NAME."
MALACHI 3:16

It's important to discuss what God has revealed, what God thinks, what God wants with your friends. The direction of your life will be more focused, more stable and more satisfying. If you don't have any friends, start smiling and doing thoughtful things for people and see if you can't make some. If your friends don't want to talk about this, get some better friends!

3. Dwell on it through the day, speak it out loud to yourself

"MY MOUTH WILL TELL OF YOUR RIGHTEOUSNESS, OF YOUR SALVATION ALL DAY LONG, THOUGH I KNOW NOT ITS MEASURE."
PSALMS 71:15

"Meditation" to Orientals may mean silently letting your mind just go blank, but to Middle Easterners like David, it's talking out loud to yourself wherever you are and whatever you're doing. So try it. Instead of reaching for the radio in the car, or the TV at home, open your mouth and declare aloud all the scripture and doctrine you can remember; then, go memorize some more for the next time. If someone hears you recounting God's amazingness, all the better! Maybe they'll start a conversation and you'll be back at number 2.

4. Do the things you know to do

"NOW THAT YOU KNOW THESE THINGS, YOU WILL BE BLESSED IF YOU DO THEM."
JOHN 13:17

Do what doctrine teaches. Forgive as you have been forgiven. Love as you have been loved. Go to church. Give as much as you can of whatever it is that you have. Visit the sick and imprisoned. Pray for your friends and your enemies. Read and memorize the scriptures and say them out loud. Welcome those far from home. Go into all the world and make disciples, baptizing them and teaching them to obey the things Jesus tells us in the Bible. Rejoice in the Lord always. His commands are the best things we can find ourselves doing.

Sure ... platitudes. It's easy to *say* we should do these things! But how do we actually <u>do</u> these things? I asked my dad how to become a great painter like him and he said, "Just throw away your first thousand paintings." In other words, you have to do something to get good at it! So let's just do doctrine without all the excuses!

5. Get involved, get engaged, get in community

"YOU YOURSELVES ARE OUR LETTER, WRITTEN ON OUR HEARTS, KNOWN AND READ BY EVERYBODY. YOU SHOW THAT YOU ARE A LETTER FROM CHRIST, THE RESULT OF OUR MINISTRY, WRITTEN NOT WITH INK BUT WITH THE SPIRIT OF THE LIVING GOD, NOT ON TABLETS OF STONE BUT ON TABLETS OF HUMAN HEARTS."
2 CORINTHIANS 3:2-3

Doctrine teaches us not just how to passively exist, but how to actively *thrive* among the people God has put all around us. It helps us to be part of our family, part of the church, part of our neighborhood, part of our world. Many people are hurting. The truth found in the study of the teachings of the Bible is powerful medicine for that pain. It's not just an intellectual exercise. With knowledge comes responsibility. The explosive truth of Jesus is meant to transform the human heart. We have tangible truth that is meant to go into all the world. Often the circumstances around us will remain unchanged, but <u>*we will be changed in the midst of the unchanged circumstance*</u> and that will make all the difference.

THE CREEDS

Creeds are nuggets of agreement among Christians. They were written, not by the Apostles, but by the church Fathers—a sort of counsel of recognized leaders. They were proposed to push back against the heresies that were attempting to destroy the truth of Christian doctrine. One such heresy claimed that Jesus never had a human body but projected an illusion of one. Another said Jesus was not God in the eternal sense, was not co-equal with the Father God. There were Gnostics who believed that sinners are not saved by the blood of Jesus, but by special spiritual knowledge. Others taught that angels had spoken to them of new ideas.

It was important to agree on what constituted mainstream Christianity. Voilà. The church Fathers got together and penned the creeds.

The creeds don't have biblical authority. They were never meant to supersede Scripture. They are not inspired by the Holy Spirit the way the Bible is. They are simply distilled doctrinal statements, carefully crafted to contain wholesome truth for the church, especially giving substance to the doctrine of the Trinity.

The creeds are quickly read, but power packed—chewable fruit-flavored Christianity tablets, if you will. Many churches use the Apostle's Creed and the Nicene Creed in weekly worship. The creeds are common ground among the sometimes warring factions of our faith, and as such, they are true treasures.

The Apostle's Creed is the older of the two, and you can recognize its influence on the Nicene Creed. These are some of the best records we have of early church doctrinal teaching! They preserve the clear and uncluttered essence of what the early church deemed to be not only orthodox but important (not the same thing!)

Major themes in the creeds have to do with the nature of the Trinity: Father, Son and Spirit, the virgin birth of Jesus Christ, the essential narrative of the Gospel, the primacy of the cross and of forgiveness, the catholic (universal) and apostolic nature of the church, and the eternal properties of the world to come.

The thing to do with creeds is to first memorize them. Use flashcards, music, record them and listen, write them on a poster and hang it by your TV! Make knowing these by heart a priority. Then think about them and discuss them with other Christians. Feel free to check them against the Scriptures to see if they line up. Chances are, you'll find them delightfully condensed versions of biblical teaching, a great place to begin any study of doctrine.

THE APOSTLES' CREED

Probably from around A.D.180

I believe in God, the Father Almighty, the Maker of heaven and earth,
and in Jesus Christ, His only Son, our Lord.

Who was conceived by the Holy Spirit, born of the virgin Mary, suffered under
Pontius Pilate, was crucified, dead, and buried;

The third day He rose again from the dead; He ascended into heaven,
and sits at the right hand of God the Father Almighty;
from thence he shall come to judge the living and the dead.

I believe in the Holy Spirit; the holy catholic church; the communion of saints;
the forgiveness of sins; the resurrection of the body; and the life everlasting.

Amen.

THE NICENE CREED

From around A.D.381

We believe in one God, the Father; the Almighty, maker of heaven and earth, and of all that is, seen and unseen.

We believe in one Lord, Jesus Christ; the only Son of God, eternally begotten of the Father, God from God, Light from Light, true God from true God, begotten, not made, of one Being with the Father.

Through him all things were made.

For us and for our salvation he came down from heaven: by the power of the Holy Spirit he became incarnate from the Virgin Mary, and was made man.

For our sake he was crucified under Pontius Pilate; he suffered death and was buried.

On the third day he rose again in accordance with the Scriptures; he ascended into heaven and is seated at the right hand of the Father.

He will come again in glory to judge the living and the dead, and his kingdom will have no end.

We believe in the Holy Spirit; the Lord, the giver of life, who proceeds from the Father and the Son.

With the Father and the Son he is worshiped and glorified. He has spoken through the Prophets.

We believe in one holy catholic and apostolic Church.

We acknowledge one baptism for the forgiveness of sins.

We look for the resurrection of the dead, and the life of the world to come.

Amen.

Made in the USA
Monee, IL
08 June 2020

32838394R00142